MEDIA AND THE GLOBAL SOUTH

What does the notion of the 'global south' mean to media studies today?
This book interrogates the possibilities of global thinking from the south in the field of media, communication, and cultural studies. Through lenses of millennial media cultures, it refocuses the praxis of the global south in relation to the established ideas of globalization, development, and conditions of postcoloniality.

Bringing together original empirical work from media scholars from across the global south, the volume highlights how contemporary thinking about the region as theoretical framework – an emerging area of theory in its own right – is incomplete without due consideration being placed on narrative forms, both analogue and digital, traditional and sub-cultural. From news to music cultures, from journalism to visual culture, from screen forms to culture-jamming, the chapters in the volume explore contemporary popular forms of communication as manifested in diverse global south contexts.

A significant contribution to cultural theory and communications research, this book will be of interest to scholars and researchers of media and culture studies, literary and critical theory, digital humanities, science and technology studies, and sociology and social anthropology.

Mehita Iqani is Associate Professor in Media Studies at the University of the Witwatersrand in Johannesburg, South Africa. Her research explores the multiple intersections between consumer culture and the media in relation to discourse, power, aspiration, identity, and global culture. She has a monograph forthcoming on the cultural politics of postconsumer waste.

Fernando Resende is Associate Professor in Culture and Media Studies at the Federal Fluminense University (UFF) in Niterói, Rio de Janeiro, Brazil. Primarily interested in the study of narratives of conflicts and diasporic movements, dealing with issues related to both physical and symbolic zones, his research focuses on theory and philosophy of communication; journalism; culture; comparative media and documentary studies; global south theory; critical cultural studies; and the impact of geopolitical discursive relations (narratives and conflicts) on the imaged geographies of East/West and, in particular, the imagination of Palestine and Africa by Brazil and England (19th and 20th centuries).

LITERARY CULTURES OF THE GLOBAL SOUTH

Series Editors: Russell West-Pavlov, *University of Tübingen, Germany* and Makarand R. Paranjape, *Jawaharlal Nehru University, New Delhi, India*

Recent years have seen challenging new formulations of the flows of influence in transnational cultural configurations and developments. In the wake of the end of the Cold War, the notion of the 'Global South' has arguably succeeded the demise of the tripartite conceptual division of the First, Second and Third Worlds. This notion is a flexible one referring to the developing nations of the once-colonized sections of the globe. The concept does not merely indicate shifts in geopolitics and in the respective affiliations of nations, and the economic transformations that have occurred, but also registers an emergent perception of a new set of relationships between nations of the Global South as their respective connections to nations of the north (either USA/USSR or the old colonial powers) diminish in significance. New social and cultural connections have become evident. This book series explores the literary manifestations (in their often intermedial, networked forms) of those south – south cultural connections together with academic leaders from those societies and cultures concerned.

Editorial Advisory Board
Bruce Robbins, *Columbia University*
Dipesh Chakrabarty, *University of Chicago*
Elleke Boehmer, *University of Oxford*
Laura I. P. Izarra, *University of Sao Paulo*
Pal Ahluwalia, *University of Portsmouth*
Robert J. C. Young, *New York University*
Simon During, *University of Queensland*
Véronique Tadjo, *University of Witwatersrand*

THE POSTCOLONIAL EPIC
Sneharika Roy

ANNOTATING SALMAN RUSHDIE
Reading the Postcolonial
Vijay Mishra

SOUTH AND NORTH
Contemporary Urban Orientations
Edited by Kerry Bystrom, Ashleigh Harris and Andrew J. Webber

TRUTH COMMISSIONS AND THE CULTURE OF
DISSENTING MEMORY
The Global South
Edited by Véronique Tadjo

MEDIA AND THE GLOBAL SOUTH
Narrative Territorialities, Cross-Cultural Currents
Edited by Mehita Iqani and Fernando Resende

For more information about this series, please visit:
www.routledge.com/Literary-Cultures-of-the-Global-South/book-series/LCGS

MEDIA AND THE GLOBAL SOUTH

Narrative Territorialities, Cross-Cultural Currents

*Edited by Mehita Iqani
and Fernando Resende*

LONDON AND NEW YORK

First published 2019
by Routledge
2 Park Square, Milton Park, Abingdon, Oxon OX14 4RN

and by Routledge
52 Vanderbilt Avenue, New York, NY 10017

Routledge is an imprint of the Taylor & Francis Group, an informa business

© 2019 selection and editorial matter, Mehita Iqani and Fernando Resende; individual chapters, the contributors

The right of Mehita Iqani and Fernando Resende to be identified as the authors of the editorial material, and of the authors for their individual chapters, has been asserted in accordance with sections 77 and 78 of the Copyright, Designs and Patents Act 1988.

All rights reserved. No part of this book may be reprinted or reproduced or utilised in any form or by any electronic, mechanical, or other means, now known or hereafter invented, including photocopying and recording, or in any information storage or retrieval system, without permission in writing from the publishers.

Trademark notice: Product or corporate names may be trademarks or registered trademarks, and are used only for identification and explanation without intent to infringe.

British Library Cataloguing-in-Publication Data
A catalogue record for this book is available from the British Library

Library of Congress Cataloging-in-Publication Data
A catalog record for this book has been requested

ISBN: 978-1-138-59552-1 (hbk)
ISBN: 978-0-429-03010-9 (ebk)

Typeset in Galliard
by Apex CoVantage, LLC

CONTENTS

List of figures ix
List of contributors x
Series editors' preface xv
Acknowledgements xvii

1 Theorizing media in and across the global south: narrative as territory, culture as flow 1
   MEHITA IQANI AND FERNANDO RESENDE

2 Imaginaries of the north and south in three Egyptian plays 17
   AMINA EL-HALAWANI

3 They are like us: race, porn, and viewing patterns in South Africa 34
   YOLO SIYABONGA KOBA

4 Popular culture, new femininities, and subjectivities: reading *Nairobi Diaries* 55
   DINA LIGAGA

5 Cartographies of Brazilian popular and 'peripheral' music on YouTube: the case of *Passinho* dance-off 72
   SIMONE PEREIRA DE SÁ

6 *Cuir* visualities, survival imaginaries 86
   RÍAN LOZANO DE LA POLA

CONTENTS

7 Risking images: the political and subjective production of images in Brazil's 2013 mass protests   105
ROBERTO ROBALINHO

8 Journalism cultures in Egypt and Lebanon: role perception, professional practices, and ethical considerations   119
ZAHERA HARB

9 Concrete poetry in Brazil and Germany: the avant-garde reviews history through new media   140
LUCA ROMANI

10 Between remembering and forgetting: memory, culture, and the nostalgia market in the Brazilian mediascape   157
ANA PAULA GOULART RIBEIRO

11 The struggle over narratives: Palestine as metaphor for imagined spatialities   170
DINA MATAR

12 Helper and threat: how the mediation of Africa-China relations complicates the idea of the global south   186
COBUS VAN STADEN

Index   203

FIGURES

3.1	Race typologies: the type of porn I watch	43
3.2	Racial demographics: the type of porn I view	44
5.1	Still from the movie: *A Batalha do Passinho*, directed by Emilio Domingos	73
5.2	Still from the movie: *A Batalha do Passinho*, directed by Emilio Domingos	73
5.3	Still from the movie: *A Batalha do Passinho*, directed by Emilio Domingos	74
6.1	*Hysteria! Revista de sexualidad y cultura*, 'Akelarre' #3	93
6.2	*Hysteria! Revista de sexualidad y cultura*, 'Carnitas' #9	95
6.3	'¡Ay hijitx!' *Maricarmen* zine. 'Activx busca pasivx. No obvixs' #2	98
6.4	'Soy una loca.' *Maricarmen* zine. 'Activx busca pasivx. No obvixs' #2	99
6.5	'Sí, tengo mucha rabia.' *Maricarmen* zine. 'Activx busca pasivx. No obvixs' #2	100
7.1	Photo by Domingos Peixoto, winner of *Esso*'s photojournalist prize 2014	106

CONTRIBUTORS

Amina El-Halawani is Lecturer at the Department of English Language and Literature at the Faculty of Arts, Alexandria University. Her PhD was on revolution in Irish and Egyptian theatres, completed within the framework of the Erasmus Mundus program 'Cultural Studies in Literary Interzones' at the Universities of Perpignan and Tübingen (2018). She is also a Fulbright Alumna (2012–2013), having spent an academic year in the United States teaching classes on Arabic language and culture, as well as comparative literature. Her current research interests include modes of resistance and revolution in theatre, performance as an act of subversion, 20th-century drama, theatre of the absurd, postcoloniality, and the global south.

Ana Paula Goulart Ribeiro is Professor at the School of Communication in the Federal University of Rio de Janeiro (Brazil) and director of the research group Media, Memory and Temporality (Memento) at the same university. She is the author of the book *Press and History in Rio de Janeiro in the 1950s* (2006) and co-editor of the collections *Media and Memory* (2007), *History of Television in Brazil* (2008), *Mikhail Bakhtin: Language, Culture and Media* (2010), *Communication and History* (2011), *Entertainment, Happiness and Memory: Moving Forces of the Contemporary* (2012), and *Television, History and Genres* (2014).

Zahera Harb is Senior Lecturer in International Journalism at City University of London. She is the author of *Channels of Resistance: Liberation Propaganda, Hezbollah and the Media* (I.B. Tauris, 2011), co-editor (with Dina Matar) of *Narrating Conflict in the Middle East: Discourse, Image and Communications Practices in Lebanon and* Palestine (I.B. Tauris, 2013), and editor of *Reporting the Middle East, the Practice of News in the 21st Century* (I.B. Tauris, 2017). Board roles include the Ethical Journalism Network and UK broadcast regulator OFCOM's content board. She is associate editor of *Journalism Practice*

CONTRIBUTORS

and member of editorial boards of several academic journals including *Journalism* and *Middle East Journal of Culture and Communication*.

Mehita Iqani is Associate Professor in Media Studies at the University of the Witwatersrand in Johannesburg, South Africa. Her research explores the multiple intersections between consumer culture and the media in relation to discourse, power, aspiration, identity, and global culture. She is the author of *Consumer Culture and the Media: Magazines in the Public Eye* (2012) and *Consumption, Media and the Global South: Aspiration Contested* (2016), and co-editor of *Consumption, Media and Culture in South Africa: Perspectives on Freedom and the Public* (Routledge, 2016), *Media Studies: Critical African and Decolonial Approaches* (Oxford University Press, 2019), and *African Luxury: Aesthetics and Politics* (Intellect, 2019). She has a monograph forthcoming on the cultural politics of postconsumer waste. She has published in journals including *Consumption Markets & Culture, Feminist Media Studies, International Journal of Cultural Studies, Social Semiotics,* and the *Journal of Consumer Culture*.

Yolo Siyabonga Koba graduated with his PhD from the University of the Witwatersrand, South Africa, in 2017. His research looks at porn consumption in South Africa with the premise that consumption practices give insight into broader formations of culture. He is the recipient of NRF and SAHUDA/NIHSS awards. Yolo's research interests include sex, sexuality, and gender manifestations in various media and art contexts. He is currently pioneering *The Sex Education Magazine*, a new South African sex education publication targeted at families to help parents and children talk about sexual matters.

Dina Ligaga is Associate Professor at the Department of Media Studies, University of the Witwatersrand, South Africa. She has published in the areas of media studies and popular culture in Africa, with a specific focus on East African popular culture. She is co-editor of *Radio in Africa* (2011) and *Eastern African Intellectual Traditions* (2012) and is currently completing a manuscript titled *Contesting the Public Gender Script: Popular Media and the Moral Narratives of Femininity in Kenya*. She has published journal articles on emerging popular cultures in the digital age, with a focus on women and agency.

Rían Lozano de la Pola is a Researcher and Lecturer in Visual Studies at the Institute of Aesthetic Research at UNAM. She did her PhD in Philosophy (Aesthetics and Art Theory) at the University of Valencia, Spain, and a postdoctoral fellowship at Rennes 2, France. Furthermore, she has done residencies at Goldsmiths College (University of London)

CONTRIBUTORS

and PUEG (University Program of Gender Studies, UNAM). Currently, she works as an independent curator and art critic. In 2010 she was part of the curatorial department of Manifesta 8 (The European Biennial of Contemporary Art). She also coordinates the pedagogical and artistic area of 'Mujeres en Espiral': a project developed with women inmates at the Santa Martha Acatitla prison, in México DF. In 2010, Lozano published her book *Prácticas culturales a-normales. Un ensayo (alter) mundializador* (edited by PUEG/UNAM), and in 2012 co-edited, together with Marisa Belasuteguigoitia, *Pedagogías en Espiral. Experiencias y Prácticas*. She is the guest editor of *Decolonial Visuality*, the last number of *Extravío. Revista de Literatura Comparada* (University of Valencia, Spain). Her work focuses on the analysis of 'abnormal' (that is, not 'normative') cultural practices and their connections to pedagogy, the creation of other epistemologies, political action, and feminisms from the South; and notions of power and representation.

Dina Matar is Head of the School of Interdisciplinary Studies at SOAS. She works on the relationship between communication, politics, and culture with a special focus on the Arab world, particularly Palestine, Lebanon, Jordan, and Syria. She is particularly interested in global media, activism; cultural politics, diasporas, and globalization; the state and the media; and Islamist politics, memory, identity, and digital politics, practices, and cultures. Before turning to academia, she was as a foreign correspondent and editor covering the Middle East, Europe, and Africa. She has published widely and is the author of *What It Means to Be Palestinian: Stories of Palestinian Peoplehood* (Tauris, 2010); co-editor of *Narrating Conflict in the Middle East: Discourse, Image and Communication Practices in Palestine and Lebanon* (Tauris, 2013); co-editor of *Gaza as Metaphor* (Hurst and Oxford University Press, 2016); and co-author of *The Hizbullah Phenomenon: Politics and Communication* (Hurst, 2014). Matar is co-founding editor of the *Middle East Journal of Culture and Communication*, which is entering its 11th year in 2018.

Simone Pereira de Sá is Professor in the Media and Cultural Studies Department and in the Graduate Program in Communication at Federal Fluminense University (UFF/Brazil). She holds a PhD in Communication and Culture Studies from Federal do Rio de Janeiro University (UFRJ/Brazil). She is Director of LabCult/UFF – the Research Lab on Urban Culture and Communication Technologies – and has been a visiting researcher at McGill University, Montreal (2008) and King's College, UK (2015/2016), sponsored by CAPES scholarship. Her research interests include pop culture in local and global contexts, Brazilian

CONTRIBUTORS

music, fandoms on social media, mediations, and materialities of the music culture.

Fernando Resende is Associate Professor in Culture and Media Studies at the Federal Fluminense University (UFF) in Niterói, Rio de Janeiro, Brazil; the local coordinator of Erasmus Mundus Joint Doctorate in 'Cultural Studies in Literary Interzones' (EACEA), and the Joint Research Project 'Literary Cultures of the Global South' (Universität Tübingen/DAAD); Visiting Scholar (CNPq) at the School of Oriental and African Studies (SOAS – University of London); and Visiting Professor at the Universidade de Coimbra (Portugal), Université Perpignan (France), Universidad Nacional Autónoma de Mexico (Mexico), and Universität Tübingen (Germany). Primarily interested in the study of narratives of conflicts and diasporic movements, dealing with issues related to both physical and symbolic zones, his research focuses on theory and philosophy of communication; journalism; culture; comparative media and documentary studies; global south theory; critical cultural studies and the impact of geopolitical discursive relations (narratives and conflicts) on the imaged geographies of East/West, and, in particular, the imagination of Palestine and Africa by Brazil and England (19th and 20th centuries). He has published numerous articles and book chapters on Brazilian media coverage and representations (press and documentaries) of the 2003 invasion of Iraq, the Israeli/Palestinian conflict, and the Afro-Muslim slaves' conflicts in Brazil.

Roberto Robalinho is a Postdoctoral Fellow in the Teach@Tübingen program at Tübingen Universität. He received his PhD in Communications from the Institute of Arts and Communications at Universidade Federal Fluminense in Brazil. His research focuses on the relation between images and their political and subjective production during Brazil's 2013 mass street protests. Roberto won the Prêmio Biblioteca UFF 2012/2013 prize and published a book on the relation between the Iraq War and image based on his master's research. He has also lectured in the Media and Cultural Studies Department at Universidade Federal Fluminense. He has directed a series of short films and is in pre-production of his first long feature film that a won an important public grant, a documentary that visits the geographical and symbolic landscape of João Guimarães Rosa's literature.

Luca Romani received both bachelor's and master's degrees in Foreign Language and Literature from the University of Milan. Afterwards, he participated in the European PhD program Erasmus Mundus Joint

CONTRIBUTORS

Doctorate, attending classes – mainly focused on experimental poetry and its relationship with new media – while developing his own research for a PhD degree in Cultural Studies in Literary Interzones. His thesis, titled 'Sound in Brazilian and German Concrete Poetry' and defended at UFF (Brazil) in 2016, aimed to return to sound poetry its physical presence and materiality. He participated in several international conferences all around Brazil and Europe and published some articles and chapters in peer-reviewed reviews/books.

Cobus van Staden is a Senior Researcher at the South African Institute of International Affairs, focusing on China-Africa relations. He is a visiting lecturer at the Department of Media Studies at the University of the Witwatersrand. He is also the co-founder of the China-Africa Project, one of the web's largest resources on China-Africa issues.

SERIES EDITORS' PREFACE

The 'global south' is a descriptive and analytical term that has recently come to the fore across a broad range of social sciences disciplines. It takes on different inflections in varying disciplinary contexts: as a mere geographical descriptor, denoting a network of geopolitical regions, primarily in the Southern Hemisphere, with a common history of colonization; driven by processes of transformation (the global south has and continues to be the site of an ongoing neo-colonial economic legacy as also of a number of emergent global economies such as India, China, Brazil, and South Africa); as an index of a condition of economic and social precarity which, though primarily manifest in the 'global *south*,' is also increasingly visible in the north (thus producing a '*global* south'); and, finally, as a utopian marker, signifying a fabric of economic exchanges that are beginning to bypass the northern economies and, gradually, a framework for political cooperation, especially from 'below,' which may offer alternatives to the hegemony of the Euro-American 'north.'

Literary cultures are a particularly pregnant site of south-south cultural analysis as they represent the intersection of traditional and modern cultural forms, of south-south (and north-south) cultural exchange, particularly via modes of translation and interlingual hybridization, and refract various discourses of knowledge in a highly self-reflexive and critical fashion, thereby demanding and enabling an interdisciplinary dialogue with literary studies at its core. Hallowed connections between literary production and the postcolonial *nation* notwithstanding, *transnational* south-south literary connections have usually marked the (anti-)colonial, postcolonial, and indeed contemporary digital epochs. Thus, literary cultures form one of the central historical and contemporary networked sites of intercultural self-articulation in the global south.

This series intervenes in the process and pre-empts the sort of bland institutionalization which has forestalled much of the intellectual force of postcolonial studies or the more recent world literature studies. It proposes

PREFACE

wide-ranging interventions into the study of the literary cultures of the global south that will establish an innovative paradigm for literary studies on the disciplinary terrain up until now occupied by the increasingly problematized areas of postcolonial studies or non-European national literary studies. The series contributes to the re-writing of cultural and literary history in the specific domain of the literary cultures of the global south. It attempts to fill in the many gaps left by Euro-American-dominated but ultimately 'provincial' northern cultural histories. The study of the literary cultures of the global south 'swivels' the axis of literary interrelations from the colonizer-colonized interface which, for instance, has preoccupied postcolonial literary studies since its inception (and which inevitably informed the 'national' compartmentalization of postcolonial literary study even when it averted its gaze from the colonizer). Instead, the series explores a set of 'lateral' relationships which have always existed but have been until now largely ignored – and which, in an age of digital communication and online cultural production have begun to emerge, once again, into their properly prominent position.

Russell West-Pavlov
Makarand R. Paranjape

ACKNOWLEDGEMENTS

The editors would like to thank Russell West-Pavlov for inviting us to lead on this edited collection, as well as all the participants in the Global South Literary Cultures network, specifically those who attended the October 2015 conference in Tübingen. We also thank Katlego Disemelo for his assistance in finalizing the manuscript.

Mehita Iqani would like to thank colleagues in the School of Literature Language and Media at the University of Witwatersrand (Wits) in Johannesburg for introducing her to the network and thereby opening up the opportunity to work on this book, as well as her colleagues and students in Media Studies at Wits, who provide daily support and inspiration.

Fernando Resende would like to thank Andree Gerland for all the support throughout the development of the Global South Project, and his colleagues and students at the Graduate Program in Communication at Universidade Federal Fluminense (UFF/Brazil) for their support and cooperation.

1

THEORIZING MEDIA IN AND ACROSS THE GLOBAL SOUTH

Narrative as territory, culture as flow

Mehita Iqani and Fernando Resende

This book is one of the first edited collections to tackle head-on the question of what the notion of the 'global south' means to media studies. Although in the study of media and communication the ideas of globalization, development, and conditions of postcoloniality have been interrogated in great detail, insufficient attention has been paid to the resonance of the idea – conflicted and fractious as it might be – of the global south. By bringing together original empirical work from media scholars from across the global south along the themes of narrative territorialities and cross-cultural currents, this book aims to interrogate the possibilities of thinking from the south in the field of media, communications, and cultural studies. In order to contextualize the diverse collections of chapters, which explore different aspects of what media mean and how they function in the global south, written by researchers from a wide variety of cultural, linguistic, and political contexts, it is useful to make a case for the particular framing of global south media that we take here, which prioritizes ideas of narrative and territory, culture and flow, and their interrelatedness. First, by way of introduction, it is necessary to take a moment to consider how the idea of the south can usefully be theorized in the context of media studies.

Re-theorizing the south in media studies

Throughout the history of cultural theory, the depiction of global politics has taken a binary shape. Starting with the rise of industrialized modernity and imperialist expansion from Europe, the idea of the rest of the world as peripheral and the origin of colonial oppressors as central became firmly established in the Western imagination. As Edward Said has shown

(1978, 1994), various forms of cultural production, from the opera to the novel, were tightly involved in the social construction of the idea of the metropole and colony and contributed directly to the political and economic expansion that took place. From this perspective, media – broadly defined as any form of cultural production or communicative technology – were intricately involved in the work of imperialism. This legacy persists. The centre-periphery binary has been re-articulated from different disciplinary perspectives. Those working in development and economics have articulated a sense of the developed and under-developed – more recently called developing – worlds. Those working in international politics have worked with ideas of the first and third worlds (originally articulated by Mao, where China and its sphere of influence was considered the 'second' world), and much nostalgia is directed towards the unfulfilled potential of the non-aligned movement during the Cold War (Craggs, 2014; Dodds, 2014). And more recently, the notion of a global north and south has emerged. The idea of the global south seeks to draw links across nations and societies that share a history of exclusion and oppression but also to highlight ways in which those histories are not necessarily confined to specific geographical boundaries (Hofmeyr, 2007; Levander and Mignolo, 2011; Prashad, 2014). The global south exists in industrialized, westernized countries (think post-Katrina New Orleans and overcrowded, under-resourced migrant camps in Calais), and the global north exists in highly unequal, developing economies (think luxury retail spaces in São Paulo and Johannesburg and the rise of middle-class groupings all over Asia, Africa, and Latin America). To what extent is this new vocabulary of the global south merely a reworking of old binaries, and to what extent does it present a new framework with which to develop our thinking about the role of media in a non-Western-centric global culture? To some extent, yes, the idea of the global north is a stand-in for the 'West,' while the 'global south' serves a similar function for 'the rest.' But arguably, the term 'global south' (which we intentionally leave uncapitalized in order to signal its non-paradigm-defining status) allows us to think with it in slightly more complex and dynamic ways than allowed by the vocabulary of 'developing' or 'third' world. Seeing 'global south' as a contradictory term, which contains within it a sense of non-alignment, or slippage (Hofmeyr, 2014), allows it to be seen as a more fertile choice of vocabulary.

> the term 'global south' is intended to summarize certain empirical commonalities, to capture the other side of western binary in an affirming vocabulary that does not depart only from a position of deficiency (as does the term, non-west, for example), that 'speaks back' by bringing together into one analytical project some of

the cross-cutting flows and tensions relevant to contexts in Asia, Africa and Latin America without homogenizing their disparate and unique characteristics.

(Iqani, 2016, p. 4)

In media studies, much attention has been paid to questions of globalization: economic, cultural, political, and social. Indeed, many writings have been published exploring these issues in great depth and making arguments about the historic and contemporary inter-connectedness between media texts and technologies and globalization (Hafez, 2005, 2013; Mazzarella, 2004; Rantanen, 2005). Similarly, significant swathes of area studies scholars have turned their attention to questions organized around the media. African, Asian, and Latin American studies have, while maintaining a focus on their particular regions, expanded to include broad questions about the consumption, production, and messaging of local, national, and regional forms and seeing the emergence of journals devoted to regional media studies, such as the *Journal of African Media Studies*, the *Asian Journal of Communication*, and *Contracampo – Brazilian Journal of Media Studies*. As well as this, a new preoccupation with questions of cultural diaspora has arisen in media studies, with growing numbers of scholars looking at the role that media play in transnational ethnic communities that have dispersed across the globe (Georgiou, 2005; Hall, 1990). Also relevant is the rise of research that looks at international communication from an intentionally non-Western bias (Ba and Higbee, 2012; Curran and Park, 2005; Wang, 2010) and a focus on international economic alliances that exclude the West, such as BRICS (Brazil, Russia, India, China, and South Africa), and the media (Thussu and Nordenstreng, 2015). From all of these perspectives, non-Western contributions to media studies scholarship have played, and continue to play, very central roles in shaping the field. Why, then, is it useful to bring in what may seem to be an overarching concept – the global south – to what is already a very vibrant and arguably dynamically de-westernizing scholarly scene?

One response could be that even though media studies are increasingly global in scope and diverse in cultural, national, ethnic, and linguistic enrichments, there is still a significant power imbalance between the north and south in the field. Western universities and scholars based there remain better funded (and receive those funds in much more powerful currencies), better supported and better resourced than scholars in the south, and as such they tend to dominate conference settings and scholarly publications, often also controlling the latter as gatekeepers and editors. Add to this the global dominance of writings in English in the academy broadly speaking, and we could argue that it remains crucial to actively seek new avenues for destabilizing the existing global power structures within the discipline while actively making space for the foregrounding of the research, writings, and theories of those still to some extent or another marginalized. Also crucial – although this volume is not able to meet this challenge – is the publishing of scholarly research in indigenous languages.

Thus far we have discussed how the idea of the 'global south' – an intentionally complex strategy of speaking back – can be useful in media studies. But arguably the converse is also true. The dynamic, ever-evolving, and consistently rich field of studies can also bring important contributions to the nascent theory of the global south itself. There has been a significant amount of writing recently that critically examines the potential of theory from the south (Comaroff and Comaroff, 2012; Connell, 2007). But very little of this has given due focus to the role of media in this new form of cultural theory. While it would be easy to write this off as a typical form of arrogance from theorists, who often come from the more 'established' disciplines and who still, erroneously, think of media studies as somehow less serious scholarship, it would be more productive to consider this gap in their thinking as an opportunity to develop it further by bringing in media-centric concepts and arguments. Contemporary thinking about the global south – an emerging area of theory in its own right – is incomplete without due consideration being placed on narrative forms, both analogue and digital, both traditional and sub-cultural. From news to music cultures, from journalism to selfie sharing, from screen forms to culture-jamming, contemporary popular forms of communication are important empirical areas that deserve ongoing theorization and study, not only from the perspective of globalization but also from the perspective of 'southern' theory.

This book aims to further explore the complexities of theories of the 'global south' through the prism of research into media and communications. Our aim in this volume is double: first, to present important research coming from southern contexts to a global audience, and second, to present important research that explores connections and flows between southern (and sometimes northern) settings. We theorize these two approaches as concerned with narrative territorialities and cross-cultural currents. In what follows, we present a framework for each of these conceptual positions and show how each of the chapters in the volume engages with, extends, or complicates each thematic. At the outset we should note that we do not conceptualize narrative territoriality and cross-cultural flow as binaries but rather as interconnected and juxtaposed in complex ways. Indeed, many of the chapters collected here succeed in demonstrating how both rootedness in specific geographies and cultures *and* exposure to influences from elsewhere are important components of global south mediations.

Narrative territorialities

It seems important to consider the points from where this book departs on what relates to the concepts of communication and media. Paul Ricoeur (2005) puts a challenge to us by stating that the enigma of communication is, after all, to make encounters happen. According to him, the paradox of communication happens somewhere beyond what one comprehends as sensory, an intriguing perspective that is based on the idea of discourse as a site where gaps are always produced.

If it is so, we argue, communication, rather than existing as an act, is a phenomenon – a potentially dialogical and collective phenomenon, which is also consistently intertextual and cultural. In different terms, we can also say communication is a phenomenon where the issue of alterity is constitutive and, therefore, a rather conflicting and somehow unpredictable gesture – a fact that makes us reflect about the gaps to which Ricoeur refers because they strongly emphasize the role played by media: to convey meanings, but more than that, to produce sensation and engage people. And for such a purpose, one understands, media is not only a technological issue but a question of how agency and intersubjectivities take place.

From this point of view, media narratives turn out to be fundamental tools that help us reflect about how and in which forms subjectivities, powers, and affects are intertwined. If one understands media narratives as important systems of representation (and we can here also argue whether media itself is a narrative in multiple modalities and forms), through which media tell us what the world is (or is not), the narratives themselves cannot be neglected.

For Homi Bhabha (2012), for instance, 'the very nature of narrative' is to raise issues on 'the otherness, power relations and contradictions/paradoxes' from a cultural/political perspective, an important argument if one is to discuss media and the production of what could (not) be south(ern) and/or north(ern). Besides all that, narratives do travel north and/or south. Either vertically or horizontally flowing, they not only portray knowledge and forms of living from elsewhere but also build, invent, and produce imagined territories.

Thus, territory becomes an important concept in order to understand the complex relation between media and the global south. Zambrano (2001, p. 29) understands territory as 'an either real or imagined space,' somehow occupied or used by a nation or a group of people that, in conflict with others, constantly produces senses of belonging. For this author, territory is 'humanized, cultivated, represented, and so forth,' and it 'generates cultural behaviours, legends, fears and toponyms.' A territory is plural, according to Zambrano, and being so, part of a constant fight because it is 'a sort of palimpsest of representations that stratifies histories, which are conflictingly juxtaposed' (2001, p. 31).

Once expanded to what Milton Santos (2014) takes as a 'territorial configuration,' territory is nonetheless a 'production of an inhabited space,' where various technologies and techniques, means of production, objects, and subjects are constantly colliding and therefore always in charge of reinventing distinct forms of existing. A sense of a dispute in the formation of a territory, in both authors, helps us understand the territorial perception as part of a structured and structuring process. In other words, a territory is never finished, and thus, within it, territorialities are constantly being produced.

If understood as what mobilizes the sense of belonging, the idea of territoriality, according to Zambrano, is fundamental in the process of the 'social construction of the territory, as it produces a phenomenon that is similar to the imagined community, a symbolic connection with the territory, which is capable of generating identification among distinct perceptions' (2001, pp. 31-32). This book takes this process of dispute as part of the problem of media and the global south in the sense that it understands narratives – and most importantly, media narratives – as significant parts of the fight.

In the media territory, as well as in the territory we all experience as part of our (everyday) lives, narratives are constantly flowing and conflicting and, therefore, inevitably producing distinct territorialities. There is an ongoing game of power and affection, where representations are always effectively mobilizing senses of belonging and non-belonging, reverberating, generating, producing, and inventing territories.

South and/or north, in this sense, are understood as cultural and political histories, narrated spaces within the realm of disputes. That is a way to understand space as part of social construction and relations (Lefebvre, 1993), and that is how we also suggest narratives to be seen: they elicit spatialities, inventing and evoking geographies (Resende, 2014). Within this framework, we intend to deal with the idea of global south as a discursive construction, which is part of a system of power relations that produces imaginaries and knowledge. Therefore, by juxtaposing this approach to narrative with the idea of space as a social phenomenon – which necessarily implies an unequal accumulation of times (Santos, 2007) – global south, from the media point of view, is here also seen as constitutive of cultural and political disputes.

The role media narratives play in this context seems to be extraordinary since it is from and within these narratives that people also interpret and build their understandings of inhabited spaces. In this sense, this book seeks to primarily discuss and present such issues from the idea that global south can be conceptualized as inscribed within a 'narrative territoriality.' The objective is to understand media and global south issues as actually being constitutive and constituent of (within and from) this territoriality, which is to say that media are not only inscribed in a territory (the global south) but are also responsible for producing narratives about it.

Amina El-Halawani's chapter, by discussing three Egyptian plays, very well presents the idea of how imaginaries (including north/south time and space configurations) are built throughout narrations. The stage frames the world, Amina El-Halawani somehow suggests, (re)producing the binary division between us and them and, therefore, reverberating and also creating and inventing territories. By comparing journalistic practices from and carefully looking at two specific countries, Lebanon and Egypt, Harb discusses similar issues through a completely different approach. Can we speak of a universal journalism culture in the Arab world, or are there specific contexts (time and space) that shape the culture and role of journalism? What is the relation between specific locations and the territorialities expressed in media practices, such as journalism?

Memory, within this framework, is by all means a very important instrument or strategy that helps us understand how and from which perspectives these collisions take place so as to configure the territory in which media narratives are inscribed. Goulart Ribeiro's chapter, for instance, places the problem from an open concept of memory, where remembering and forgetting are both parts of the same coin, and this way helps us build this argument by referring to media and its 'diverse mnemonic practices' as part of a 'nostalgia market.' There is a certain territoriality being produced by (and within) this process, which seems to be important to consider in terms of our understanding of certain roles media play in the context of Brazil.

Reinforcing this same framework and argument, Koba's reflection, by proposing a discussion about issues related to power and porn, puts emphasis on the fact that there is a straight connection between race and pornography. The narrative territoriality being built from this perspective, which is grounded in and involves specificities related to South Africa, trespass physical boundaries, not only because consumption is seen as part of a power game but also, and more than that, because the promiscuous relations between media and capitalism are thus uncovered. Though not a South African invention, in that particular territory, one may gather, such relation finds its own forms of subsistence. Is there a south in that? And if so, from which extent, and more importantly how, is it global?

Further inquiries, discussing media and geopolitical interests, are certainly needed. But this book also suggests the recognition of a certain narrative territoriality does not imply defining and limiting physical geographical locations. It is the way the relation is built, within and from a mediatized and geopolitical system, which is somehow the focus of our understanding about how the global south is also part of an invented process.

From Pereira de Sá's piece, YouTube in Brazil becomes a site from where this territoriality is built. Along with the idea of an 'aesthetic cosmopolitanism,' an approach that guides us to certain ways through which global south is produced, the narrative territoriality invented by funk music in Rio de Janeiro, enables us to understand, as the author says, how 'informational territories [. . .] produce symbolic, affective and economic belonging.' This chapter, for the purpose of this book, helps us become aware of how close the relation is between media (locative and mobile, in that case) and the production of a territory.

Such an approach suggests that media and global south be seen as co-related instances; they activate the problems into which we place our research issues. For this reason, this framework puts the question of arguing upon a relational epistemological position, one that deals with the 'anthropos,' as suggested by Mignolo (2003). By counterpointing 'humanitas' as a universal principle that helped build a system of knowledge production affected by the perspective of a modern/colonial world, Mignolo indicates that in order to critically think from a decolonial project, one ought to argue about how to account histories not only from inside the modern world but also, and mainly, from its borders. For such a purpose, Mignolo argues, there are no fixed categories but social/cultural/political contexts and power relations within which a certain thought must be regarded and produced.

This means being critical towards the 'epistemic obedience' – which has long been part of the process of implementing colonialities of power – and at the same time proposing a thought much more connected to what he understands as a 'geopolitics of sensing and knowing' (Mignolo, 2011). The 'anthropos,' as a perspective that considers the presence of the other, and therefore the complex relations between local histories and global projects, by raising questions related to enunciation processes, knowledges, and practices, for instance, would be an effective theoretical and epistemological path.

Thus, some basic questions to follow the whole argument within the framework of this book are: Would an epistemological question need to be raised when it comes to thinking about media and global south? Would there be any need to think about any particular problem concerning the global south, and are there specificities in such a case? Or instead, would one need to be aware of a specific media theme and/or problem, and only then ask about the territory from where it comes?

Lozano de la Pola's and Robalinho's chapters might give us some clues, as they both discuss topics related to (and derived from) a certain 'epistemological problem.' Lozano de la Pola, by making what she calls a 'visual criticism' on images taken from independent Mexican publications, discusses the need of building theoretical tools 'from' the south, so as to enable 'other bodies be made to appear.' Her reading of the '*cuir*' images (a word, which refers to queer, but closer, as the author proposes, to Latin American linguistic context) is an important way to think about south as a territory, which is built (and therefore invented) from and with linguistic and theoretical concerns.

On the same direction, but from a distinct thematic and location, Robalinho proposes an epistemological perspective that considers the risk of being in what the author understands as a transcrossing position: one that regards images as located in a certain context (the 2013 Brazilian protests, in his case), and as part of a process that understands politics, subjects, and space as aesthetically produced. Both Lozano de la Pola and Robalinho, therefore, are worried about ways to consider the complex relation between subjects/objects, as they claim the need for us to understand the process of producing a narrative territoriality demands, many times, deepening the question about knowledge production.

The fact that Robalinho also puts a question from issues related to capitalism ('would this need to be reconsidered from the perspective of a south?') and that Lozano de la Pola argues upon issues related to queer and gender concerns takes us straight to Ligaga's 'new femininities and the neoliberal world.' According to Said (1994, p. xviii), 'the power to narrate, or to block other narratives from forming and emerging, is very important to culture and imperialism, and constitutes one of the main connections between them.' Once again, narrative territorialities, when considering media and the global south, demand close looks at contexts and grounded terrains, but in no way may they disregard the fact that this terrain is made of various layers of power and affection.

Cross-cultural currents

As discussed up to this point, a number of chapters in this volume highlight well the conceptual framing linked to questions of the intersection between narrative and territory. But these same chapters also show how the book is also concerned with questions to do with the flow of media narratives, forms, and practices *across* boundaries.

Goulart Ribeiro's chapter discusses nostalgia as a global media thematic and shows how it cuts across national and linguistic boundaries. A variety of global media texts, those that originate in the West as well as in important global south nodes such as Brazil, are increasingly treating historical narrative as a basis for escapism but also commentary on contemporary society.

The cross-border flow of these texts highlights an important aspect to the role that global south markets and audiences play in the global media economy and also suggests that some narrative thematics cut across geographic, cultural, and linguistic boundaries.

Similarly Lozano de la Pola's chapter, which presents a new vocabulary for theorizing queer identity and experience in Latin America, argues that, without discounting the importance of vernacular forms of naming and the need to decolonize theories rooted in the West, queerness is a condition that is at once universal to all human societies and indigenous to many global south contexts, rather than something imported. In the context of threats to LGBTQIA individuals and communities in some global south countries, this argument takes on a pressing urgency.

Ligaga's fantastically rich chapter provides an interesting counterpoint with its focus on gender performance. We are invited to conceptualize *Nairobi Diaries*, a television reality show that follows the lives of seven Nairobi-based 'socialites' in Kenya, as an iteration of a global media genre organized around the postfeminist sensibility. From this perspective, although the TV show is rooted in specific vernacular culture, the influence of global cultural flow is a key to unlocking its social significance. The television show positions the women as global, neoliberal subjects who are on par with similar women in the West, without undermining their unique Kenyan and African qualities.

Koba's piece on the consumption of pornography in South Africa raises the question of how media products that become global through their broad, digital distribution around the world are enthusiastically received and consumed regardless of the viewer's own ethnic identities or personal racial preferences in relation to sex. Although the chapter provides detailed empirical insights into only one national and cultural setting, it links in with global audience and porn studies by centring the question of the role of race in the consumption of sexually explicit material, something that is by no means restricted to specific nations.

Pereira de Sa's study of YouTube video clips from the funk scene in Rio de Janeiro, Brazil, shows how even media or cultural practices that are rooted in very specific localities become cross-cultural and globally accessible precisely due to their digital mediation. This raises the possibility of extending south-south cultural connections and understanding through shared affinities for popular culture forms and increasingly accessible digital platforms. Similar thematics are explored in Luca Romani's chapter on concrete poetry and the avant-garde across Germany and Brazil.

Roberto Robalinho's chapter argues that protest is a form of spectacular political action which, when visually mediated, can enter mainstream discourses and shift structures and relationships of power. Although social

MEDIA IN AND ACROSS THE GLOBAL SOUTH

discontent grows in many countries in the world, often expressed through protest, through media representation, inherently global as it is, connections can be made between struggles that may otherwise seem separate. The knitting together of precise local dissatisfactions into a bigger fabric of resistance against neoliberal culture is perhaps the most exciting possible outcome of increasing cross-cultural flow within and across the global south. These chapters remind us that questions of cross-cultural flow and global media culture do not displace those of narrative territoriality, or vice versa, but they exist in a complex and dynamic tension.

That said, there are also inherently transnational and cross-cultural media forms that animate the condition, culture, and politics of the global south. As theorized by Arjun Appadurai, the postmodern, postcolonial global landscape is defined by a number of cultural, financial, and media flows (Appadurai, 1996). There is a long-standing tradition in media studies that is concerned with transnational comparative research, which in media and communications research is increasingly important and complex. As Livingstone argues, communication does not 'respect national boundaries' and as such careful thought needs to be given to the salience and necessity for transnational approaches to doing research in the field (Livingstone, 2003, p. 478). Indeed, many might argue that media are inherently transnational. Global and national media companies are deeply invested in the international media economy, the trading and syndicating of media commodities, and the selling of audiences to advertisers. The political economy of media is inherently globalized: not only do Western media corporations continuously seek new markets in the global south, but corporations within the south – such as Brazil's Globo, South Africa's Multichoice, Qatar's Al Jazeera, and China's Alibaba – are increasingly engaged in cross-border trade and marketization. 'Informal' economies, such as the Nollywood video industry, are also booming, and the production and dissemination of media material in modes unique to non-Western contexts are receiving increasing attention from scholars.

Audiences of certain global media products are transnational, sometimes even unified around specific media events (such as huge sporting competitions). Southern audiences are voracious consumers of media narratives produced in the global north as well as locally and regionally produced images. But there is also a south-south flow in discourses and fandom, which requires deeper theorization. Mexican and Turkish soap operas are hugely popular in the Middle East. Japanese cartoons were dubbed into Afrikaans in apartheid-era South Africa. Teenage girls all over Africa idolize Beyoncé but also their own local stars, all the while producing and sharing their own selfies over a variety of social media networks. The rise of a plethora of social media platforms has allowed citizens to mediate their identities and lives in ever more creative ways, all of which have global reach.

11

If we accept that all media cultures are inherently global, be it due to global production processes, and/or the trans-nationality of audiences whether actual or potential, an important question arises as to the extent to which south-south flows constitute that globalness. What happens when media objects, narratives, or practices (in addition to forms of media production and capital) cross borders and flow in unique ways globally – be it only across the global south or between the north and south? What kinds of ideas flow, and how do different origins and destinations affect not only the routes but also the trajectory, speed, and influences of those media movements? Many forms of media (objects, texts, practices) are global both in terms of their narrative content and in terms of their technological form, and this 'globalness,' contested and fractious though it might be, needs to be given due theoretical consideration. What this volume brings to the conversation about the inherent globalness of media is ways of thinking about that globalness as not inherently directed or defined by the north.

Amina El-Halawani's chapter on narrative in three Egyptian plays may at first seem to fit best with the theme of territoriality, but in fact it examines an age-old thematic in global cultural politics. By exploring in detail how north-south geopolitical and historical relations are represented in the plays, an important contribution is made to thinking about how cultural imperialism is re-loaded in postcolonial times. It also forces us to keep our definitions of media intentionally broad and to see theatre as a powerful form of popular communication.

Zahera Harb's chapter presents findings from research with journalists in Lebanon and Egypt. These important and original empirical perspectives help to develop our existing understandings of how journalists see their work, both in general in a context of increasing pressure on newsrooms around the world, and in the specific setting of the Middle East. This study shows that although there are really important 'territorial' aspects to media research in global south settings, there are also often cross-cutting cultural issues that need to be taken into account.

Cobus van Staden presents a summary of how China-Africa relations have been mediated in two broad strokes, where China is presented as both helper and threat to Africa, as both ally and neo-imperial colonizer. He argues that this case study forces us to rethink what we mean by the global south, as China itself straddles the status of developed and developing. Indeed this argument could be applied to other nations, like Brazil, India, and South Africa, which all exhibit a wealthy elite and growing middle class alongside persistently poor masses. These case studies show that the categories of global north and south do not follow geographical boundaries but are fractured across them and evident always within all nations, which forces us to think more carefully about how to theorize the role of media in those fracturing processes of division and alignment. As such, although it is useful to an extent to think about the global south as mediated either from the position of territory or from the position of cross-territorial flow, we argue that it is more useful still to think about these conditions as juxtaposed, inseparable, and interrelated.

Flowing narratives, cross-cultural territories: concluding remarks

Dina Matar's chapter explores how Palestine serves as a metaphor for imagined global south spatialities. Here we see the idea of cross-cultural flow in full force, as the discursive operations of media and culture combine to create a powerful set of ideas that are inherently international in scope and humanist in ethics. In a propositional approach, once it goes beyond the common sense in which is based the criticism towards the Israeli/Palestinian conflict, Matar also helps us understand how territories, for the reason of being plural, are at the same time cultural and political.

Narratives on and about that specific conflict, for its long-term duration and cultural effects it produces, for the power and affection inscribed in that specific territory, and for the reason of being accounts derived from the perspective of a violated geography (Resende, 2017), might perhaps help us comprehend how both narrative territoriality and cross-cultural flow are key aspects to theorizing both media and the global south – as co-related instances.

It is the intersection of these ideas that activates the problem into which we contextualize the research issues examined in the book. From this perspective, the book suggests that reflecting about these issues and the questions depends on the ways in which they are approached (the theoretical frameworks and analytical tools) and the means through which they propagate and are produced. In order to do that, this book also suggests that

> opening the map of the so-called 'global south' from the perspective of the Middle East, Africa, Latin America, and many other 'souths' around the globe might be very productive, once from there, the global south can be seen as part of a complex spatiality. From this point of view, the gesture of understanding the term should also be the act of mapping existences and differences, which have constantly been disregarded by the games of power. This perspective, as it has been suggested, might be a way of unfolding narratives, and it certainly requires suspicious acts and willingness to produce different writings.
>
> (Resende, 2014, n.p.)

The book is, in this sense, the effort of staging different ways of approaching problems and issues related to media studies and the global south, taking into account the ideas of 'narrative territoriality' and 'cross-cultural currents' as fundamental for considering media's representation and the production of meaning. The chapters that follow are organized so as to begin with the ideas of narrative territoriality and then to progress into international comparisons and on towards global imaginaries. These boundary-crossing studies will allow the reader to 'follow the media object' and understand more about the many types of flow that constitute global south media cultures today.

This is not to suggest that there is some kind of magic explanatory power to the idea of the global south that can be easily deployed in media studies. But there is something interesting that comes up when we shift attention away from old paradigms of power and think about how narrative is rooted and flows in different ways – south to south, within and across languages, in translation or through the global language of the image – and by so doing brings into being a new kind of global culture which is not necessarily, at all, dependent on a northern power differential.

As the collection of work here shows, there is always something 'global' about a media phenomenon that exists within a specific territory, be it imagined, cultural, or political. And so too is the converse true: there is always something inherently rooted to a specific place and time in media phenomena that insistently transgresses national boundaries and enters into global media culture. In order to fully explore and theorize what the status of global south thinking does for media, and what media theory in turn does for the concept of the global south, it is necessary to extend an analytical framework that can hold both the idea of flow and territory and which does not allow one to cancel out the other. As research and scholarship in media and communications increases in popularity, scope, and intensity throughout the world, and as more and more scholars from global south positions make their important contributions to global debates, we should expect to see an ongoing shift not only in the canon of key theories and ideas but in the very manner in which we conceptualize the world as mediated. This volume goes some way towards engaging that future conversation.

References

Appadurai, A. (1996). *Modernity At Large: Cultural Dimensions of Globalization*. Minneapolis, University of Minnesota Press.

Ba, S.M., and Higbee, W. (2012). *De-Westernizing Film Studies*. London & New York, Routledge.

MEDIA IN AND ACROSS THE GLOBAL SOUTH

Bhabha, H. (2012). Homi Bhabha e o valor das diferenças. *Jornal O Globo*, Rio de Janeiro, Brasil (http://blogs.oglobo.globo.com/prosa/post/homibhabha-o-valor-das-diferencas-426300.html)

Comaroff, J., and Comaroff, J. L. (2012). Theory from the South: Or, how Euro-America is Evolving Toward Africa. *Anthropological Forum*, 22(2), 113–131. https://doi.org/10.1080/00664677.2012.694169

Connell, R. (2007). *Southern Theory: The Global Dynamics of Knowledge in Social Science*. Cambridge, Polity Press.

Craggs, R. (2014). Development in a Global-Historical Context. In V. Desai and R. Potter (Eds.), *The Companion to Development Studies*, Third Edition (pp. 5–10). London & New York, Routledge.

Curran, J., and Park, M. J. (2005). *De-Westernizing Media Studies*. London & New York, Routledge.

Dodds, K. (2014). The Third World, Developing Countries, the South, Emerging Markets and Rising Powers. In V. Desai and R. Potter (Eds.), *The Companion to Development Studies, Third Edition* (pp. 5–10). London & New York, Routledge.

Georgiou, M. (2005). Diasporic Media Across Europe: Multicultural Societies and the Universalism – Particularism Continuum. *Journal of Ethnic and Migration Studies*, 31(3), 481–498. https://doi.org/10.1080/13691830500058794

Hafez, K. (2005). Globalization, Regionalization and Democratization: The Interaction of Three Paradigms in the Field of Mass Communication. In *Democratizing Global Media: One World, Many Struggles* (pp. 145–163). Maryland: Rowman & Littlefield.

Hafez, K. (2013). *The Myth of Media Globalization*. Cambridge: Polity.

Hall, S. (1990). Cultural Identity and Diaspora. *Identity: Community, Culture, Difference*, 2, 222–237.

Hofmeyr, I. (2007). The Black Atlantic Meets the Indian Ocean: Forging New Paradigms of Transnationalism for the Global South – Literary and Cultural Perspectives. *Social Dynamics*, 33(2), 3–32. https://doi.org/10.1080/02533950708628759

Hofmeyr, I. (2014). Against the Global South. In *WITS-Michigan Workshops*. Johannesburg, WISER, University of Johannesburg.

Lefebvre, H. (1993). *The Production of Space*. Oxford: Blackwell. 3a ed.

Levander, C., and Mignolo, W. (2011). Introduction: The Global South and World Dis/Order. *The Global South*, 5(1), 1–11. https://doi.org/10.2979/globalsouth.5.1.1

Livingstone, S. (2003). On the Challenges of Cross-National Comparative Media Research. *European Journal of Communication*, 18(4), 477–500. https://doi.org/10.1177/0267323103184003

Mazzarella, W. (2004). Culture, Globalization, Mediation. *Annual Review of Anthropology*, 33, 345–367.

Mignolo, W. (2003). *Histórias Locais/Projetos Globais – Colonialidade, Saberes Subalternos e Pensamento Liminar*. Belo Horizonte: UFMG.

MEHITA IQANI AND FERNANDO RESENDE

Mignolo, W. (2011). Geopolitics of Sensing and Knowing: On (De)Coloniality, Border Thinking, and Epistemic Disobedience. EIPCP – European Institute for Progressive Cultural Politics (http://eipcp.net/transversal/0112/mignolo/en)

Prashad, V. (2014). *The Poorer Nations: A Possible History of the Global South*. London and New York: Verso.

Rantanen, T. (2005). *The Media and Globalization*. London: SAGE.

Resende, F. (2014). The Global South: Conflicting Narratives and the Invention of Geographies. *IBRAAZ – Contemporary Visual Culture in North Africa and the Middle East*. 008/November (www.ibraaz.org/essays/111)

Resende, F. (2017). Imprensa e Conflito: narrativas de uma geografia violentada. In Ana Teresa Peixinho and Bruno Araújo (Eds. e Org.), *Narrativa e Media: géneros, figuras e contextos* (pp. 105–136). Coimbra: Imprensa da Universidade de Coimbra.

Ricoeur, P. (2005). Discours et communicacion. In *Cahier de L'Herne Ricoeur*. Paris: Editions de L'Herne, n.81.

Said, E.W. (1978). *Orientalism*. New Delhi: Penguin Books India.

Said, E.W. (1994). *Culture and Imperialism*. New York City: Vintage.

Santos, M. (2007). *Pensando o espaço do homem*. São Paulo: EDUSP.

Santos, M. (2014). *Metamorfoses do espaço habitado*. São Paulo: EDUSP.

Thussu, D.K., and Nordenstreng, K. (Eds.). (2015). *Mapping BRICS Media*. London: Routledge (www.sponpress.com/books/details/9781138026254/)

Wang, G. (2010). *De-Westernizing Communication Research: Altering Questions and Changing Frameworks*. London: Routledge.

Zambrano, C. (2001). Territorios plurales: cambio sociopolitico y gobernabilidad cultural. *Boletim Goiano de Geografia*, 21(I), 9–49, jan/jul.

2

IMAGINARIES OF THE NORTH AND SOUTH IN THREE EGYPTIAN PLAYS

Amina El-Halawani

Halt, friends, both! Let us weep, recalling a love and a lodging
by the rim of the twisted sands between Ed-Dakhool and Haumal,
Toodih and El-Mikrát, whose trace is not yet effaced
for all the spinning of the south winds and the northern blasts;
there, all about its yards, and away in the dry hollows
you may see the dung of antelopes spattered like peppercorns.

–Al-Qais, Imr (1957)

This is how Imru' al-Qais[1] starts his Mu'allaqa,[2] which dates back to the sixth century AD or earlier, by invoking space, place, geographies, time, and memory.[3] In what becomes a typical Arabic poetic tradition of starting an ode by *alboka' ala alatlal* or weeping over the traces of the tribes of their loved ones, Imru' al-Qais asks his friends to stop and weep. When the poem starts we are already in motion in both time and space, and his 'Halt' puts everything on pause while he moves in a different temporal spatiality 'recalling' his beloved and her home. In other words, despite accurately naming the places to which he refers, Imru' al-Qais is not merely lamenting a specific spot in the vast desert, or its geographical coordinates, but rather enacting a commemoration of his loved one and her dwelling place, which to him is what gives meaning to this locale, in an almost Lefebvrian sense. Hence, even the 'dung of antelopes' becomes a rich and important element in producing the space, which he constructs out of the camp traces that persist despite the winds of time. Time and space are inseparable here as Imru' al-Qais teaches us, but more importantly narrating them is a subjective process of continuous construction and deconstruction, as the northern and southern winds continue to work their way on the ruins while he tells the tale.

Although Imru' al-Qais's northern and southern winds were purely a natural phenomenon out to efface the traces left of his beloved's tribe as they roamed the deserts of Arabia to find a new campsite, the north and south in our contemporary world have become themselves spatial constructs, which carry within themselves narratives of conflict, effacement, and change. I say that with the realization that in a postmodern world it has become accepted to view history too as a narrative of time, space, and subjectivities, often conflicting and continuously in flux, where postcolonial voices incessantly challenge the prevalent hegemonic colonial narratives that have persisted for centuries. This chapter, hence, aims to address the issue of contested temporalities and threatened territorialities in three Egyptian openly anti-imperialist plays, namely, Saad Eldin Wahba's *El Masameer* (1967) [*Nails*], Mahdy Youssef and Mohamed Sobhi's *Mama Amrika* (1998) [*Mother America!*], and Lenin El-Ramly's *Bel Araby el Faseeh* (1992) [*In Plain Arabic*].

Theatre with its public audience can be argued to be the world's first form of mass media, yet what really differentiates it from other forms of media is its immediacy as an art form, which makes its discussions of spaces and temporalities all the more interesting. Theatre centres on bodily presence. Both performers and audiences have to exist in a shared space, and as such it is momentary and immediate. As a performed art, even though it may often be reliant on text, and in Egypt was even frequently televised, it still in very literal terms comes to life in a certain space and holds the present captive in the moment of the performance. What does it mean, then, when the theatre evokes the past, revisits it, and quite literally brings it into the present? This fusion of what has already taken place and what is happening now brings us to another essential question: What is past and what is present? And how much of the past is actually present? According to Edward Said,

> Appeals to the past are among the commonest of strategies in interpretations of the present. What animates such appeals is not only disagreement about what happened in the past and what the past was, but uncertainty about whether the past really is past, over and concluded, or whether it continues albeit in different forms.
>
> (Said, 1994, p. 3)

This highlights the centrality of history to the understanding of the world today. In other words, understanding colonial history and tracing the exercise of power coupled with the Euro-centric intellectual tradition for centuries, which have been studied thoroughly by postcolonial

IMAGINARIES OF THE NORTH AND SOUTH

theorists including Said, is a means of interpreting the present world order. As the world moved away from colonial times and former colonies have been acknowledged as independent states, world balance has not yet been restored. As West-Pavlov reminds us, '*Post*-colonialism is clearly a misnomer in a world in which colonialism lives on in neo-colonialism, and imperialism continues under another flag' (2013, p. 160).

What was often accomplished solely by military power in the strive for territory and dominion is in a way translated into economic advantage in a capitalist world. This entails a shift from a West/East dichotomy into a hierarchical classification of countries into North and South, where the South, as opposed to the rich North, bears all the baggage of the older 'oriental' subject, as ignorant, poor, and incapable. In his foreword to Fanon's *The Wretched of the Earth*, Homi Bhabha writes that 'With few exceptions, the cartography of the global south follows the contours of the Third World' (2004, p. xxvii)[4] and explains that 'Although times have changed [. . .] [n]ew global empires rise to enforce their own civilizing missions in the name of democracy and free markets' (Bhabha, 2004, p. xiv). It is through the creation of dual economies – inherent in the capitalist system that followed the Cold War – that some societies are left poor and vulnerable.

This reminiscing over lost pasts, akin to Imru' al-Qais's lamentation, and a reflection on a distorted world balance is a main concern of this chapter, particularly in the Middle East, where economic and territorial issues rise to the surface once a discussion of any future is at stake. As Bhabha suggests, 'The critical language of duality – whether colonial or global – is part of the *spatial* imagination that seems to come so naturally to geopolitical thinking' (2004, p. xiv) and as such keeps the world at odds, held in an everlasting tension between binary opposites, be it North and South, East and West, occupier and occupied, rich and poor, civilized and uncivilized, peaceful and violent/terrorist, and the list goes on.

Setting the stage

Identifying the spatial position from which one approaches the issue is thus important, because where these questions seem most polemic is of course in the South (the former East). So where is the stage on which such narratives are framed? Looking at three Egyptian plays as a case study, this chapter focuses on *El Masameer* (1967) [*Nails*], *Bel Araby El Faseeh* (1992) [*In Plain Arabic*] (trans. 1994), and *Mama Amrika* (1998) [*Mother America!*], and their representations of space and time in relation to the North and South.

Although Saad Eldin Wahba's play seems to belong to a different era (the late 1960s), it represents a turning point in both the theatre and the politics of Egypt and the whole region. The 1950s in Egypt were filled with much hope when after the 1952 revolution President Gamal Abdel Nasser had started propagating his ideals of a Pan-Arabism, which would not only liberate the Arab world from the grip of the West but would also free Palestine and promise the welfare of all. After all, the movement by the Free Officers 'was the culmination of seventy years of nationalist agitation that gripped Egypt since 1882, when another group of soldiers under the leadership of Ahmed al Urabi rebelled against the Egyptian monarchy,' as Cook puts it (2012, p. 12). And as such, the nationalization of the Suez Canal in 1956 was an important statement of liberty for the Nasserite regime. The act, however, was not taken lightly. The nationalization of the canal resulted in the Tripartite Aggression where Israel, joined by France and England, attacked Sinai in an attempt to seize control of the canal, but as the cities around the canal continued to resist and the UN pressured the aggressors to stop the war, the 1956 War was more a demonstration of the geopolitical makeup of the region than an actual loss. The war had made it clear that France and England had aligned their interests with the newly founded state of Israel against Nasser, who was now turning towards Russia.

The Arab defeat by Israel in 1967, however, was a different story. More of Palestine was lost; Israel had seized East Jerusalem, the Gaza Strip, and the West Bank, along with the Golan Heights in Syria and the Egyptian Sinai Peninsula; so there were already a handful of Arab countries physically involved in the conflict. The Defeat, or as it is known in Arabic, the 'Naksa' [setback], was the second darkest day in modern Arab history after the Nakba [the catastrophe] of the first occupation of Palestine in 1948, and hence the moment had its weight on the identity and the morale of the pan-Arab nation, as dreamt by Egyptian President Nasser, if ever such nation was meant to exist.

History re-told

Wahba's play was written right after the setback to epitomize the Egyptians' realization that not much on the global scene had actually changed, and that their dream of liberty was sabotaged with this new player in the region, who not only occupied Palestine but who also continued to show hostility and threaten further expansion. Directed by Saad Ardash, the play *El Masameer* [*Nails*] was staged in Cairo as a reaction to the Egyptian and Arab defeat in 1967 by Israel, and thus it has signs of frustration though it is also full of fervour for resistance, for the return of the land to its rightful owners, and for the overthrow of the occupier. The play evokes the national spirit of Saad Zaghlul and his belief in 'the final triumph of immanent justice' (Paris Peace Conference, 1919–1920).

IMAGINARIES OF THE NORTH AND SOUTH

Thus, instead of directly treating the recent war, the defeat, or even the foundation of the state of Israel, Saad Eldin Wahba chooses to set his play in a turbulent Egypt that is still demanding freedom from the British imperialist rule during the 1919 revolution. Wahba bases the work on two historical incidents mentioned in Abdel Rahman El Rafei's chronicle of the 1919 revolution, Kafr el Sheikh and Nazlet el Shobak (1987, p. 246, 295, 296). In Kafr el Sheikh, the British troops were looting the village and imposing a tax on the villagers in the form of daily flogging sessions to break their pride; while in Nazlet el Shobak, the British soldiers had seized the village, pillaged it, assaulted and raped women, and later took the village chief, his brother, son, and some other villagers, half-buried them in the sand, and then executed them without trial.

In choosing these incidents, Wahba is asking the very same question Said was suggesting: 'Is the past really past?' Wahba's play points to the continuity of history by digging out the British colonial 'past' and linking it to the present. Moreover, Wahba's trope equates the humiliation and loss of dignity associated with the flogging to the Egyptian and Arab defeat in 1967, which resulted in the occupation of the land.

More than 20 years later, one would expect things to have really changed, and yet we still find *In Plain Arabic* and *Mother America* to be hitting the same chords, though this time with a more bitter tone of frustration and much less of a fighting spirit. Much of the fervour for the cause is gone, and their portrayals of the Arab nations' relationship with the West/North is pinned upon more complicated views oscillating between self-blame and conspiracy theories to present a quasi-schizophrenic relationship between the South and the North, where the latter is often portrayed as villainous and cunning and at the same time as educated, cultured and civilized. The South literally *looks up* to the North for its prosperity and *looks down* on itself for its own disappointments and economic defeat vis-à-vis the North. In both plays, Arab nations are portrayed as petty, interest-driven rivals bickering amongst themselves and dragging one another down.

'Our land has been planted with nails' (Wahba)

In Wahba's play, the image of the 'land' in the relationship between oppressor and oppressed is central. The play is set in a village called Kafr, close to which the British soldiers have set a camp. The situation is already volatile; we learn that they have been killing villagers, raping some of their women, looting their goods, and so on. And we are told that the villagers have been resisting and causing casualties in the British lines as well. This constant image of endless violence in the play is solidified in the 'tax' the British impose on the villagers; 25 of them are to be flogged from morning to sunset every day. When the villagers get ready to defend themselves in the face of the next British attack, they are badly defeated and three of them are captured. And as in the historical incident of Nazlet el Shobak, they are buried alive and executed the next morning without any formal trial.

'El masameer' [nails], in the title, refer to the occupation, which Fatma, the main character, calls 'shoka fi dahrena' [a thorn in our back] in the prologue of the play. After Fatma's prologue, the curtains open to the villagers who are gathered to negotiate what should be done with those English soldiers who have killed some of their men. Some think that they should pursue their own interests and keep quiet, while others headed by Abdallah, Fatma's husband, and Salem, Fatma's uncle, refuse to give in. They think the only way out is to continue to resist and free the country. Evoking the damage that the British military presence has already caused, Abdallah continues his attempt to convince the villagers:

> Everything beautiful in our country is either lost already, or will be lost. The green plants that had covered the land are gone. They have planted the land with nails. Our land has been planted with nails, MEN! Nails! If we walk, we walk over nails, and if we eat we eat nails, and if we breathe the nails get stuck in the throat of every one of us to choke him and kill him. Fellow men, let's put our hands together to uproot the nails from the land so it can turn green again.
>
> (1.1, translation mine)

The image is a concrete one, in which the colonizer is seen as responsible for the decay of every beautiful thing in the country, and the land, which represents territory, home, and livelihood in the form of agriculture, is not only taken away but completely ruined. The empty space of the stage, occupied by the characters, some scattered trees, and a forsaken water mill, bears witness to Abdallah's words, which lament the now arid land's bountiful past.

Power is most obviously in the hands of the British, while the villagers seem tired and torn apart, even at times portrayed as womanly and weak when they show signs of despair. Wahba seems to equate manliness with power and the ability to fight back. Hence, while the manliness of the British soldiers themselves in not contested, because they hold the power, that of those who follow them from the Egyptian side is. Those who continue to resist, who get flogged, who stand for their rights are the 'men,' and though seemingly defeated are triumphant; while the others, who in Wahba's view have sold out on their land and their right, are heavily ridiculed (1.1). Even Fatma, whose valour is compared to that of a hundred men, is presented as more manly than Zeydan Bey, the pro-British landlord, his follower, Rashwan, or even Ramzy Effendi, the enlightened schoolteacher. Manliness in Wahba's dictionary becomes a sought-after category only achieved by those worthy of it, and those are the powerful and the brave. Sab'awy chooses to get flogged instead of others who can pay him, a subtle criticism of the dynamics of economic means within the society, but he also puts himself in the place of those who he thinks should not be flogged whether out of respect or pity for their health or age. However, taking a flogging as a job in lieu of tilling the land of a pro-British landlord, Sab'awy is seen as a figure of resistance. And yet the most powerful character in the whole play is Fatma El Halawani. There is a saying in Egypt, 'He who built Egypt was originally a *Halawani* [a pastry maker],' so the name becomes synonymous with Egyptian history, and Fatma becomes a metonymy of Egypt. Her strength, rebellious nature, and resistance withstand any form of colonial intervention, and thus there is hope for the country to recover from the fate that has been inflicted on it, despite the colonizer's momentary 'supremacy': Egypt will rise from the setback, which it did in 1973 under President Sadat.

The execution scene, though agonizing by being based on a true story, becomes a theatrical fulfilment of the return of the land, which now, having witnessed the sacrifice of its people, has started producing fruit, symbolized by the berry or sycamore tree Wahba describes in the setting. When Salem and two others are caught and asked to dig their own graves and then to stand inside them, the image of rootedness and unity with the land is hard to miss, and the stage becomes a glaring outcry for the right to the land; it is almost the land that is speaking through Salem's mouth, while George, the British representative, asks them in his broken Arabic why they kill British soldiers.[5]

GEORGE: Why you fight the British?
SALEM: I wish . . .
GEORGE: You wish what?
SALEM: I wish I could have gotten any of them, I would have crushed them with my teeth.
GEORGE: Why fight the British?
SALEM: Why the British fight us?
GEORGE: Because 'us' fight the British.
SALEM: The British are there. . . . Their country is at the other end of the world. . . . Why did they leave their country over there to come and fight us over here?
GEORGE: British come here to make a 'Human Being' out of you.
SALEM: No, I have seen everything.
GEORGE: What have you seen? (3.2, translation mine)

And Salem starts to enumerate all the atrocities he has seen committed by the British soldiers, from murder to robbery to rape.

These lines pose the deepest questions in the simplest logic. According to George's narrative, it is Salem and his brethren who are fighting the British. Salem confronts his executioner when he resorts to geographical referents to ask what seems like a simple question: what brings the British to their land anyway? Confounded by the answer, George reiterates the colonial discourse of a 'civilizing mission'; not only that, but in his worldview, the villagers/Egyptians are not even human beings per se, but they have to be turned into ones by their British patrons.

The obvious division of 'us' and 'them', or what Fanon describes as a compartmentalized colonial system, becomes even clearer in the portrayal of the British sympathizer Ramzy Effendi, an Egyptian teacher who is fascinated by British culture, civility, and progress. Ramzy Effendi is assured by his compatriots that while the British may have a great cultural repertoire, he may never be considered one of them or even worthy of listening to, and to his dismay they turn out to be right. Ramzy Effendi ends up in prison, not for complaining about the villagers' flogging but for complaining about his civilized friends' turning the school into stables for their horses.

Rashwan, who works for Zeydan Bey, and the right hand of the British forces, also ends up being flogged like the rest of the villagers. Even his master Zeydan Bey is humiliated and threatened with flogging as well, but then, as one of the characters suggests, the British seem to have found him still of use, and until they don't need him anymore he will remain in their good books. This suggests that the colonizer in the play is also perceived as an opportunist, who is not to be trusted due to being driven by interest and nothing else.

Wahba very much sees the world divided, and though there is a clear contestation of colonial legitimacy in Salem's discourse, in the scene right after the villagers' defeat there seems to be a questioning of their strength in comparison to that of the British. How could they beat us so badly? They blame themselves for trying to stand against the British unprepared for the havoc this would cause, which in a way illustrates a subconscious affirmation of, if not even admiration for, the 'military' supremacy demonstrated on their part.

Double vision and the new world order

Unlike Wahba's direct treatment of colonial times, Mohamed Sobhi's *Mama Amrika* [*Mother America*], a joint writing project with Mahdy Youssef but often referred to as Sobhy's because he was also the director of the work as well as the lead actor, shows us that not much in the

IMAGINARIES OF THE NORTH AND SOUTH

discourse of the 'self' and 'other' has changed, although the 'other' in this case becomes America – the character of Amira Kamel, and you can hear the pun, of course – and its political support for the state of Israel. In this play as well as in *In Plain Arabic*, to be discussed later in this chapter, the issue of the Arab self-portrayal becomes very complex. First staged in 1998, the play is a political satire, delivering some heavy-handed criticism of US Middle East policy, to the extent that it is said to have upset the US ambassador at the time. What is interesting about the play, however, is that it is as much critical, if not even more critical, of the Arab nations too. Like *El Masameer* the play also finds respite in a distant past, when the family of Manafe' [benefit/interest], which represents the disintegrated Arab states who now each care only for their own individual interests, gather to open their late father's will to discover that he had owned 'land' – so again mention of territory – which he distributes amongst them unequally and with one hitch. The land has long been 'stolen,' which in this case is an allegory for the loss of Palestine. Yet there is also a lament over the more remote years of colonization by Western forces, which left all these brothers divided and poor, with the exception of Brother Aboud, who represents the rich oil-producing countries. And within this frame, the whole play pivots on the brothers' attempt to revive their past and regain their right to their inheritance.

Especially in *Mama Amrika*, there seems to be a schizophrenic relationship between the South and the North (traces of which can already be seen in *El Masameer*). This is most evident in the scene where Amira Kamel, the rich businesswoman, arrives with her entourage, and Ayesh looks around with much fascination and identifies her part of the stage as America (rich) and his own part, which is filled only with a box of straw for a desk, as Somalia (i.e., poor), highlighting the gap between the two worlds. The play opens with an image of the Statue of Liberty in the background and a song that works like a prologue for the whole play, juxtaposing occidental and oriental music patterns, one referring to the United States and the other to the Arab world. The song, however, announces that the play presents the story of this young man who is fascinated by the American dream, in which the United States is presented as a conscience for the world and a holder of peace and justice. This is the dream Ayesh holds on to while facing the disintegration of his family house whose harmony is now disturbed because of the death of its patriarch and the loss of their family estate.

The names are very interesting in this respect. Sobhy plays the lead role of Ayesh Shehata Manafe', which literally translates into 'living on charity,' who is supposedly the educated brother, although he has been unsuccessfully trying to get a degree in law for seven years. Being a law student, Ayesh is in charge of retrieving the family's inheritance, and yet we know that he has long quit his studies, and he now has four different jobs. Besides working as a taxi driver on the family-owned cab, he also works at a bakery and at the sewage department, as well as a percussionist with a belly dancer, all incomparable to the much respected status of a lawyer, which points to the idea of failure which we are going to discuss further later on. Allam [the knowledgeable] represents the forgetful consciousness of the nation. He is always high on drugs and forgets everything. He is a history teacher, who over and over keeps mentioning episodes from the Arab history in Andalus and repeatedly expresses his will to write a book called *Wah Andalusah!* [*Ode to Al-Andalus*], an act of lamentation much like the older Arab odes, but unlike such poets he never manages to remember the events or the narrative he wants to chronicle. There is a clear notion here that the answers to contemporary questions are to be found in history, but the problem lies in our forgetfulness of it. This almost echoes Peter Burke's idea that only the winners 'can afford to forget,' 'whereas the losers are unable to accept what happened and are condemned to brood over it, relive it, and reflect how different it might have been' (2013, p. 54). Suspended between past and present temporalities, Allam keeps going back to that moment in history, Al-Andalus – a moment when the Arabs were at the centre and not the periphery, where they made a proper contribution to humanity in terms of knowledge production and were not merely at the receiving end, as well as having been affluent and not torn apart by poverty as they are here portrayed.

History and its interpretations become central in the play's treatment of the current state of confusion the brothers are in. Allam, speaking of Ayesh's inability to get his law degree, says 'I have often advised him to drop the Law and study History instead, history is also full of discourse on *rights*, but lost ones' (translation mine) – alluding, of course, ironically to their own right to the land their father had lost. Unlike the grand narrative of the victorious, however, Allam's history book mulls over the past only to narrate losses, defeats, and failures.

Even the family's attempts at success always arrived 'too late,' a tagline that runs throughout the play. The father has always been trying hard to catch up but remained out of date, Ayesh tells us. When he used to manufacture flags, he made 20,000 Egyptian flags, the green one with the three stars, from when Egypt was a kingdom, and he wouldn't sell them until it was too late. By that time, the 1952 revolution had taken place, and he lost everything. The following time, he made 30,000 flags in red, white, and black, and before he sold them it was again too late. Now the unity between Egypt and Syria meant two stars had to be added, which is what he did. Yet again before he sold them, Yemen had joined the unity, so he added a third star, and before he sold any, the unity was broken altogether. The father then made 50,000 flags with 22 stars. 'Poor thing,' says Ayesh, 'he was waiting for the Arab unity' (translation mine), a dream often lamented upon and never realized, and as the play develops we understand that it is quite unlikely to ever materialize.

Ayesh finds a saviour in the figure of Amira Kamel, the rich businesswoman, who represents the United States in the play. Amira Kamel is portrayed as a capable businesswoman who also has a relief organization for donkeys. Ayesh is fascinated by her charm and culture and thus is easily fooled by her sweet talk. He believes that she can help him and his family to retrieve their right to their inheritance, and in the process, he falls in love with her to later find out that she has been fooling him and collaborating with the enemy instead. As they plan to get married, Amira Kamel's team convince him of his sexual weakness and of his need for treatment. They start giving him the steroids used for donkeys, which allegedly cause brain damage. The whole scheme turns out to be a big thwart not only to his intelligence but also to his sense of masculinity.

And in the final scene, when Ayesh travels to the United States and starts admiring the Statue of Liberty, it falls apart in front of him, and despite his repeated declarations 'I love America! I love peace!' enumerating presidents, famous actors, and American products in an attempt to show his love for the country, for the police, he is instantly accused to be a 'terrorist' owing to his Egyptian and Arab identities, which he naively confuses with the word 'tourist.' 'I am Egyptian, yes, I am Arab yes, *Erhaby* (Terrorist) no!' he finally declares when he eventually understands the situation, an interesting episode of an all too common image in contemporary media, though it is worth noting that this play in fact precedes the events of 9/11.

Although a clear sense of othering is demonstrated in the play, we should not forget that we are throughout following Ayesh's story driven by his desire to travel to the United States and live the dream of democracy and liberty, which he cannot find at home. So while the play may demonstrate a certain stand against US foreign policy, it seems to still find American life, translated into notions of success, hard work, liberty, and luxury, to be desirable and worthy. Hence, while imaginaries of the North and South seem to collide once territory and space are contested, the North remains desirable and the northern way of life remains a dream to be sought.

Framing the present and juxtaposed spatialities

Although *In Plain Arabic* chronologically precedes *Mother America* in its production date, I find it a good place to bring some threads together and bring us closer to the main focus of this volume. The play was first staged in Cairo in 1991, also starring Mohamed Sobhi. It was published in Arabic the following year and translated into English in 1994. According to Ibrahim Dawood, the play 'simultaneously represents a commendable effort within the dramatic genre, a valuable contribution to the art of satire, and a major addition to works dealing with cross-cultural encounters' (Dawood, 1996). The play enjoyed huge success and was even recommended by the Egyptian Ministry of Culture to a number of festivals around the Arab world.

The play is a framed narrative in quite concrete terms, a commentary not only on theatre and the theatrical but also on all kinds of media representations, which no matter how much they claim or even sincerely attempt to capture the 'truth,' will continue to fall short of it. The stage is viewed as a medium just like any other, framing the world from a very specific place, and hence never unbiased. The play centres on a fictitious television crew commissioned by the Arab authorities to go to London to follow the story of 14 Arab students, representing the different Arab countries, in an attempt to dispel stereotypes about Arabs in the West. The television program sharing the same title of the play itself, *In Plain Arabic*, offers a sarcastic reality show heavy on montage, censorship, and didacticism, while the audience is made aware time and again that the play is framed within a fixed lens, presenting a single, even distorted over-sympathetic perspective.

F. ANNOUNCER: We set out with intentions of honesty, truth, and accuracy...
M. ANNOUNCER: But after filming a portion of the program...
F. ANNOUNCER: We realized that the recorded picture did not reflect the whole truth. (1994, p. 1. Prologue)

And that is why they tell us that they have decided to present the audience with everything that happens behind the camera. Accordingly, the audience are constantly made aware of all the selective and theatrical processes involved in producing the show, as well as the play, which from the very beginning appears to be outright staged, as the director starts putting words into his guests' mouths.

El-Ramly makes it clear that any form of media representation, even the seemingly documentary, can never be unbiased, while poking fun at the Arab's special case of self-censorship. The director himself blurts out quite assertively, 'you can't convey the truth on camera!' which of course goes for the stage too, and goes on to explain that 'as soon as an Arab sees a camera he immediately goes into a schizophrenic trance and says anything but what he feels' (1. Prologue). This makes the cameraman suggest they follow the students' stories through a hidden camera in order to be able to capture the real essence of their lives. The attempt is still fraught by the many debates the crew have amongst themselves throughout the play.

IMAGINARIES OF THE NORTH AND SOUTH

The first collective feed they film of the Arab students appears to be staged, and their picture as a united group looks fake. They all declare that they are in London on a mission to pursue knowledge and resist 'the debauchery of the West with full will and determination' (7). Thus, from the very beginning we are once again faced with the divided worldview of Arab and other, though this time the characters are displaced in the West. The frame the cameraman shoots of the students in unity, however, happens to also include an English policeman, causing the dismay of the director. The policeman in the picture acts like a figure of authority who seems to haunt the Arab dream of unity and to remind the Arab consciousness of their history as colonized peoples. Yet the juxtaposition of place, where it is in fact quite natural for an English policeman to exist on English soil throws us back to Wahba's logic in the scene of the trial – a logic revisited several times in the play, where the Arab students keep calling the English 'foreigners' regardless of the fact that they are in London and hence *they* are the foreigners themselves. This highlights their inaccurate perception and undermines their over-sympathetic depiction of themselves.

Through commenting on this group picture of the students and how it is representative of Arab unity and the long-awaited Arab awakening, the audience is already anxious of what El-Ramly really has to say. When soon enough Fayez, the Palestinian student, disappears, they all vow to find him in the name of solidarity yet refuse to ransom him when they get a call from his kidnapper. It is interesting to note that even before his abduction the students had been working on a play called *Woe Ye Arabs*, a clear reminder, or rather foreshadowing, of Allam's *Wah Andalusah!* but this time it is about the abduction of their Palestinian friend, which of course symbolizes the loss of Palestine and foretells the actual disappearance of Fayez.

Like Ayesh, the disappeared Fayez is accused of being a terrorist and burning down a bookstore which sells anti-Arab works. When the inspector questions the students about the incident, however, instead of defending Fayez and telling the inspector that they spent the night at the nightclub, they all refuse to testify in fear for their reputations. In other words, they all choose their own interests in protecting their misconstrued reputations over saving their so-called brother.

In the second act, we see even more of that broken unity. When the students meet to discuss what they are going to do about Fayez's case, all they do is fight over who chairs the meeting and forget altogether why they had gathered in the first place, most of them deciding to simply withdraw from the meeting altogether. When Professor Wisdom – an interesting name for an English orientalist – invites them to discuss Fayez's case with their Western colleagues, they insist on censoring the discussion like they do in their own gatherings, where no talk of sex, politics, or religion is allowed. When the other party insists on freedom of speech, however, the Arab students withdraw from the debate and refuse to have a dialogue. This behaviour is an indication of an oversensitivity as a result of a constant state of threat. The Arab students are displeased not only with anyone who rejects their opinion but also with anyone who refuses to take their side, and they perceive it as a failure to oversee justice. Professor Wisdom refuses to take sides when asked about his support for Israel, calling himself 'neutral' on the matter, though when it comes to conflict over the ownership of the land, what can one make of neutrality? Silence for El-Ramly seems to support further injustice, which makes it impossible for Fayez to return, contesting the whole logic (or 'wisdom') of Professor Wisdom and the institution behind him.

It is clear thus that again the issue of Palestine and the Arab-Israeli conflict keeps coming up in any discussion of a relationship between the Arab nations and the West, giving way to diverse reactions from accusations of grand conspiracy theories to attempts at reconciliation to even episodes of self-flagellation, which El-Ramly's play had been accused of. However, El-Ramly explains why his play seems too radical on all fronts, pleasing no one and unveiling all sorts of extremist views to the point of ridicule, by putting words in the mouth of Jassir, who is as Mustafa calls him the 'critic' of the student troupe:

JASSIR: I believe that acting is an opportunity to exaggerate and go to extremes to teach the audience and explain to them . . . (2.3).

Jassir's presumption of the role of theatre seems in line with Schechner's description of how aesthetic drama can transform its spectators' worldview:

by rubbing their senses against enactments of extreme events, much more extreme than they would usually witness. The nesting pattern makes it possible for the spectator to reflect on these events rather than flee from them or intervene in them. That reflection is the liminal time during which the transformation of consciousness takes place.
(2003, p. 193)

And that reflection and its outcome is also the 'opportunity' El-Ramly describes in his attempt to make audiences reflect on their contemporary condition with all its complexity.

Constructed imaginaries as performed resistance

It is through this divided paradigm that the postcolonial subject in all three plays looks at the North as a place to be dreamed of, as a potential friend and ally, but then comes the question of land/territory problematizing the issue, bringing about nostalgia to a lost past and a deep sense of injustice. While subjective spatial and temporal consciousness loom large in the background, it seems difficult to find a balanced position from which to dismantle the binary reality of 'self' and 'other,' and while El-Ramly comes very close to portraying the distortion that occurs to any event once it starts being framed in narrative, even in his play we still see the world in sharply categorized compartments. There are the Arab students against the West and its hegemony not only over them but also over their very image, even when they make fools of themselves.

In both *In Plain Arabic* and *Mother America!* we get a more nuanced view than that presented in *El Masameer*, where things are seen more in terms of black and white. However, the nationalist cause seems to have also dissipated and is no longer urgent or at least no longer feels as such, though the centrality of the right to the land remains at the heart of the discussion in all three plays. Hence, by comparing the three works, their obsession with history, rights, territory, the ills of capitalism, and world economic imbalance is a clear statement of rejection of a world order that seems more inert than we think, even if its workings had been in flux.

However, the works' reproductions of these schisms in their imaginaries of the North and South should not be disregarded or perceived simply as a failure to capture the complexity of the world in which we live. Instead, they can be placed in the larger contexts of their precise historical moments. Their awareness and acknowledgement of their own positionalities in both time and space allows them to avoid the pitfall often facing postcolonial writers who simply refute one master narrative for another, while they seem to remain suspended between the different temporalities which make up their today. The playwriters' acts of writing are attempts at performing a resistance that is directed not only towards colonial powers but also towards empty nationalist discourses that seem to only enlarge the cleft between these geographies while providing no apparent solutions. At the very moment that they reject colonialism, they also reject to 'Halt' and 'weep' at 'the spinning of the south winds and the northern blasts' as Imru' al-Qais does.

Notes

1 I prefer this spelling of the name to the one used in Arberry's translation, 'Imr Al-Qais,' because it is more faithful to the original pronunciation of the poet's name.

2 Al-Mu'allaqat are a collection of seven pre-Islamic Arabic 'qasidas' [odes] considered to be among the best poems ever written in Arabic. Each Mu'allaqa was created and recited by a different poet and they were only later written down and collected. Legend, though many have denied its truth, holds that they have gained their name of Mu'allaqat [hanging poems] since they were written in gold and hung on the walls of the Ka'ba in Mecca. However, regardless of the legend's truth, the preciousness and centrality of these poems remains uncontested.

3 This poem, which has stood for centuries as one of the best and most central pieces ever written in Arabic verse, pioneered a long tradition of Arabic poems which start with a lament of times gone by, an ode to a love lost, and a place that was. It is believed that this tradition of lamentation, which became famous in poetry all over Arabia and the Arabic speaking world up to contemporary times owes its origin to Imru' Al-Qais's Mu'allaqa.

4 An interesting map related to this cartography is published by the Bartlett Development Planning Unit at UCL's project 'Thinking Across Boundaries: Planning Dilemmas in the Urban Global South', in which the world is divided into the 'Rich North' and 'Poor South.' Australia is excluded from the South. Map available at www.bartlett.ucl.ac.uk/dpu/news/Thinking_across_boundaries_RGS.

5 I have tried to render the same effect of George's broken Arabic in my translation, both for its comic effect and because it works very well in condensing the message so it is not missed. Uttering the most problematic words of the play, George does away with all functional words that might distract.

References

Al-Qais, Imr (1957). Mu'allaqa of Imr al'Qais (A. J. Arberry, Trans.) *The Seven Odes: The First Chapter in Arabic Literature* (pp. 61–66). London: George Allen & Unwin Ltd.

Al, Rafei A. (1987). *Thawrat 1919: Tareekh Misr AlQawmy Men Sannat 1914 ila Sannat 1921* [The 1919 Revolution: Egypt's National History from 1914 to 1921]. Cairo: Dar AlMaaref.

Bartlett Development Planning Unit, The. (2013). Thinking Across Boundaries: Planning Dilemmas in the Urban Global South. [Map]. Retrieved from www.ucl.ac.uk/bartlett/development/news/2013/sep/thinking-across-boundaries-planning-dilemmas-urban-global-south

Bhabha, H. K. (2004). Foreword: Framing Fanon (R. Philcox, Trans.) *The Wretched of the Earth* (pp. vii–xli). New York: Grove Press.

Burke, P. (2013). *Varieties of Cultural History*. na: Wiley. Retrieved from www.ebrary.com

Cook, S. A. (2012). *The Struggle for Egypt: From Nasser to Tahrir Square*. Cairo: American University in Cairo Press.

Dawood, I. (1996). In Plain Arabic: A Play in Two Acts by Lenin El-Ramly and translated by Esmat Allouba. *World Literature Today*, 70(1), 233–234. https://doi.org/10.2307/40152015

IMAGINARIES OF THE NORTH AND SOUTH

El-Ramly, L. (1994). *In Plain Arabic: A Play in Two Acts* (E. Allouba, Trans.). Cairo: American University in Cairo Press (originally in 1992).
Fanon, F. (2004). *The Wretched of the Earth*. (R. Philcox, Trans.). New York, NY: Grove Press.
Paris Peace Conference. (1919–1920). Egyptian Delegation to the Peace Conference, Collection of Official Correspondence from November 11, 1918, to July 14, 1919; Twelve Appendices Containing Verbatim Transcriptions of Official Egyptian Reports, Correspondence, Depositions of Victims and Eye-Witness, and Photographs of Atrocities Committed by British Troops in Egypt. (1919). Retrieved 24 March 2017 from https://archive.org/stream/egyptiandelegati00pari
Said, E.W. (1994). *Culture and Imperialism* (1st ed.). London: Vintage Books.
Schechner, R. (2003). *Performance Theory*. London: Routledge.
Wahba, S. (1967). *ElMasameer* [Nails]. Cairo: Dar AlKatib AlAraby liltiba'a Walnashr.
West-Pavlov, R. (2013). *Temporalities*. Abingdon: Routledge.
Youssef, M. and Sobhy, M. (1998). *Mama Amrika* [Mother America; Television recording]. Cairo: Egyptian TV.

3

THEY ARE LIKE US

Race, porn, and viewing patterns in South Africa

Yolo Siyabonga Koba

Hester (2014, p. 16) states that 'if pornography isn't always corrupting, violent or oppressive, neither is it always progressive, healing or liberating.' By transcending the pro-porn/anti-porn dichotomy, I draw on the capacity of pornographic imagery to both oppress and liberate.

This chapter is interested in how liberties of South Africa's 'libidinal economy' avail both sexual freedom and censure by zooming in to how porn consumers use and understand raced sexual images. Wilderson (2010, p. 9) describes 'libidinal economy' as 'the economy, or distribution and arrangement of desire and identification (their condensation and displacement), and the complex relationship between sexuality and the unconscious.' Porn access and consumption practices constitute a unique set of 'distributions and arrangements of desire' whose salient features can be mapped out onto the larger body of consumer behaviour. How the libidinal economy or these set of distributions of desire yield to various pornographic representations of race is the focus of this chapter. In examining South Africa's 'libidinal economy,' I seek to explore how various sexual liberties in modes of porn consumption collide with various racial power structures. This chapter shows that pornographic images can help bridge racial divides through demystifying racial myths. It also shows that porn images can also retrench racial stereotypes.

The question of race and racial preference in South African porn consumption is a poignantly pertinent one since social life, economic resources, and political discourse are predominantly fractured along racial lines in the country. The history of apartheid in South Africa means all aspects of life are defined by systematic racial segregation. Wealth, resources, municipal services, types of entertainment, and living arrangements still have identifiable racial demarcations even in 2017.

A divisive legal system like apartheid, which segregated human beings purely on the fallacies of race, did much to educe and fortify corrosive national imaginaries which impugned the value of life based on colour. Castoriadis (1997) has argued that social imaginaries (the manner in which particular people 'imagine' and define themselves) are directly responsible for all aspects of culture. This includes the manner in which various groups within such imaginaries characterize and perceive their role and value within the 'nation.' There is no doubt that black people within the order of apartheid were treated differently to whites. However, occupying the same national imaginaries as their white counterparts, they also believed this difference to be true.

In his paper 'Introduction: What Is "Media Imaginaries"?' Anthony Uhlmann asks 'How do new technologies of communication affect the ways in which we perceive the world and ourselves as well as the ways in which we are governed?' In short, various media technologies and representations can help us reshape, revise, review, and remodel our imaginary schematics in relation, but not limited to, sex and race. This chapter demonstrates that porn, a unique and powerful media form, can rupture or sustain rigid conceptions of racial and sexual difference.

This chapter relies on data I collected in 2013 for my PhD research at the University of the Witwatersrand, Johannesburg. The study garnered 676 survey responses and 25 in-depth interview respondents. The sample frame of this study mandated that all research participants be 18 years and older, be living within South Africa, and be porn consumers. Those who participated were first screened. All participants were guaranteed their ethical right to anonymity and confidentiality. Interview respondents were granted aliases. Methodological details relating to the data and collection process are presented in the next sub-section.

Methodology

This study utilized a mixed method approach, a large anonymous survey, and a smaller number of in-depth interviews. This led to the recruitment of 676 complete South African survey responses and 25 interview respondents. All research participants (both from the survey and interviews) had to confirm they were 18 years old or older. Table 3.1 represents the number of respondents who participated in the national survey by gender, race, and age.

The survey questions were developed using a seven-fold thematic framework: demographics (age, race, gender), beliefs/perceptions (how people perceive porn and their porn consumption), feelings (how porn makes consumers feel), practices and preferences (how people consume porn and which porn they like), uses (why people consume porn), and associations (how porn consumption intermediates consumers' interactions with other people). The qualitative research instrument was an interview schedule with 38 questions, subdivided into five theme-based sections/segments: 'introductory questions,' 'feelings,' 'practices and preferences,' 'uses/interactions,' and 'personal beliefs.'

The sample frame of this research demanded participants met three conditions. They had to have watched porn within the last six months of their participation in the study, they had to be residing in South Africa at the time of the research, and they had to be of legal age (18 years or older). The first requirement was important because the study sought to investigate consumption practices and opinions of porn consumers, not of the general public. The second sampling category aimed to sift out people who were not living in South Africa due to the study's primal focus being on idiosyncratic consumption patterns *within* South Africa. The last requirement pertained to the national legal regulatory framework, The Film and Publication Act, which mandates that only adults should have access to pornographic material (Watney, 2005). The survey was digitally instructed to exit any respondent who indicated they did not meet any of above criteria. All porn consumers who wished to be interviewed also had to confirm age, location, and porn consumption.

The questionnaire was made available through an online survey software such that time and location posed no hindrance to respondents who wished to participate. All survey and interview respondents were people from all provinces and parts of South Africa. Interview respondents who indicated a desire to participate could choose to be interviewed via online live chat, a telephone call at my cost, WhatsApp mobile chat, or a face-to-face interview with me. Out of the 25 interview respondents, three chose to be interviewed online, another three through WhatsApp, 10 chose to have a telephone call, and nine requested a face-to-face interview. All participants were guaranteed confidentiality and anonymity. Pseudonyms were used to protect identities of the interview respondents. Table 3.1 represents the details of all the 25 interviewees who chose to participate in the research.

They are like us: how porn can bridge racial lines

In South Africa, the pre-democratic dispensation that existed prior to 1994 instigated a draconian legislative framework on matters pertaining to sex and pornography. One of the many prohibitory statutes through which

Table 3.1 Biographical information of interview participants (anonymized)

Respondent	Gender	Race	Age	Mode of interview	Relationship status	Brief bio
Themba	Male	Black	27	Phone call interview; 38 minutes	Married	Works as a security guard officer in Eastern Cape
Tina	Female	White	30	Face-to-face interview; 31 minutes	In long-term relationship	Not working; studying towards a master's degree in linguistics
Joe	Male	Black	37	Phone call interview; 32 minutes	Married	Lives and has an office job in Johannesburg; has two children
Suraj	Male	Indian	23	Online live chat interview; 14 pages	Single	Working and staying in Durban
Duma	Male	Black	23	Face-to-face interview; 41 minutes	Single	Home in Mpumalanga but studies in Johannesburg; completing master's degree in economics
Senzo	Male	Black	31	Face-to-face interview; 1 hour 40 minutes	Single	Lives in Soweto and works at a debt-collecting company in Johannesburg
Litha	Male	Black	26	Online live chat interview; 26 pages	Single	Works as an actor in the South African TV industry
Joseph	Male	Black	45	Online live chat interview; 15 pages	Married	Information not available
Zethu	Female	Black	22	Face-to-face interview 27 minutes	Single	Not working; final year student in politics
Sheila	Female	Black	25	Face-to-face interview; 53 minutes	Stable relationship	Working
Tara	Female	White	50	Phone call interview; 47 minutes	In long-term relationship	Retired
Danny	Male	Black	18	Phone call interview, 1 hour	Single	Final year in matric

(Continued)

Table 3.1 (Continued)

Respondent	Gender	Race	Age	Mode of interview	Relationship status	Brief bio
Elam	Male	Black	30	WhatsApp mobile interview; 7 pages	In long-term relationship	Information not available
Brian	Male	White	63	Phone call interview; 30 minutes	Married	Working at a TV/music studio
Simon	Male	Black	31	WhatsApp mobile interview; 7 pages	Married	Information not available
George	Male	Black	40	WhatsApp mobile interview; 7 pages	In long-term relationship	Information not available
Thabo	Male	Black	22	Phone call interview; 1 hour 19 minutes	In a relationship	Information not available
Pule	Male	Black	22	Phone call interview; 1 hour 15 minutes	In a relationship	Works as a security guard in Kwazulu Natal
Lihle	Male	Black	27	Phone call interview; 1 hour 26 minutes	Single	Looking for employment
Elrod	Male	Coloured	60	Phone call interview; 1 hour 4 minutes	Married	About to retire
Ndoda	Male	Black	18	Phone call interview; 47 minutes	Single	Final year in high school
Dave	Male	White	42	Face-to-face interview; 2 hours 38 minutes	In long-term relationship	Works as a call-centre agent
Kholo	Male	Black	29	Face-to-face interview; 1 hour 4 minutes	Engaged	A script-writer freelancer
Emmanuel	Male	Black	29	Face-to-face interview; 1 hour 31 minutes	Engaged	Unemployed
Sam	Male	Black	36	Phone call interview; 44 minutes	Engaged	Information not available

the state attempted to police sexual bodies was the Immorality Act of 1927 (later amended in 1950) to ban all sexual interactions and marriage between different races in the country, especially between white and black people (Glücksmann, 2010). Other laws such as the Group Areas Act No. 41 of 1950 'forced physical separation between races by creating different residential areas for different races' (Glücksmann, 2010: 14). Essentially, this meant different racial groups had very little exposure to each other apart from approved working encounters. What many people knew about 'the other' race was what the government said or what they read in newspapers or saw on television (when television finally made it to South Africa in 1976). Even when dialogue and physical interaction occurred, sexual engagements were illegal.

It was in such a politically ominous milieu that pornography covertly bridged the gap of normalized social separation between different races, perhaps even in a way that most media forms couldn't. Simon (31, black male), for example, who started seeing porn at age 16, says that he and his friends were shocked and amused at the sight of naked white bodies.

> We were laughing 'cause we never saw whites naked before. It was funny 'cause we could see they were like us . . . because where I'm from that time there was no white people so seeing them fucking and naked it felt so good.

Simon mentioned the place he grew up is Bushbuckridge, a small town in the Mpumalanga Province. The authors Raamutsindela and Simon (1999) confirm that Bushbuckridge was a black residential region that harboured feuds and simmering hostilities between the Pedis, Shangaan-Tsonga, and the Pulana ethnic groups. Growing up in such an environment, Simon would have been aware of the ethnic rivalries of the region: the clashes for linguistic preferences in schools, protests over land claims, and condemnation of interethnic romance (Raamutsindela and Simon, 1999). With these being the most pressing issues of the time, Simon at age 16 wouldn't have had much reason to be bothered about white people since there were no whites around him. He would have seen white people mostly from popular American action movie figures such as *Rambo* and Jean-Claude Van Damme, but he would never had known, or perhaps imagined, what exactly they looked like naked. In South Africa, black and white people even had separate TV channels with black television featuring black content. Most white content accessed by black people was mainly from the United States. Given the level of geographical, institutional, cultural, and social segregation that had, over the decades, deprived South Africans of racial acquaintanceship, only a sense of mystery and superstition could prevail. The theory of 'contact hypothesis' can be used to explain this:

> Social psychological research on segregation has mainly worked within the theoretical framework of the 'contact hypothesis.' This hypothesis holds that the mutual isolation of groups encourages the development of negative attitudes and stereotypes.
> (Dixon, Tredoux, and Clack, 2005, p. 403)

The contact hypothesis also proposes an inverse of this: that is, when different groups people of regularly interact, prejudice, ignorance, and stereotypes are reduced. Nevertheless, the segregation that defined apartheid was predicated on racial difference and the bioculturalist distinction of racialized bodies. Posel (2001, 53) speaks of bioculturalist as referring to 'aligned readings of bodily difference closely with differences of class, lifestyle and general repute.' It was perhaps bound to happen that whatever misconceptions and myths that Simon and his friends had about white people would be premised on cultural and even bodily difference. According to Posel, the apartheid project sought to entrench a façade of human difference based solely on bodily deviations (mostly pigmentation) with the extraction that corporeal differences were the cause of all other socioeconomic dissimilarities and injustices.

> The ideological logic of Apartheid depended upon thinking about all blacks as essentially different from all whites and coloureds, and, correlatively, all blacks as sharing essential features that united them into one race.
> (Posel, 2001, pp. 64–65)

The apartheid state institutionalized the deification of bodily difference as an index of all other differences. One was relegated to a sub-standard level of existence simply because one *looked* darker than everyone else. Given this logic, black children and teenagers, in particular, had reason to believe there must have been something ineradicably different between the bodies of white and black people to merit the vast existential gap between them. It is not really clear *how* Simon and his friends had envisioned white bodies to vary from their own. What is clear is that they had expected to see inimitable differences between their bodies and white people's bodies. The realization that white people 'looked like us' (had bodies and genitals that looked like theirs) was not only revelatory to them but most probably became a bathetic demotion of 'whiteness' from its exalted social pedestal to an inoculating reality of white people's routine normalcy. It makes sense they would laugh, having expected to see a lofty spectacle only to discover the commonly familiar.

Not only did different racial populations of South Africa dwell in separate geographical locations but they were granted separate services (bathroom, benches, transport, diners, etc.) even in spaces where they worked side by side. A stark portrait of South Africa's jagged social, cultural, and economically landscape is given by Dixon, Tredoux, and Clack (2005, pp. 396, 397). As a visual record of the multifarious forms that racial separation assumed during the apartheid era, we find illustrations, for example, of urban apartheid, the homeland system, the racial organization of institutions of education, industry, transport, and many other areas of social life. At one level, the apartheid system was famously impressed upon the global organization of urban life in South Africa, taking the form of group areas, infrastructural barriers, buffer zones, and other features of the apartheid city.

Suffice to say that this nationwide segregationist arrangement imposed by the state turned South African people into strangers whose encounters, even after the democratic dispensation, became marked by constant fear and suspicion (Nattrass and Seekings, 2001). Dave (42, white male) admits that even at age 22 (year 1994) he did not have any black friends or personally know any black people. Dave's first sight of a naked African human being was through pornography.

> and I started to notice things about African guys then that I . . . I didn't or wouldn't have noticed before, you know . . . I mean stuff that I would obviously notice on white people. So, then I started to notice these things like wow, you know, made observations that I never made before . . . I mean like how dark skinned are you, like how light skinned are you. Uhmm . . . like, how much hair does he have on his head. I never had the opportunity to look at a Black guy naked before. The crowd that I mixed with was basically heterosexual and white.

Dave's romantic and sexual liaisons since this encounter have become mostly black, a clear indication that in some way, this experience significantly impacted his predilections. Of more significance is the way that such images drastically altered his perception of black bodies and black people. Stuart Hall (2005, p. 445) accents that the stereotype 'all black people are the same' or that 'you can't tell the difference because they all look the same' is 'a predicate of racism.' Therefore, in confessing that he never saw or noticed variations in the physiological features of black people Dave is fundamentally admitting the manner in which he had typecast black people as being all the same.

However, in the kind of sexually and racially separationist and repressive society epitomized by old South African laws, Dave's psychological myopia was, perhaps, to be understood, maybe even to be expected. This is why his life-changing epiphany vis-à-vis black porn is a critical embodiment of the contestations between the restraints of power and the recourses of pleasure. Porn acts as a bridge between the institutionalized racial divide of 'strange' bodies, allowing each safe familiarization to the socially unattainable and bringing an experience of sexual and racial novelty that's been deprived in the real politicized world. Evidently, porn does what no other media genre can do: expose all our raw corporeal truths so plainly that all veils of mysticism about other people's 'anomalies' are stripped away. Porn reveals the profound yet basic truth that no matter how estranged people may be to each other (poor, privileged, brown and light alike), they are all human, connected by the undeniably common bodily features and structures that define all bodies and all humans. In light that Dave's experience led to a change in his love life, friendships, and entire social organization, we can safely conclude his sexual 'awakening' became his social transformation.

Dave and Sam's accounts about how, for the first time in their lives, they saw the human in the estranged racial other are antithetical to writings which have claimed that porn promotes viewers to see sex in racist terms. Stager (2003, p. 54) for example reveals the three ways in which porn characters are labelled and promoted in their videos: by their body types, their race, and their age. Similarly (Dines, 2006) agrees that mainstream pornography seeks to deliberately construct a racially polarized sexual universe defined by eroticized black and white bodies engaged in sexual intercourse: 'dominant performers are black men and white women with titles such as *Black poles in white holes, Huge black cock on white pussy*, and *Monster black penises and tight white holes*' (Dines, 2006, p. 285).

Admittedly, the porn industry does often thrive and capitalize on racially centred body difference. For this reason, there is significant merit in studying porn texts since 'questions of power and the political have to be and are always lodged within representations of textuality' (Hall, 2005, p. 15). However, there is no evidence that consumers are somehow hoodwinked into reducing other human into sexualized black or white bodies. Though it is unclear how many porn consumers in South Africa as a whole may have similar stories as Dave's and Sam's, exposure to different bodies proves the ability to bring consumers closer to the perception of those (different) bodies as human, in Sam's words, as being 'like us.' I now turn my attention to the ways in which pornographic images in South Africa contribute to racial hegemony and exclusivism.

White porn, white domination: why most South Africans consume white porn

With 90 percent of the entire 676 survey respondents indicating they frequently viewed white porn, it is clear that white pornography is very popular porn in South Africa. Figure 3.1 shows the different-raced porn categories watched by the survey respondents.

When these figures are demographically apportioned, however, the story of which porn type is consumed by which racial group the most becomes even more telling as illustrated by Figure 3.2.

A number of observations from the cross-tab are worth noting. White porn is very popular among all population groups, even more so amongst white and coloured respondents, all peaking above 92 percent. Black porn is most popular only amongst black consumers and is watched by white and Asian consumers the least. Lastly, white porn (at 90 percent) and interracial porn (at 85 percent) are the two most watched porn types across all racial groups. The universality that underscores white porn, in particular, as a staple sexual commodity is worth discussing.

Considering that most available porn in South African adult stores is predominantly white, it is of no surprise that the majority of South African consumers frequently view white porn. This is unfortunately the same for porn accessed from the internet. The ubiquity of white bodies on the internet makes it highly unlikely for black people to only watch black porn, even

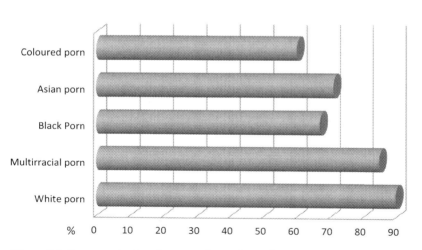

Figure 3.1 Race typologies: the type of porn I watch
Source: Yolo Koba

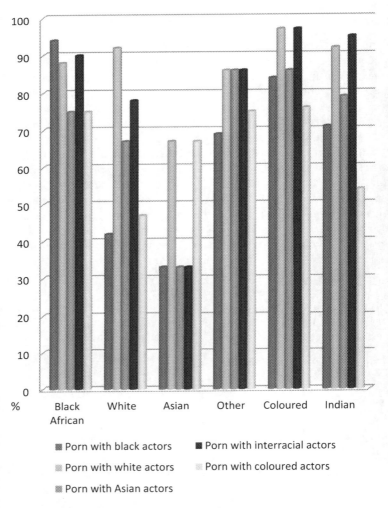

Figure 3.2 Racial demographics: the type of porn I view
Source: Yolo Koba

if they wished. As Dines (2006, p. 296) points out, 'white ownership of media and pornography has defined and continues to define the contours' of porn production and by extension consumption. Referring specifically to gay porn, Litha (26, black male) pointed this out when he said: 'Just search the words *gay porn*, and you're bombarded with white men. In fact, you can even leave out the word *porn*: white gay men RUN THIS.' To extend on Litha's remark, the patterns of production ownership that permeate the gay porn industry globally and in South Africa are patterns that replicate themselves in the heterosexual porn business where white producers dictate the types of content to be mass produced for consumption. Dines (2006, p. 289) further notes that 'While there are both black and white pornography producers and directors, the audience for internet porn is overwhelmingly white.' Litha's statement 'you can even leave out the word *porn*' puts emphasis on the fact that in South Africa specifically, the 'whiteness' of gay porn can be linked to the whiteness of commercial gay culture generally (Sonnekus, 2013; Livermon, 2012; Milani, 2014). Sonnekus and Van Eeden (2009, p. 84) argue that 'by not transgressing the acceptable norms within which gay culture gains social significance by heteronormative, capitalist role-players, the overwhelming presence of white, middle-class, "straight"-acting gay men inevitably reproduces traditional (raced) power relations.' One of the most symbolic epitomes of white dominance over South African commercial gay culture was the notable clash between the mostly white-led Gay Pride contingent of 2012 with black gay activists. The white-led procession wanted to parade the streets of the city in the usual extravagant celebratory fashion, but the black demonstrators felt the Gay Pride march should have taken a more politically conscious stance by stopping and keeping a moment of silence to honour all brutally murdered lesbians (McLean, 2013). Threats, insults, and chaos ensued when these two gay camps refused to accommodate each other's demands. Unsurprisingly, members of the more resourced white-led group made threats to members of the less resourced black group.

According to Shome (2000, p. 367), 'whiteness remains the organizing principle of the social fabric and yet remains masked because of the normativity that this principle acquires in the social imaginary.' Global media forms have deified whiteness as the default standard of beauty through the unrelenting frequency with which white bodies are exhibited and favoured above other raced bodies. Porn is no exception to this. Even when internet users unwittingly come across porn through pop-ups, those images tend to be white. A simple browse through porn sites is most telling of this 'hegemonic everydayness' (Shome, 2000, p. 367) of whiteness where racial difference is accorded niche status and exoticized exception worth its own separate category, such as 'Asian porn,' 'black porn,' and 'Arabic porn.' 'White porn,' on the other hand, has no special category because most porn is de facto white and by extension normal. In many ways this means white bodies, with their ability to be everything, to be everywhere, disguised under facile values of individualism and meritocracy, are hardly avoidable. For this reason, it is understandable that 90 percent of the porn sample watched white porn. For most interview participants, for example

(Sheila, Duma, Litha, Zethu, Dave, Elrod, Suraj, Sam, Tara, Joe, Kholo, Brian, Lihle, Tina, Senzo, Elam, Simon), the first porn they were exposed to was white.

Beyond the power dynamics of media ownership and production and how these shape porn consumption, I wondered if elements of racist bias or stereotyping could have been an additional factor in the manner in which consumers preferred one race typology over another. By racist stereotyping, I mean the proclivity to negatively or positively prefer one racial group based on reductionist race-based epithets. According to Jost (2005, p. 498), not all stereotypes are negative, but even those 'favourable in content are yet prejudicial in their consequences.' Why, for example, is black porn one of the least watched amongst *all* porn types? Note that there are more white survey respondents who view interracial and Asian porn than those who view black porn. Why do white participants exhibit such little interest in black porn?[1] For the most part, each racial group found its own race more sexually appealing and arousing than other races. Notice how 92 percent of white people view white porn and 94 percent of black people view black porn. The exceptions are that coloured respondents watched more white porn and interracial porn than their own respective race caterings, and Indian respondents consumed the same amount of white porn as white consumers (92 percent). Asian, Indian, and coloured respondents have a greater predilection for white porn than their respective porn caterings while interracial porn has the second largest viewership amongst all races. These numbers require an exploration of more than simple questions of unequal porn production and distribution disparities. Questions regarding the provenance of sexual preferences also need to be raised.

As much as white porn has been established as the most pervasive of all porn types, the internet still provides a pornotopic mixture for all different sexual tastes, providing 'different strokes for different folks' (Williams, 1999, p. 6). Consumers therefore have a huge degree of choice. This means answers to questions about favoured racial porn types have to include considerations of personal preferences. The thorny issue of racial preference can thus not be avoided. It is substantially pertinent to explore particularly because of the significance of the historical relations between white and black South Africans.

I asked interview participants what they thought about their own race preferences. Many interviewees claimed to have no particular racial preference in selecting porn even though, on further probing, they all admitted to watching one particular race more than others. Interview respondents rejected the idea that predilections for one race porn type over another had anything to do with a racist outlook. Most of them pointed to personal sexual preference as an explanation for race-based porn selection.

SHEILA: Well, do you think its racist for a person to say that I, a white person, 'I *only* date white girls?' It's . . . it comes down to preference . . . again. Honestly, it's somebody's preference. As long as he is not asking you for your Pass and . . . and making you call him 'Bass' whatever, you know what I mean? As long as he is not infringing on your God-given human rights . . . well, state-given human rights . . . then whatever . . . to each his own . . . whatever. It's not my problem. I don't really care. You watch whatever you wanna watch. You see. . . . The line between racism and preference is so thin . . . Uhm . . . but I mean if it's an honest-to-God preference, it's an honest-to-God preference.
ELAM: No, I don't think its racist, it's just one's taste, just like you might prefer watching English soccer to the South African league.
DUMA: No, I don't think it's racist at all, uhm. . . . People like different things and don't necessarily mean that because you like this or that you're this way . . . Uhmm . . . I have a friend who just watches black porn. He doesn't like . . . I mean my neighbour . . . neighbour slash friend. He says he likes just black porn, uhm . . . which doesn't mean that you're racist because he's had white girlfriends and stuff like that.

There is scholarly evidence to substantiate the views of these respondents. As Duma points out, 'People like different things' and, in Elam's words, have the right to prefer 'English soccer to the South African league' even if they themselves are South African. Curra (2010) points to the fluidity of human sexuality as reason against 'normalising' people's sexual preferences. He states that:

> If anything natural or 'normal' can be found in human sexuality, it is that we humans find a great many things sexually arousing and that our sexual identities are subject to a great deal of flexibility and variability [. . .] shared sexual identity is not identical to shared sexual experience. People pigeonholed in the same sexual identity category (e.g., heterosexual or homosexual) are characterized by a range of different experiences, outlooks, and temperaments.
> (Curra, 2010, p. 227)

The aim therefore of exploring this question of racial preferences is not to advocate a prescriptive standard on how raced bodies ought to sexually respond to other raced bodies. Homogeneity in sexual identity or racial identity can lend itself to heterogeneous racial and sexual proclivities as pointed out by Curra (2010). Note, for example, how Duma's black friend prefers black porn yet has had white girlfriends.

On the other hand, it is evident that racial identity is strongly associated with sexual preferences, for example, for particular kinds of raced porn sub-genres. Recall black respondents watch more black porn and white respondents viewed white porn the most. Writers have called this 'same race sexual preference' (Mendelsohn et al., 2014; Durrheim et al., 2011; Fishman and Iyengar, 2008). Mendelsohn et al. (2014, p. 3) states:

> literature on interpersonal attraction would likewise lead to the expectation that romantic relationships between blacks and whites would be rare. It is well established that proximity and similarity are positively associated with attraction and liking. . . . Both are likely to be substantially greater within than between ethnic/racial groups.

In South Africa, most ethnic and racial groups still inhabit racially and ethnically designated geographical spaces bequeathed to them by the apartheid government (Human Development Report, 2015). Since proximity and similarity help shape subjects' sexual race preferences, the prospect that whites would sexually prefer whites and blacks sexually prefer blacks seems almost inevitable. In this context, Sheila's view 'to each his own' makes perfect sense. Nonetheless, as someone who lives in one of the most racially divided countries in the world, one whose 'society is obsessed by race' (Durrheim et al., 2011, p. 276), I find it necessary to probe deeper than the ostensible paradigm of 'similarity and proximity.' Are there any dimensions of racist bias (note *racist*, not *racial*) that exist in the racial selection of porn material? Some of the data and literature seem to suggest so.

In South Africa, questions of racist bias merit an examination for a number of reasons. Literature indicates that perceptions of white people tend to be negative and prejudicial towards their black counterparts. According to Durrheim et al.'s 2011 study, which collated quantitative research data findings on racial perceptions in South Africa from 1934–2011:

> Not only did black groups express lower levels of prejudice toward outgroups but their attitudes were not clearly race based. Whereas the attitudes of English and Afrikaans speaking white respondents was marked by a 'colour bar' – reflecting positive attitudes toward all white groups and negative attitudes toward all black groups.
> (Durrheim et al., 2011, p. 264)

The year 2016 saw a deluge of racist incidents being exposed by the South African online media. These incidences reveal that many white South Africans still secretly perceive black South Africans as inferior. Examples of these are: Realtor Penny Sparrow calling black people monkeys on Facebook; High Court Judge Mabel Jansen claiming child rape is normal in black culture; 26-year-old Matthew Theunissen angrily labelling black people 'a bunch of kaffirs,' 'black fucking cunts' who should go 'fuck themselves'; a white guest-house owner who admitted denying blacks residence because they are not people (SABC, 2016). This increase in the visibility and exposure of racist attitudes in South Africa underscores deeply rooted racial fissures amongst the country's citizens. At an ostensible level, the survey data also seems to suggest that white South African porn consumers adopt a 'colour bar.'

Recall the survey statistics from Figure 3.2 revealed that 88 percent of black respondents viewed white porn. In sharp contrast, only 42 percent of white respondents indicated that they view black porn. Even in their sexual proclivities, white consumers mostly avoid black porn. Earlier, I noted the 'everydayness' of white porn and its suffusing hegemonic presence on the web. However, this everydayness is in parallel existence to an infinitesimal online galaxy of pornotopia. Therefore, *all* porn types, including different racial typologies such as 'black,' are profligately accessible to any internet user. Why, then, would white South African respondents show such little interest in black porn? Clearly, the question is no longer one of non-availability of porn or distance versus proximity. Tara (50, white female) was honest enough to admit that her preference for white porn as a white woman had racist attachments:

TARA: Being born and bred as a white South African, uhm . . . I'm probably inherently or . . . at some level racist myself, uhm. . . . So for me if Indian people *only* want to watch Indians, well then, somewhere in my sub-conscious . . . somewhere in my genetic make-up that's normal and if . . . if Chinese people *only* want to watch Chinese people, well then, that's normal, so if black people *only* want to watch black then it's normal.

What Tara says is profoundly revealing. It shows that porn consumers can deploy the legitimacy of 'sexual preference' as a means to rationalize their own feelings of race distancing, that is, I prefer *only* white people in porn, therefore others (Chinese, Indians, and blacks) can do the same if they wish. It's normal. However, as I have pointed out, black people in particular are auspiciously diverse in their sexual tastes, with 94 percent watching black porn, 88 percent white porn, and 90 percent interracial porn. They do not watch *only* black porn. It is this racial exclusivity, which rejects other races, that I find worth questioning. Sue (2013, p. 23) defines racism as 'any attitude, action or institutional structure or social policy that subordinates a person or group because of their colour.' The word *subordinate* can be applied in numerous contexts. There is physical subordination. There is sexual subordination. There are also professional subordinates. In this instance of porn consumption, however, I am referring to attitudes of consumers that subordinate blackness to precincts perceptual of strangeness and ugliness, the belief that black bodies – black porn – does not merit attention. Any conscious wholesale rejection of particular raced bodies or wholesale elevation of *one* constitute a form of racial subordinating as stated by Dave:

> I would say it's racist because you are excluding a possibility of anybody else being a sexual stimulation for you. . . . So I would say, Ja. I would say that is basically racist because then you are *only* preferring one and your own.

Tara's attempts to justify her exclusion for other races as sexual stimuli is telling of her denial to accept that she's probably more than just 'probably racist.' The fact that she is willing to admit to a 'probability' of racism and still brand choices stemming from that as 'normal' reveals her acceptance of racism as a customary part of life for a white South African person. It's normal.

Sheila earlier conceded that each person has the right to watch what she wishes: 'to each his own.' Later on, however, she also admitted: 'You see. . . . The line between racism and preference is so thin . . . Uhm . . . but I mean, if it's an *honest-to-God* preference, it's an honest-to-God preference.' The idea that there are 'honest-to-God' preferences suggests there are 'not-so-honest-to-God' preferences. The slippery slope of race and sexual attraction are difficult to thread precisely because, for the most part, people do not choose what they find sexually attractive. Still, while we must fully respect porn consumers' sexual preferences, even those consigned to racial types, it is also useful to question the provenance of raced sexual preference in porn consumption. Race-based sexual preferences are not supernaturally allotted to individuals from the ether. They are assimilated through socio-cultural osmosis, just like a human cell is infused with solvent molecules from its surrounding environment. Levin (2003) proposes that sexual desire is mechanized by the confluence of three factors – biology, psychology, and culture. Biology composites physiological anatomy and hormonal bodily regulation; psychology encompasses moods and interpersonal affection/

connection; and culture comprises cultural mores, societal expectations, school teachings, family influences, and media exposure. Since biology does not encode racialized sexual preference, it is the structures of culture and psychological connections that coagulate ways of sexual perception and arousal that needs focus. Litha confirms this when he says:

> Our fantasies are structurally shaped by institutions. This means that in many ways we erotisise power. So, that's why certain bodies aren't glorified in our culture; for so many, sexiness is equated with physical perfection, which is inherently unfair. One of the biggest lies ever sold to us is that beauty is something one can see with the naked eye. But one can't see it, because beauty is a social construct; we are all maimed and disfigured by heterosexism, patriarchy, and white domination. I guess porn illustrates those very tensions within us. Our porn won't change if we don't.

Litha's statement that 'we erotise power' forms the pivot of this chapter. His observation about the circumscriptions of beauty, heterosexism, and whiteness articulate the inevitable indictment of power imposed on the pleasures of porn consumption. Richard Dyer (2008, p. 9) asserts that 'racial imagery is central to the organisation of the modern world [. . .] it is never not a factor, never not in play.' This statement proves itself true even for the topic of porn where whiteness is so dominantly omnipresent that it is 'not seen as whiteness but as normal' (Dyer, 2008, p. 12). Litha's poignant statement 'we are maimed by white domination' illustrates how people's preferences are formed in the grip of unrelenting pervasive structures which venerate whiteness. Litha's own first porn exposure, for example, was shaped by the reality of dominant white porn. The maiming effect of whiteness is seen, for example, in its monopolizing ubiquity but also in everyday practices and discourses that locate blackness as its opposite, inferior other. Sexual preferences, especially racial ones, even when manifest in the selection of porn by consumers can never be 'innocent' or free from collusions of power (Ciclitira, 2004).

Conclusion

Consumption theories which shed light on how people acquire, use, and dispose of products can be used to explain the various ways people attain pornography. From this, we can glean an understanding of people's sexual preferences, motivations, beliefs, and needs. This chapter limited its scope to the consumption of raced explicit media and the various bearings they can have on porn consumers.

Porn does what no other media genre can do: expose all our raw corporeal truths so plainly that all veils of racial mysticism about other people's bodies are stripped away. As such, porn can act as a bridge between structured racial divides by allowing each race safe acquaintanceship to the socially unattainable. On the other hand, the ubiquitous dominance of white porn in South Africa has the socio-culturally maiming effect of 'naturalising' whiteness and white bodies as the standard of beauty. This maiming effect has the capacity to entrench a sense of racial 'cageism' that robs most South African whites from viewing 'other' bodies as seen from the data presented in this chapter.

In the introduction of this chapter, I argued that porn can help us reshape, revise, review, and remodel social imaginaries. The potential of porn in particular is that it can rupture or sustain rigid conceptions of racial difference. If we consider Castoriadis's (1997) words that social imaginaries are directly responsible for all aspects of culture, we need to consider whether or not the swarms of pornographic images in circulation today are inviting us to review and reshape apartheid-like imaginaries of sex, gender, and sexuality. Is our porn ultimately contributing to a vision for a better equitable culture, a vision for a better us?

Note

1 I am choosing to focus on white respondents because although Asians watched black porn the least, with only three Asian survey respondents their number is statistically insignificant.

References

Castoriadis, C. (1997). *The Imaginary Institution of Society*. Cambridge, MA: MIT Press.

Ciclitira, K. (2004). Pornography, women and feminism: Between pleasure and politics. *Sexualities*, 7, 281–301. https://doi.org/10.1177/1363460704040143

Curra, J. (2010). *The Relativity of Deviance*. Los Angeles, CA: Sage Publishers.

Dines, G. (2006). The white man's burden: Gonzo pornography and the construction of black masculinity. *Yale Journal of Law and Feminism*, 18, 283–297. Retrieved from http://digitalcommons.law.yale.edu/cgi/viewcontent.cgi?article=1250&context=yjlf

Dixon, J., Tredoux, C., & Clack, B. (2005). On the micro-ecology of racial division: A neglected dimension of segregation. *South African Journal of Psychology*, 35(3), 395–411.

Durrheim, K., Tredoux, C., Foster, D., & Dixon, J. (2011). Historical trends in South African race attitudes. *Psychological Society of South Africa*, 41,

263–278. Retrieved from https://journals.co.za/content/sapsyc/41/3/EJC98655

Dyer, R. (2008). The matter of whiteness. In P.S. Rothenberg (Ed.), *White Privilege: Essential Readings on the Other Side of Racism* (pp. 9–14). London: Worth Publishers.

Fishman, R., Iyengar, S.S., Kamenica, E., & Simonson, I. (2008). Racial preference in dating. *Review of Economic Studies*, 1, 117–132. https://doi.org/10.1111/j.1467-937X.2007.00465.x

Glücksmann, R. (2010). *Apartheid legislation in South Africa*. Accessed May 2015. Retrieved from http://goo.gl/3MLHVt

Hall, S. (2005). *Critical Dialogues in Cultural Studies*. New York: Routledge.

Hester, H. (2014). *Beyond Explicit: Pornography and the Displacement of Sex*. Albany, NY: State University of New York Press.

Human Development Report. (2015). *United Nations Development Programme*. New York. Retrieved from goo.gl/nd5u6Acontent_copy

Iqani, M. (2016). *Consumer Culture and the Media: Magazines in the Public Eye*. London: Palgrave Macmillan.

Levine, S. B. (2003). The nature of sexual desire a clinician's perspective. *Archives of Sexual Behaviour*, 32(3), 279–285.

Livermon, X. (2012). Queering freedom: Black queer visibilities in post-apartheid South Africa. *GLQ: A Journal of Lesbian and Gay Studies*, 18(2–3), 297–323.

McLean, N. (2013). Digital as an enabler: A case study of the Joburg Pride 2012 clash. In: *Feminist Africa: E spaces: E politics*. Cape Town: African Gender Institute.

Mendelsohn, G. A., Shaw Taylor, L., Fiore, A. T., & Cheshire, C. (2014). Black/white dating online: Interracial courtship in the 21st century. *Psychology of Popular Media Culture*, 3(1), 2–18.

Milani, T. (2014). Queering masculinities.' In S. Ehrlich, M. Meyerhoff & J. Holmes (Eds.), *The Handbook of Language, Gender and Sexuality* (pp. 240–259). Chichester: John Wiley & Sons.

Nattrass, N., & Seeekings, J. (2001). Two nations? Race and economic inequality in South Africa today. *Daedalus*, 130 (1), 45–70.

Posel, D. (2001). What's in a name: Racial categorizations under Apartheid and their afterlife. *Transformation*, 47(1), 50–74.

Raamutsindela, F. M., & Simon, D. (1999). The politics of territory and place in post-Apartheid South Africa: The disputed area of Bushbuckridge. *Journal of Southern African Studies*, 25(3), 479–498.

SABC. (2016). Retrieved, June 2016, from www.sabc.co.za/news/tag/Racism

Shome, R. (2000). Outing whiteness. *Critical Studies in Media Communication*, 17, 366–371. https://doi.org/10.1080/15295030009388402

Sonnekus, T. (2013). 'We're not Faggots!': Masculinity, homosexuality and the representation of Afrikaner men who have sex with men in the film Skoonheid and online. *South African Review of Sociology*, 44(1), 22–39.

Sonnekus, T., & Van Eeden, J. (2009). Visual representation, editorial power, and the dual 'othering' of Black men in the South African gay press: The case of gay pages. *Communicatio: South African Journal for Communication Theory and Research*, 35(1), 81–100.

Stager, P. (2003). What men watch when they watch pornography. *Sexuality and Culture*, 7, 50–61.

Watney, M.M. (2005). Regulation of the Internet pornography in South Africa. *Journal of Contemporary Roman Dutch Law*, 227–237. https://doi.org/10.1111/j.1468-5906.2011.01630.x

Wilderson, F. B., III. (2010). *Red, White & Black: Cinema and the Structure of US Antagonisms*. London: Duke University Press.

Williams, L. (1999). *Hardcore: Power, Pleasure and the Frenzy of the Visible*. Berkeley, CA: University of California Press.

Wing, Sue D. (2013). *Overcoming Our Racism: The Journey to Liberation*. San Francisco, CA: Jossey Bass.

4

POPULAR CULTURE, NEW FEMININITIES, AND SUBJECTIVITIES

Reading *Nairobi Diaries*

Dina Ligaga

In this chapter, I discuss a local television show recently introduced on Kenyan television called *Nairobi Diaries*. Within an emerging scholarship on the global south, I argue that local productions such as television, radio, and other digitalized shows make it possible to glimpse the intricate ways in which cultural productions both shape and are shaped by global interfaces and interactions. I want to show how a local television production, in the age of globalization, engages and re-articulates everyday narratives of femininity in Kenya in ways that are located and specific to this African nation. Linguistically and referentially, *Nairobi Diaries* signals local cultural practices around femininity and the aspirational desires of those who participate in specific urban cultures. The show brings together well-known celebrities but also makes use of young men and women who encompass the daily experiences of aspirational cultures in Kenya's capital, Nairobi. While the show in itself provides a rich case study, it offers an opportunity to map out how local practices of class and desire are encompassed within narratives of femininity within an African city and, in the case of this chapter, a space to re-examine the idea of agency within the context of heteronormative media practices.

Nairobi Diaries is a television reality show that follows the lives of seven Nairobi-based 'socialites' in Kenya. Among the all-female cast is popular video 'vixen' and entrepreneur, Vera Sidika. The show also features other less well-known women who nonetheless showcase themselves as fashion-forward, classy, global subjects. This is indicated in the way they dress, what they purchase, how they look, and even how they speak. I am interested in re-engaging the idea of agency of these women within a show that essentially presents itself as a 'global' show in the way that it seems to mimic existing shows in the global north such as *The Real Housewives* franchise. However, as Arjun Appadurai (1995), Joyce Nyairo (2004), Stephanie Newell (2000), and others have variously noted, what appears to be mimicry is often complex in its connections with local cultures. In this chapter, I consider the hypervisibility of the female subject against a competing discourse of morality through which femininity is read in Kenya. Hypervisibility is both a way of proclaiming presence and also a way of reading the women as global subjects in a neoliberal world. I focus on the first season of *Nairobi Diaries*, which aired in December 2015. Importantly, while the show is a television show, I analyze the archived videos of the show on YouTube and take into account a different public addressed through the show. Through a narrative, visual, and discourse analysis of the kinds of femininities showcased in the show, I hope to make an argument for agency, while recognizing the location of these women as global, neoliberal subjects.

Hypervisibility or the representations of black women

This chapter is premised on the idea of hypervisibility as an agentic strategy in reading the representations of African women in Kenyan popular culture. In black feminist studies, the idea of hypervisibility is juxtaposed alongside that of invisibility to refer to the stereotyping of black women's bodies as abnormal, hypersexual, and deviant (Mowatt et al., 2013). In other words, the black woman is often either absent completely from discourse, or when she comes into view, it is as a source of spectacle (Mowatt et al., 2013). In fact, Rasul Mowatt et al. argue that the sexism and racism that black women experience in the academy has contributed significantly to the invisibilizing of black women subjectivities in research. This is, of course, in addition to the marginalization of black women as participants in research. Christine Obbo (1980), carrying out research on African women, similarly laments about the lack of women as researchers and participants in African historiographies, leading to a lopsided view of the social realities that affect them directly. As such, Mowatt et al. (2013) urge for an approach to any research of black women's bodies that recognizes the intersectional politics of race, class, and gender and how these impact the inclusion of black women in research. In this chapter, I take into cognizance the context in which I read black women's bodies as a crucial factor in interpreting the practices and choices that the women I analyze engage in. I recognize the location of the research in an African country where gender, class, and sexual politics collide to influence how women are represented or self-represent. The location of culture is important in situating and exploring the social realities of gender, race, sexuality, and class that define black women's bodies in productive ways (Mowatt et al., 2013). Women's (in)visibility in Africa has historically been a social threat that needs managing. Within literature and the media, in particular, two dominant modes of representations have prevailed (Cornwall, 2005; Tamale, 2011). They have either been represented negatively as the voiceless victims of multiple oppression (see Cutrufelli, 1983) or as wild, eroticized, feisty, self-reliant, and threatening to the family unit (Cornwall, 2005; Kanogo, 2005; Obbo, 1980; Mutongi, 2007). In the case of the former, the African woman is ruralized and contained within myths of femininity that domesticate and reintegrate her into the dominant narrative of family and nation (Mupotsa, 2014). The ideal African woman in both the colonial and the postcolonial states was the one who stayed in the rural spaces performing gender-normative roles. The African woman as mother is hence a colonial and postcolonial invention during a period of social anxiety. The myth was reproduced within a paternalistic logic on the role of womanhood (Cutrufelli, 1983). In her review of literature on motherhood in African literature and culture, Remi Akujobi (2011) concedes that the 'maternal ideals . . . entrenched and valorized in all cultures . . . present a woman's central purpose to be her reproductive function and so motherhood and mothering become intertwined with issues of a woman's identity' (2011, 4), generating the female archetypes of Virgin, Venus, and Mother Earth. From such myths, the African woman as mother becomes appropriated much later in narratives of nationhood for instance, in which these women become selfless cradle-rockers, nurturers, and goddesses (Akujobi, 2011, 3). The African woman who travelled to urban spaces and embraced modernity is painted as antithesis to the ideal woman. Christine Obbo's (1980) work, for instance, shows how the economically independent young woman who was unmarried but sexually active was presented as a social threat that needed to be disciplined. The woman in such a case is considered a distraction to men, a threat to the family unit, and generally a disruption to colonial and postcolonial social and political orders (Obbo, 1980). Such women enter into circulation in the newspaper press and popular culture as 'good-time girls' or 'modern girls' (Modern Girl Around the World [MGATW] et al., 2005; Newell, 2002; Obbo, 1980). The 'modern girl' is identified by her 'explicit eroticism' and use of specific commodities, 'wearing provocative fashions and pursuing romantic love' (MGATW et al., 2005, 245). It is generally accepted that her independence means that she is also promiscuous, is dressed inappropriately to lure unsuspecting men, and brings unwarranted competition for men at the workplace (Obbo, 1980). She is blamed not only for creating 'male confusion and conflict over what the contemporary roles of women should be, but for dilemmas produced by adjusting to rapid social change' (Obbo, 1980, 11). She is the bearer of sexual diseases and the cause of broken marriages. Popular cultural narratives carry warnings of such 'good-time girls,' whom young men are advised to stay away from (Obiechina, 1972). While men are able to access opportunities created by the colonial economy, women are not (Kanogo, 2005). In fact, as Kanogo argues, 'being a woman in the highly gendered colonial spaces precipitated a plethora of conflicts, contradictions and negotiations' (2005, 3). In this respect, the lives of African girls and women become, as Kanogo argues, sources of 'public spectacle' (2005, 3). Calls for laws banning certain kinds of female dresses considered to be 'injurious to public morale' (Obbo, 1980, p. 11) are made constantly through media reports 'condemning the exhibition of the female body, and maintaining that it should be a private thing, especially if a woman was attached to a particular man' (Obbo, 1980, p. 11). Such reports and public discussions encourage the violent abuse of women's bodies in public spaces, if the woman was deemed to be dressed indecently (Mwangi, 2013). Women become the moral bearers of culture with a concerted effort to 'reverse or hinder possible changes in the power and authority relations between men and women' (Obbo, 1980, 15). Tabitha Kanogo, reading women in the colonial Kenyan context, has argued that women were subjected to unwarranted public surveillance and sanction, such as the forceful removal of an 'undocumented and unaccompanied rural woman' from a city-bound vehicle (2005, 3); the abduction of girls from school for 'compulsory' clitoridectomy (genital excision); and other forms of public performances that ensured women remained within the constraints of colonial and African traditional practice (Kanogo, 2005). Through judicial laws, 'uneasy alliances' emerged between 'official and unofficial groups that were determined to shape the lives of African girls and women' (Kanogo, 2005, p. 4). Whether invisible (rural) or visible (urban), women's presence in Africa can be understood as problematic and in need of interrogation.

'Wicked woman': stereotypes in African popular culture

Within popular culture, the narrative of the urban woman is captured within the stereotypical representation of the wicked city woman. I read popular culture as ubiquitous forms that 'flourish without encouragement or recognition from official cultural bodies, and sometimes in defiance of them' (Barber, 1987, p. 1). They include art, music, theatre, paintings, and sculptures to name a few, as well as 'decorated bread labels . . . portrait photography . . . jokes', rumour and gossip, as well as numerous other similar forms (Barber, 1987, p. 5). Popular culture participates in narrativizing everyday life, using language recognizable by those who consume it and familiar plotlines that help to generate lessons (Gunner, 2000). Agnes Muriungi (2007) has argued that by critically engaging with popular literature, it is possible to read how these texts dramatize specific themes drawn from everyday realities, such as 'sex, gender, sexuality, marriage, commercial sex/prostitution, widowhood, single parenthood, love and romance, orphanage. . . [and] morality' (2007, p. 7). By extension, these popular texts open up 'new possibilities of thinking about human sexualities and understanding . . . society in general' (Muriungi, 2007, p. 7). The popular, according to her, is informed both by its style as well as its thematic content. Tom Odhiambo, who reads popular literature as an urban phenomenon, defines it as that which 'borrows its subject matter from the public on issues of contemporary importance' (Odhiambo, 2004, p. 33). The temporal relevance of popular art is combined with its generic orientation – thrillers, romance, adventure story, mystery, and rumour – to argue that such categorizations enable the popular forms to perform multiple functions of entertaining, educating, informing, and instructing, while paying close attention to people's 'worries, questions, experiences and lives' (2004, p. 33). The popular is thus intertwined with the everyday lives of the ordinary Kenyans who read, produce and reproduce, and use them. They are laden with the stereotypical thinking, anxieties, and other social and economic realities of these people.

Stereotypes become an important marker for identifying how popular cultural texts work. A stereotype, according to Chris Barker (2004, p. 188), is a 'vivid but simple representation that reduces persons to a set of exaggerated, usually negative character traits and is thus a form of representation which essentializes others through the operation of power.' Within African popular culture, the stereotype of the wicked city woman highlights an undesirable character who has to be avoided if one is to survive in the city. Onitsha Market literature pamphlets most exemplify this argument. These pamphlets were produced in the 1960s in Nigeria and sold in the then thriving market of Onitsha. These pamphlets were produced by local presses and have been celebrated variously for their connection with the real lived experiences and anxieties of audiences (Newell, 2000). They mainly consisted of stories, plays, advice, and moral narratives and were designed to give advice to young men who were moving into cities.[1] Young women were marked as dangerous, and they either had to be taught to become good wives and girlfriends or be treated as pariahs. In most of these booklets, these young women were merely 'good-time girls' in need of money to purchase various consumer items without really bringing much benefit to the man. Commenting on the male authorship of this literature, Jane Bryce (1997, p. 118) observes, that popular fiction displays 'sex-and-violence sensationalism with aggressively macho heroes, and women represented as seducers or sex objects.' Citing the work of popular Kenyan novels such as John Kiriamiti's *My Life in Crime* and Charles Mangua's *Son of Woman* as examples, Bryce explores the different ways in which these figures are constructed as degenerates who occupied the city spaces in strategic ways (1997, p. 119). Alongside the stereotype of the wicked city woman was that of the 'proper woman.' Most of these were rural women who were 'represented only as wives and mothers . . . the polar opposite of the wicked urban woman. She is a bridge to a pure past, a talisman which the beleaguered urban man holds up before him to ward off the temptations and obstacles of town' (Newell, 2002, p. 111). She is, as Florence Stratton observes, the 'Mother Africa trope' (1994, p. 39), a point that I make earlier in this chapter.

New femininities, (hyper)visibility, and presence

In exploring new representations of femininity in Kenya through the theme of hypervisibility, I acknowledge existing representations of women and femininities in the African context. Yet, in light of emerging literatures on new femininities on the continent, I want to argue, following Simidele Dosekun's assertion, that there is a need for 'new terrains of enquiry . . . to better keep up with and critique the deeply political and contradictory cultural logics of globalization' (2015, p. 962). Making an argument for understanding postfeminism as transnational culture, Dosekun argues that this enables a better understanding of what she terms 'spectacular new femininities' in Africa and other non-Western locations (2015, p. 962). Dosekun's call comes in the wake of recognition of new femininities within neoliberal cultures (McRobbie, 2009; Tasker and Negra, 2007; Gill and Scharff, 2011; Gill, 2007, 2008). These studies recognize 'the cultural sensibility proclaiming that women are "now empowered" and celebrating and encouraging their consequent "freedom" to return to normatively feminine pursuits and to disavow feminism as no longer needed or desirable' (Dosekun, 2015, p. 960). These women defy clear-cut, stereotypical fittings as good/bad, rural/urban, and so on but invite a critique of them as neoliberal subjectivities. In a context such as Kenya, however, where gender and sexuality are still heavily policed through the propagation by, among other avenues, the media, of what it means to be a proper woman, I find that the mere critical reading of how women are represented is itself important. I look at the new femininities represented through shows like *Nairobi Diaries*, and the cultures embraced by the women therein, as commenting and intervening in existing morality discourses that insist on fixing women's identities in the public sphere.

POPULAR CULTURE, NEW FEMININITIES

Nairobi Diaries is a television reality show that was premiered on 14 December 2015 for the television station K24 in Kenya. Premised on an already familiar typology made popular through shows such as *The Real Housewives of Atlanta*,[2] the show portrays a group of women as dramatic, raunchy, sassy, and 'ratchet.'[3] Among its original cast is popular video vixen Vera Sidika. Sidika is a Kenyan socialite who became famous after her appearance in a music video of the song 'You Guy' by a popular Kenyan music group called P-Unit. Despite drawing a lot of negative attention due to her choices (breast augmentation, skin-lightening procedures), she remains in the public eye, showing off her body, her lifestyle, and accompanying material gains or both (see also Iqani, 2016). Other cast members of the first season of the show include fellow socialite and singer Pendo; musician and actress Ella Ciiru; Gertrude Murunga, a student; Kiki Diang'a, an architect; Marjolein Blokland, a fitness instructor; and Sylvia Njoki, a fashion stylist.

The opening shots of the show project these women as middle class through signifiers of success, money, education, beauty, and upward mobility.[4] This is depicted through their modes of dress, postures, and speech. Each of the women is dressed in fashionable outfits that mark their positions within global trends. They each have heavy make-up on, and nearly all of them have weaves – again depicting their location as postfeminist subjects (see Dosekun, 2016). At the end of the opening credits, a single still visual shot features all cast members facing the camera and communicating confidence and even defiance. The background is largely dominated by red clouds depicting stormy weather, perhaps preparing its audience for melodrama. The background also features iconic buildings that signify Kenya's city centre, Nairobi, such as the Parliament Building and the Kenya International Conference Centre. Despite the visual promise of a show on middle-class culture, here read as respectability, of these Nairobi-based women (see my reading of Skeggs, 1997, later in this chapter), the preview to the show (at the start of the opening shots) and the text of the final shot just as the programme begins signal a complication and contradiction of the meaning of class as social practice through its focus on dramatic characterization and melodramatic plotlines. In true reality television fashion, the show is previewed as full of drama. The calm voiceover narrator who introduces the show is juxtaposed with the shrillness and melodrama presented through the characters who promise scandal, back-stabbing, betrayals, gossip, and physical fights. It promises to give the audience an insider view of the lifestyles and leisure activities of young women in Nairobi.

To speak of their hypervisibility is to draw attention to the choice to showcase these women as synonymous with Nairobi city. The cast members of this show in many ways evokes the popular parlance *manzi wa Nairobi* to refer to a particular kind of woman who specifically aligns with urban femininities in Kenya. While the phrase has existed in informal popular lore on and about Nairobi, it was made popular in hip-hop tunes such as Kenya's Nonini's (Herbert Nakitare) now famous tune 'Manzi wa Nairobi' (Mwangi, 2007). Nonini's song captures the image of the 'Nairobi chic' (*manzi wa Nairobi*) in sexually loaded lyrics that include depictions of a slick, confident, well-dressed young woman who is guaranteed to drive men crazy.[5] Nonini's music is part of a proliferation of a new style of music that enters into the Kenyan scene from the mid-1990s that begins to revise the narrative of the city as a degenerate space that breeds seedy characters (Mwangi, 2007; Nelson, 2002). In revising this earlier narrative, this popular form signals the effects of 'intense globalization, the spread of computer technologies, and the onset of multiparty politics since the 1990s' in Kenya (Mwangi, 2007, 321). In the earlier narrative, patriotism and African racial pride were concomitant with rural identities and location (Mwangi, 2007). In the new discourse, the musicians 'seem to have fallen in love with the city despite its myriad problems' (Mwangi, 2007, p. 321). In this music, artists seems to be celebrating 'their unsure identities in the city in a grammar that seems impatient with notions of national purity and rural stability and that seems more liberal in talking about topics earlier considered off-limits' (Mwangi, 2007, p. 321). 'Manzi wa Nairobi' therefore occupies a new discourse of freedom and progress. Even then, scholarship on popular music in Kenya seems to suggest a heavily masculinized vision of what a 'manzi wa Nairobi' should be (Thiong'o, 2015; Wasike, 2011; Mwangi, 2004). Echoing Evan Mwangi (2004), who argues that the city space is a masculine space interpreted through masculinist lenses, Chris Wasike asserts that Kenyan hip-hop artists, mostly male, use their lyrics to emphasize their masculine identities (2011). Their music, Wasike argues, is violent and sexist in ways that signal hard-core American rap and hip-hop music (2011). In her analysis of male artist depiction of women in popular music, Kanyi Thiong'o similarly points to tendency of male musicians through Kenya's postindependence history to portray the 'liberated' woman as 'rotten,' even while fixing their gaze on her sexualized body (2015, p. 10). Within these contradictory scholarships – reading Nairobi as a progressive space versus negative portrayal of women in male-dominated hip-hop music scene – the women of *Nairobi Diaries* emerge as glaring anomalies, rightfully located in a global cosmopolitan space but in the face of continued moralizing discourses and hegemonic masculinities.

Consumerism and class in *Nairobi Diaries*

If the women of *Nairobi Diaries* emerge as contradictions, it is because they occupy the nexus between class and consumerism. As Beverly Skeggs

(1997) reminds us, class is marked by the notion of respectability, which influences 'how we speak, who we speak to, how we classify others, what we study and how we know who we are (or not)' (p. 1). Respectability is central to structuring class identities and categorizing social groups (Skeggs, 1997). Just as we are reminded in Linda Nead's work, respectability was worked into visual representations of femininity and moral judgement of women in 19th-century Victorian England (1988). Respectability, as a marker of class, is what is historically recognized as categorizing through standardization of behaviour and social decorum, towards which those who want to gain entry into classed social circles must aspire (Skeggs, 1997). It is such classed categories that create perceptions of inequality (Skeggs, 1997). Against what is read as classed women of society, or the ladies of leisure, the opposite figure of the working-class women is projected as 'contagion, pollution, danger, distaste and excess heterosexuality' (Skeggs, 2005, p. 966). Reading hen parties in the UK, Beverly Skeggs (2005) demonstrates the manner in which the working-class woman is represented in the media vis-à-vis national public morality discourse. She discusses the public ways in which white working class women are 'forced' to display their lack of moral values within emerging neoliberal cultures where the lack of display of class and affect. Skeggs emphasizes the manner in which this class of women visually refuses to conform to the neoliberal sensibility of a well-manicured, polished look, a result of the regimes of self-care (Skeggs, 2005). Instead, she is known for her vulgar language and sensibility, loud and aggressive personality, and her disregard for other people's moral sensibilities (Skeggs, 2005). This pathologizing of the working class is crucial in locating how working-class morality has been used in moments of crisis and social disorder (Skeggs, 2005).

If, according to Skeggs, the respectable and the working-class women are in tension, how can we read the women of *Nairobi Diaries* and understand them as hypervisible subjects? For one, *Nairobi Diaries* presents its female characters as ladies of leisure, projected as such mainly through their consumerist practices. This occurs primarily through the locations in which the show is shot and where the women socialize, through their choices of intimate partners, through their leisure activities, how they dress, and where they shop and how they speak. I use the phrase 'ladies of leisure' to signal the very deliberate ways that the show projects these women's lifestyles in material terms. It also loosely signifies their aspirational desire towards gentrification, while at the same time, the negation of that desire through their relationships to each other. Ladies of leisure as aspirational speaks to how these women locate themselves within the city space, as educated, professional women with access to money and expensive lifestyles. For instance, in the first episode of the first season, Pendo and Marjolein meet for brunch at the lavish Karen Connection, in Nairobi's posh Westland suburbs. During this meeting, in which they share a meal, they discuss other aspects of their leisurely engagements, including joining friends for cocktail parties later and participating in a karaoke event at a friend's high-end bar. In a different shot, we see Pendo and Ella meet up to go shopping together at what is scripted in as an expensive boutique. Though small, this and other boutiques that the women visit in the duration of the show project themselves as expensive through items that are sold for large amounts of money. Pendo, for instance, in episode two, buys a pair of shoes for 13,000 shillings (about $200). This is steep for an ordinary Kenyan's budget, but in the context on the show, this is how Pendo 'spoils herself.' Another way in which these women are distinguished as ladies of leisure is through what is purportedly polished, educated English language accents. All the women speak with an accent that marks them as not only belonging to an educated category of young black women but also as women who have grown up in the comfortable suburbs of Nairobi. Pendo, for instance, born and brought up in the Swahili-speaking town of Mombasa, nonetheless feels it is important to mention that she was educated at the prestigious Kenya Girls High School.[6] All of the women in the show have been to university, even though it is not clear how many have obtained their degrees from the institutions as most are either still registered students or dropouts. Needless to say, these women seem to epitomize the real women of Nairobi who have access to finances.

The contradiction created by these cast members comes in the form of the genre itself and what it generates. In what Pier Dominguez (2015, p. 156) terms

> The docusoap money shot, a kind of trashy, antisublime moment of intimacy and negative affect that interpellates viewers through the production of thrilling anxiety . . . the performance and representation of anger, envy, and other forms of affect that are coded as feminine and/or low class, such as jealousy and unwarranted pride, and that reproduce gendered racial imaginaries, such as the figure of the 'angry black woman,' are, paradoxically, very much in character for the cast and expected by the docusoap viewers.

Dominguez's reading of *The Real Housewives of Atlanta* points towards the contradiction embodied by the characters through the endless gossip and backbiting, shouting matches, sex scandals, foul language, name-calling, and other kinds of 'ratchet' behaviour (2015). For Dominguez, it is such moments, what he calls 'getting out of character' moments (meaning, not performing for the camera), that create tension for the viewers by dwelling on the predictable unpredictability (2015, p. 156). This is a moment of hypervisibility, which according to Kristen Warner (2015) epitomizes the ratchetness of black womanhood representations. According to Warner,

> ratchetness, a disposition characterized by foolery that is more tacky than ghetto and more world-worn than camp, is a fitting descriptor for many of the women on reality series such as VH1's *Basketball Wives* (2010–13) and *Love and Hip Hop* (2011–) and their respective spinoffs, *Basketball Wives LA* (2011–) and *Love and Hip Hop: Atlanta* (2012–).
>
> (2015, p. 129)

The trashiness that both Warner and Dominguez refer to above is an important tool for understanding *Nairobi Diaries*. In pursuit of reputation, these women, rather than occupy much neater, sanitized roles that align with discourses of respectability demanded by their apparent class status, instead locate themselves in their stereotyped selves. In this way, they remain aligned to earlier narratives of the city woman as a cesspool of evil that is carried in popular cultural lore. Kristen Warner, however, argues that this hypervisibility of the black woman, rather than be automatically read as negative, can be the beginning of a new narrative of agency. In her argument, 'the analysis rests on an understanding of the liminality of their performance of ratchetness as a means of ensuring a material wage and maintaining visibility in a medium where black women's bodies are often rendered invisible' (2015, p. 129). Beyond the argument of settling, that Warner seems to be intimating here, I also want to argue that occupying the space of negative comment and feedback, with regard to dominant moralizing discourse, is in itself an act of self-assertiveness and reinvention of the image of black womanhood. Pendo, for instance, shares with the viewer through a strategy of reality television in which cast members speak directly and intimately with the viewer (Dominguez, 2015) details of her intimate life. She mentions that she is currently seeing a very rich West African man who funds her lifestyle, in many ways, imitating the lifestyle of co-cast member and socialite Vera Sidika.

Postfeminist selves

In exploring the question of postfeminism, one of the dominant aspects of this culture is the emphasis placed on regimes of self-care in order to enhance and project senses of beauty. Each cast member is projected as jet-setting, successful, and wanting for nothing. In fact, their egos and pride that make them so entertaining is supposedly drawn from their confidence in their wealth (see Dominguez, 2015). In the show, each of the women is projected as a successful celebrity figure who is already swimming in wealth. The choices made in the show in this way are not accidental. In her article on the web series *An African City*, Grace Ogunyankin (2016) argues, for instance, that the projection of the series as a world-class city is part of a need to reframe the discourse of Africa as already belonging to the world. These women project a worldliness that places them in the same league as any other woman anywhere in the world, shattering 'the usual Western portrayal of, say, the woman with the child on her back and a load on her head, who appears to care little about fashion' (Ogunyankin, 2016, p. 42). The cast members are fashionable, and this, as Ogunyankin argues, places them as agentic subjects able to make decisions that affect them at personal levels (2016).

Take for instance cast member Vera Sidika. Sidika is a 26-year-old video vixen and fashion model for plus-size women, famous for her big bottom and for publicly acknowledging that she has undergone a skin-lightening procedure. Her first encounter with the public is through the music video for the hit song 'You Guy (Dat Dendai)' in 2012, performed by the hip-hop group P-Unit.[7] Arguably the star of *Nairobi Diaries* in its first season, Sidika signifies a postfeminist culture in which the sexy body is the ultimate mark of feminine identity. This body, while presented as a woman's source of power, is also constantly in need of 'surveillance, discipline and re-modelling' (Gill, 2007, p. 149). Modern cultures have epitomized regimes of self-care that impose notions of beauty on men and women that need maintenance through consumer spending. Vera Sidika's glossy, well-polished look is an end product of this disciplinary regime. Her lightened skin and augmented breasts emphasize the 'sleek, toned, controlled figure' considered 'essential for portraying success' (Gill, 2007, p. 150). In the show, she always appears dressed in expensive clothes that depict glamour, gloss, and high-end living. Mehita Iqani (2016), reading Sidika and other female celebrities, has referred to this practice of representation as commoditized beauty in the global south. Sidika also participates in the postfeminist culture through the constant citation of individualism, choice, and sense of empowerment that allows her to use her body to earn money. In a radio interview recorded during the show, Sidika maintains that she has no problems with how her body navigates the public space. In a different television interview with Kenyan NTV anchor Larry Madowo, for instance, she says, 'Looking good is my business, my body is my business, nobody else's business but mine.'[8] She goes on to confirm that she lightened her skin because her 'body is a moneymaker.'[9] She was also featured on *BBC*

Trending where she defended her choice for lightening her skin, claiming that it was her choice to do so.[10]

The other cast members equally embrace postfeminist cultures that make prominent their embrace of transnational cultures of postfeminism (see Dosekun, 2015, 2016). They become markers of aspiration while still locating themselves within existing discourses of the 'wicked city woman' so circulated in popular culture. However, in this chapter, I urge for a look beyond this stereotype in order to consider what visibility means in the context of agency and African subjectivities. Echoing Warner (2015), it is possible to begin to explore new avenues of agency within existing discourses. In the first episode of the first season, there is a screenshot of Gertrude, the university student, and Marjolein, the fitness instructor. Born of a Dutch father and a Kenyan woman, she is naturally lighter in tone than the other women and her hair remains natural. Both women have make-up on, although Gertrude's appears to be more heavily applied. The 'girls' are in yet another high-end restaurant, gossiping and catching up with each other, giving off an air of nonchalance about this leisurely practice. They each have on fashionable dresses with chandelier earrings, each cutting a figure of a cosmopolitan woman. Gertrude is later seen in a different shot in the opening of her charity event for the girl child, projecting not just success but social responsibility for the less fortunate. Again, this plays on stereotypes that flatten African women (Ogunyankin, 2016).

Nairobi Diaries therefore plays with ideas of choice and freedom of these women, projected variously through modes of dress, speech, and leisure in order to locate them as powerful subjects who conquer the city. However, they are working within the genre of a reality TV show, which in many ways falls back to stereotypical aspects of femininity (Dominguez, 2015). Similarly, their embrace of consumerist cultures as their location of freedom is also problematic precisely within the context in which the show is shot. As Iqani has argued elsewhere, the social and economic realities within which these postfeminist figures exist should be taken in to account in defining success and, in the case of this chapter's argument, agency.

Conclusion

Within a broader matrix of scholarship on the global south, it is interesting to follow local articulations and productions that point us towards specific cultures that define the character of such locations. Popular cultural narratives are one way into this complex matrix, as they provide a link between what is perceived through visual presentation and what is implied through cultural associations. This is the case of *Nairobi Diaries* discussed here.

The chapter has mapped out the thematic of hypervisibility of black women's bodies in a popular television production, leading us to consider ways in which agency can be read and understood within such a local production. In the chapter, while the global subjectivities of these women remain important, the ways in which their locations are marked through visual and narrative texts points us towards a better understanding of narrative territoriality in Kenya.

Notes

1 For a sample of material, see Onitsha Market Literatures (2018). Retrieved from http://onitsha.diglib.ku.edu/index.htm.
2 The Real Housewives of Atlanta (2018). Retrieved from www.bravotv.com/the-real-housewives-of-atlanta.
3 www.urbandictionary.com/define.php?term=Ratchet&defid=6710768. For a full definition of *ratchet* in urban lingo. Also see tabloid announcements of the show when it premiered: www.sde.co.ke/m/pulse/article/2000185750/fans-expect-nothing-but-drama-as-nairobi-diaries-kenya-s-new-reality-show-premiers.
4 K24TV (2015). Nairobi Diaries Episode one. Retrieved from www.youtube.com/watch?v=vR4day_jgL8&list=PLbQ7LA0_TqGJCURcy-3WjX75r1-Rul3bdX.
5 Nonini MgengeTrue (2013). Manzi wa Nairobi. Retrieved from www.youtube.com/watch?v=HlxtZ-jLOTQ.
6 Historically, Kenya Girls High school has been marked a national school, meaning that in a system of meritocracy, only the very best girls from all over the country qualify for a place in the school. It is located in Nairobi's Westlands area, in Kileleshwa, and is one of the oldest schools in the country.
7 KenyanPoetsLounge. P-Unit. 'You Guy' YouTube video: www.youtube.com/watch?v=DE-MtRUsp9E. Date accessed 2 May 2016.
8 As is the nature of online material, the original interview has been removed due to third-party copyright infringement. It now appears in snippets online. However, one can still find a few videos that reference the original such as this: www.youtube.com/watch?v=1YEdTBh0Y3c.
9 Ibid.
10 BBC Trending (2014). #BleachedBeauty Vera Sidika Speaks out. Retreived from www.youtube.com/watch?v=6RoIjOBzVAU.

References

Akujobi, R. (2011). Motherhood in African Literature and Culture. *Comparative Literature and Culture*, 13(1), 2.
Appadurai, A. (1995). *Modernity at Large: Cultural Dimensions of Globalization*. Minneapolis, MN: University of Minnesota Press.
Barber, K. (1987). Preliminary Notes on Audiences in Africa. *Audiences in Action*, 67, 347–362. https://doi.org/10.2307/1161179

POPULAR CULTURE, NEW FEMININITIES

Barker, C. (2004). *The SAGE Dictionary of Cultural Studies*. London: SAGE Publications.
Bryce, J. (1997). Women and Modern African Popular Fiction. In Barber, K. (Ed.). *African Popular Culture* (pp. 118–124). Bloomington, IN: Indiana University Press.
Cornwall, A. (Ed.). (2005). *Readings in Gender in Africa*. Bloomington, IN: Indiana University Press.
Cutrufelli, M. R. (1983). *Women of Africa: Roots of Oppression*. London: Zed Books.
Dominguez, P. (2015). 'I'm Very Rich, Bitch!': The Melodramatic Money Shot and the Excess of Racialized Gendered Affect in the Real Housewives Docusoaps. *Camera Obscura: Feminism, Culture, and Media Studies*, 30, 155–183. https://doi.org/10.1215/02705346-2885486
Dosekun, S. (2015). For Western Girls Only? *Feminist Media Studies*, 15, 960–975. https://doi.org/10.1080/14680777.2015.1062991
Dosekun, S. (2016). The Weave as an 'Unhappy' Technology of Black Femininity. *Feminist Africa*, 21, 63–74. Retrieved from http://agi.ac.za/sites/agi.ac.za/files/fa21_standpoint_1.pdf
Gill, R. (2007). Postfeminist Media Culture Elements of a Sensibility. *European Journal of Cultural Studies*, 10 (1), 147–166. https://doi.org/10.1177/1367549407075898
Gill, R. (2008). Empowerment/Sexism: Figuring Female Sexual Agency in Contemporary Advertising. *Feminism & Psychology*, 18(1), 35–60. https://doi.org/10.1177/0959353507084950
Gill, R., and Scharff, C. (2011). *New Femininities: Postfeminism, Neoliberalism, and Subjectivity*. London: Palgrave Macmillan.
Gunner, L. (2000). Wrestling with the Present, Beckoning the Past: Contemporary Zulu Radio Drama. *Journal of Southern African Studies*, 26, 223–237. https://doi.org/10.1080/03057070050010084
Iqani, M. (2016). *Consumption, Media and the Global South: Aspiration Contested*. London: Palgrave Macmillan.
Kanogo, T. (2005). *African Womanhood in Colonial Kenya, 1900–50*. Oxford: James Currey.
McRobbie, A. (2009). *The Aftermath of Feminism: Gender, Culture and Social Change*. London: SAGE Publications.
Modern Girl Around the World [MGATW] Research Group, Barlow, T. E., Dong, M. Y., Poiger, U. G., Ramamurthy, P., Thomas, L. M., and Weinbaum, A. E. (2005). The Modern Girl Around the World: A Research Agenda and Preliminary Findings. *Gender and History*, 17, 245–294. https://doi.org/10.1111/j.0953-5233.2006.00382
Mowatt, R., French, B., and Malebranche, D. (2013). Black/female/body Hypervisibility and Invisibility: A Black Feminist Augmentation of Feminist Leisure Research. *Journal of Leisure Research*, 45, 644–660. https://doi.org/10.18666/JLR-2013-V45-I5-4367
Mupotsa, D. (2014). *White Weddings* (Unpublished doctoral thesis). University of the Witwatersrand, Johannesburg.

Muriungi, A. (2007). 'Chira' and HIV/AIDS: The Reconstruction of Sexual Moralities in Kenyan Popular Fiction. In Ogude, J., and Nyairo, J. (Eds.). *Urban Legends, Colonial Myths* (pp. 281–305). Trenton, NJ: Africa World Press.

Mutongi, K. (2007). *Worries of the Heart: Widows, Family, and Community in Kenya.* Chicago, IL: University of Chicago Press.

Mwangi, E. (2004). Masculinity and Nationalism in East African Hip-Hop Music. *Tydskrif vir Letterkunde*, 41, 5–20. Retrieved from www.ajol.info/index.php/tvl/article/viewFile/29671/22617

Mwangi, E. (2007). Sex, Music, and the City in a Globalized East Africa. *PMLA*, 122, 321–324. https://doi.org/10.1632/pmla.2007.122.1.321

Mwangi, W. (2013). Silence Is a Woman. *The New Inquiry.* Retrieved 2 November 2016, from http://thenewinquiry.com/essays/silence-is-a-woman/

Nead, L. (1988). *Myths of Sexuality: Representations of Women in Victorian Britain.* Oxford: Blackwell.

Nelson, N. (2002). Representations of Men and Women, City and Town in Kenyan Novels of the 1970s and 1980s. In Newell, Stephanie (Ed.). *Readings in African Popular Fiction* (pp. 108–116). Oxford: James Currey.

Newell, S. (2000). *Thrilling Discoveries of Conjugal Life: Ghanaian Popular Fiction.* Oxford: James Currey.

Newell, S. (Ed.). (2002). *Readings in African Popular Fiction.* Oxford: James Currey.

Nyairo, J. (2004). 'Reading the Referents': (Inter)textuality in Contemporary Kenyan Popular Music (Unpublished doctoral thesis). University of the Witwatersrand, Johannesburg.

Obbo, C. (1980). *African Women: Their Struggle for Economic Independence.* London: Zed Press.

Obiechina, E. (1972). *Onitsha Market Literature.* London: Heinemann.

Odhiambo, T. (2004). *The (Un)popularity of Popular Literature in Kenya: The Case of David Maillu* (Unpublished doctoral thesis). University of the Witwatersrand, Johannesburg.

Ogunyankin, G. (2016). 'These Girls' Fashion is sick!': An African City and the Geography of Sartorial Worldliness. *Feminist Africa*, 21, 37–5. Retrieved from http://agi.ac.za/sites/agi.ac.za/files/fa21_feature_3.pdf

Skeggs, B. (1997). *Formations of Class & Gender: Becoming Respectable.* London: SAGE Publications.

Skeggs, B. (2005). The Making of Class and Gender through Visualizing Moral Subject Formation. *Sociology*, 39(5), 965–982. https://doi.org/10.1177/0038038505058381

Stratton, F. (1994). *Contemporary African Literature and the Politics of Gender.* London: Routledge.

Tamale, S. (Ed.). (2011). *African Sexualities: A Reader.* Nairobi: Pambazuka/Famahu.

Tasker, Y., and Negra, D. (Eds.). (2007). *Interrogating Postfeminism: Gender and the Politics of Popular Culture.* Durham, NC: Duke University Press.

Thiong'o, K. (2015). Portrayal of Women in Selected Songs of Kenyan Male Artistes. *Journal of African Women's Studies Centre*, 1, 66–78. Retrieved from http://journals.uonbi.ac.ke/

Warner, K. J. (2015). They Gon' Think You Loud Regardless: Ratchetness, Reality Television, and Black Womanhood. *Camera Obscura: Feminism, Culture, and Media Studies*, 30(188), 129–153. https://doi.org/10.1215/02705346-2885475

Wasike, C. (2011). Jua Cali, Genge Rap Music and the Anxieties of Living in the Glocalized City of Nairobi. Muziki. *Journal of Music Research in Africa*, 8(1), 18–33. https://doi.org/10.1080/18125980.2011.570073

5

CARTOGRAPHIES OF BRAZILIAN POPULAR AND 'PERIPHERAL' MUSIC ON YOUTUBE

The case of *Passinho* dance-off

Simone Pereira de Sá

For almost 30 years, funk music has been one of the favourite musical genres among low-income youngsters in the city of Rio de Janeiro, Brazil. Funk is the soundtrack of everyday life in the favelas and outskirts, and going to a funk party is one of the preferred nightlife options on weekends and holidays.

Although it originated in Rio de Janeiro's favelas (slums) and suburbs in the 1980s,[1] this musical genre has extended its visibility far beyond its territories over the last decade by being posted on the internet.

In this context, this chapter analyzes a phenomenon called *Batalha do Passinho* (*Passinho* Dance-Off), a 'challenge' between youngsters from the favelas and outskirts of Rio de Janeiro who perform complex dance steps, blending funk and other genres such as *frevo* (a traditional dance from northeast Brazil), tango, and even the famous Michael Jackson move known as the moonwalk. They dance to the sound of mobile phones, film the performances, edit them in an amateur fashion, and post them on the internet, as shown in the Figures 5.1 through 5.3.

Spread quickly on YouTube, the 'battles' gained visibility beyond their original territory thanks to the organization of a championship sponsored by the Rio de Janeiro's mayor's office in 2011[2] and then through performances on TV shows of wide audience such as *Esquenta*, aired by Rede Globo on Sundays and hosted by a Brazilian popular actress, Regina Casé. Other initiatives such as the documentary film *Batalha do Passinho*, by Emilio Domingos,[3] also contributed to the diffusion of this cultural expression to the point that the *passinho* dance featured in the opening ceremony of the Rio 2016 Olympic Games along with other musical representations of Rio de Janeiro.[4]

Figure 5.1 Still from the movie: *A Batalha do Passinho*, directed by Emilio Domingos
Source: Photographed by João Xavi and courtesy of Emilio Domingos and João Xavi

Figure 5.2 Still from the movie: *A Batalha do Passinho*, directed by Emilio Domingos
Source: Photographed by João Xavi and courtesy of Emilio Domingos and João Xavi

Figure 5.3 Still from the movie: *A Batalha do Passinho*, directed by Emilio Domingos

Source: Photographed by João Xavi and courtesy of Emilio Domingos and João Xavi

Dance moves performed by 'ordinary' people and shared through social media are today one of the biggest phenomena of entertainment culture in digital platforms, forming a category of videos still little explored by audio-visual studies. Therefore, considering YouTube and the social media as a 'cultural system' (Burguess and Green, 2009), this chapter discusses this funk trend according to the following three sets of related issues:

- The role of mobile and locative media to reshape territorial boundaries
- The use of mobile phones and the ways of spreading this subgenre on the social media, especially on YouTube
- In the context of the global south perspective, the way it addresses the notions of centre/periphery, global/local, and especially world/favela – taking each of these pairs not as dual categories or excluding pairs but as connected signifiers.

Mobile media and territories of funk

Definitely, as we disconnect our machines from wires and cables, as mobile phone networks, Bluetooth, RFID or

CARTOGRAPHIES OF BRAZILIAN MUSIC ON YOUTUBE

> Wi-Fi turn our cities into unplugged and wireless communication machines, paradoxically, we create projects that seek exactly the opposite: territorialisation, anchorage in physical spaces, linkage to things, places, objects.
> (Lemos, 2007, p. 135)

The extensive discussion on the relations between media, technology, space, and place is consolidated in communication studies and have been approached by many authors such as Castells (1999), Virilio (1995), Wertheim (2001), Adams (2009), Couldry and McCarthy (2004), and Mitchell (1995), among others. In Brazil's context, the human geography perspective, especially Milton Santos's prolific work (Santos, 1978), also promotes productive dialogue. More specifically in the field of the relations between mobile, locative media, territories, and the urban space, many authors such as Lemos (2007, 2010), Santaella (2008a, 2008b), and Zeffiro (2012) analyze the appropriations and re-significations of space through these artefacts, mostly the mobile phone, highlighting a significant 'spatial turn' in cyberculture studies nowadays. Thus, although our relationship with cyberspace regarded place as irrelevant at first – since we were able to connect to the internet in a dematerialized and anonymous way – the idea that place, space, territory, and environment are central elements in the context of digital media has gained strength with the development of projects related to *ubiquitous computing* through *pervasive media*.

According to Galloway (2003), the expression 'locative media' was proposed first by Karlis Kalnins at RIXC – Center for New Media in Riga, Latvia, based on the ideas presented in the Headmap Manifest by Ben Russell (1999). The expression refers to the development of artefacts or applications containing location-based features such as smartphones, GPS, wireless connection, augmented reality, and radio frequency identification (RFID), allowing the offering of suitable services for each place. Using Google Maps for orientation in a less familiar part of town or tagging the location in a social media post are examples of such experience (Santaella, 2008a; Lemos, 2007; Brotas, 2013; Andrade and Pereira de Sá, 2012; among others).

It is worth mentioning that the developing of these artefacts and services is inspired by the paradigm of ubiquitous and pervasive computing proposed by Mark Weiser (1991). In the communication model envisioned by the author, machines would be less visible as possible and computers would be infiltrated in objects and disseminated in the human environment, intertwining to everyday life. In his later works, Weiser (1994) proposes that computing should not be understood as restricted to desktops and notebooks that centralize the user's attention *in machines on the table*, but it is also related to various devices connected to the web. In this sense, computers disseminated in the environment, equipped with sensors, would be capable of detecting and extracting data in various locations, making it possible to control, arrange, and adjust applications according to the users' needs. Similarly, each machine in this group would be able to detect the user's presence and other devices, interacting automatically with them and building a smart environment to its application. Sterling (2005) calls the later developments of this perspective the 'web of things,' and this is the foundation of mobile media endowed with locative functions analyzed here.

Based on this discussion, Lemos (2007) proposes the notion of 'informational territory' to circumscribe the reconfiguration of urban spaces from this type of technologic mediation. The informational territory is a 'hybrid, in motion' space that emerges from the intersection between cyberspace and urban space through the mediation of mobile and locative media. For example, the wireless access spot in a park is an informational territory, different from the physical space of the park and the electronic space of the internet. By accessing the internet through this Wi-Fi network, the user enters an informational territory interwoven in the physical territory (and political, cultural, imaginary, etc.) of the park and the telematics network space (Lemos, 2007, 128).

Informational territories are configured by social activities that produce symbolic, affective, and economic belonging and are articulated to places and physical territories through complex relations. Thus, it is possible to state that mobile and locative media contribute to the reconfiguration of our relationship with space and territory in at least three aspects: (1) transforming abstract spaces into symbolically significant places; (2) amplifying the connection and communitarian usages; and (3) allowing different experiences and singular appropriations of the urban space. Therefore, it is possible to reflect on the tensions between local and global aspects of music scenes from the multiterritorialities perspective (Haesbaert, 2002, 2004; Herschmann, 2013) that articulate and challenge the parameters of territorialization. These dimensions stand out in the multifunctional usages that actors of the *Passinho* Dance-Off make from their mobile phones. At first, the device is the sound source for the dancers' performances. In most of the videos they dance – solo or in a group, on the street or at home in the favela – to the sound of their mobile phones that also record the performance that will be later uploaded to YouTube. This way, the mobile phone allows the demarcation and reconfiguration of the daily space of the favela for recreational use and sociability. The alleyway that one minute earlier would only serve as the transit of pedestrians or the family kitchen are spaces that can be reconfigured as improvised dance floors where the dancers perform their moves, often in front of an audience formed by friends who applaud, whistle, and cheer. Therefore, the mobile phone connected to the internet registers the performance and allows the upload to YouTube, shaping this space as an *informational territory* constituted by the complex and hybrid network that connects the local territory and the dancers' presential performance to the amplified web. By activating the device's geolocation feature, the video is posted with an identification of the place where it was made. It is, therefore, one among many types of performance mediated by digital technologies, reconfiguring the presential experience that is conceived to be recorded with the mobile phone.[5]

Considering that the use of mobile phones with internet connection is a crucial aspect of this practice, allowing the almost immediate uploading of the videos to YouTube, we are going to reflect now on some characteristics of this platform in order to better understand its role in the process.

Mobile media and YouTube as a cultural system

YouTube was created in 2005 by designer Chad Hurley and the computer engineers Steve Chen and Jawed Karim as an amateur video channel. However, the easy and powerful interactions provided by this tool were so intense that, within a short while, it became an extremely successful platform based not only on the possibility of broadcasting but also on ranking, recommending, saving of videos, and creating personal channels. Apart from that, it is worth mentioning another important element of the platform: the classification, recommendation, and thematic aggregation system that presents to the user a set of related videos each time we insert a keyword in the search system. Therefore, YouTube is an example of a new class of business for the entertainment industry, which has given up any attempts at producing its own content in order to assemble content produced by a variety of sources. It is, then, a metabusiness based in participatory culture – whose principles are cooperation, interaction, and sharing – as its main product (Jenkins, 2008; Burguess and Green, 2009). The platform inserted in the context of Web 2.0 is at the same time a space for storage of amateur and professional videos, a media archive, and a social network. It has greatly modified the way people relate to the internet, to intellectual property, entertainment, audiovisual content and, mostly, with one another on the internet (Jenkins, 2008; Burguess and Green, 2009).

In Brazil, this consolidation coincides with the increase of internet access, particularly after the emergence of new consumers from the lower classes due to the expansion of mobile telephony. According to the Instituto Brasileiro de Geografia e Estatística (Brazilian Institute of Geography and Statistics, 2016), in 2014, the number of Brazilian households with internet access has increased more than a half (54.9 percent). The same survey has shown that, more than computers, mobile phones were the most used devices to connect to the internet.[6] Different research reveals that Brazil occupies the fourth position in the world ranking of social media users and the second one of Facebook users, behind only the United States. Also, among the most accessed websites in Brazil, Facebook occupies the second place, with YouTube in fourth place.[7] In comparison to other countries, the data become even more significant since the speed offered by broadband and mobile telephony companies in Brazil is one of the worst among the 20 researched countries.[8] Thus, with a population of 200 million inhabitants, Brazil represents the eighth largest internet audience in the world and the larger community of Latin America in absolute numbers – despite all the mishaps and inequities in revenue distribution and, consequently, digital access.

The implications of this reconfiguration remain analytically challenging. Nevertheless, we can bet on substantial impacts in a media system based on a highly centralized model, which has been consolidated during the 1970s, marked by a strong predominance of broadcast television as the primary source of information (Muzakami et al., 2014, p. 12).

YouTube's features

Burguess and Green highlight YouTube's 'own logic,' with some features that characterize this digital platform as a system with its own aesthetic and technical values. The first one is what became known in common sense as a 'YouTube video,' which means the category of videos featuring 'low-tech' aesthetics and based on a few technical components such as (a) amateur and witnessing videos, (b) short videos, (c) technically limited or denoting improvisation, and (d) low resolution. Besides this feature, the second component of YouTube's cultural logic is its pedagogical dimension. As we already know, it is possible to learn, after a brief search, the most unimaginable tasks, crafts, and skills. Apprenticeship develops primarily in informal, amateur, peer-to-peer, and little-institutionalized ways. The third component is the encyclopaedic character of the platform, since YouTube is the largest melting pot of visual memory and pop culture currently available.

Finally and more broadly, this set of practices points towards an extended sense of literacy. Therefore, YouTube's specific skills are learned and mobilized through participation in its very social network. On *passinho* dance-off videos, some of these features are easily observed. These videos are mostly recorded by their own protagonists, showing scenes shot with mobile phones to be rapidly uploaded, hence emphasizing the performances' details: dancers' bodies in close-up, details of the 'dance floor,' always implying the occupation of the neighbourhood spaces.

However, it is the invitation to participate – which is implicit in the dancer's mimicking their counterparts' dance moves – that sparks the sharing. From this point, the possibility of classifying and assembling videos in the same array is what allows the construction of a network of users who watch, comment, and upload 'responses,' hence extending the network far beyond their local territories.[9]

In this sense, the construction of a virtual audience is definitely connected to the live performance in the party venues in the favelas. The strong sense of belonging to a particular territory – the favela – is not opposed to their virtual exhibition 'to the world.' 'It all begins with the funk party,' they say in Domingos's documentary film. A second important aspect is that their choreographies are based on a creative mix of transnational pop references – from Michael Jackson to hip-hop and street dance – with traditional Brazilian dance genres, such as *frevo* and *samba*, again reinforcing the links among global and local cultural traces. Such references were absorbed directly from YouTube because these youngsters were not even born when Michael Jackson was a hit. Apart from that, peer learning through videos of friends and neighbours is also a practice to be considered. The third aspect is that the aesthetic bricolage commonly seen on YouTube videos is a crucial element to the creation of the *passinho* dance steps, marked by the combination of moves from different music genres. Its main characteristic is the intrinsic hybridism arising from YouTube itself and that helps building the dancers' performance.

Ultimately, this set of practices points out to the broader sense of literacy highlighted by Burguess and Green (2009).

> Being a 'literate' in YouTube context means not only to be capable of creating and consuming video content, but also being able to comprehend the way how YouTube functions as a set of technologies and as a social network. [. . .] What counts as 'literacy' is partially specific to YouTube culture.
>
> (2009, p. 101)

Thus, the specific competencies are learned and mobilized through the participation in the social network.

The video *Tutorial do Passinho* (*Passinho Tutorial*) made by Maycon Ângelo is an example. The 10-minute video contains all characteristics of the YouTube videos described earlier and presents didactically 'all the steps from the very beginning until the most recent,' according to the opening caption, presenting a brief history of the dance moves and teaching how to perform them in increasing levels of difficulty. Down the page, it is possible to read comments from users thanking for the free class and saying that the video is 'kick-ass.'[10]

The video demonstrates the expertise that only a well-versed user of YouTube has: perceiving the *passinho* videos as part of a whole that has a history and evolution and that belongs to a set of choreographies that should be taught and shared. Also, the manner in which the tutorial is constructed – with captions that imitate the Star Wars opening sequence – also inserts it in another sub-group of YouTube tutorials that has rules shared among the users. Therefore, it points out to a social-technical network (Latour, 2005) formed by a set of audiovisual fragments that interact with each other and expands the senses of the various productions involved in the composition of this collective. According to Railton and Watson, it is 'a distinct media form with its own patterns of production, codes and conventions of representation, and complex modes of circulation, and, on another level, as a key site through which cultural identities are produced, inscribed and negotiated' (2011, p. 10).

Aesthetic cosmopolitanism in local and virtual music scenes

In this process, how does the *passinho* contribute to our discussion about cultural identities in the context of the 'global south'? Motti Regev, in his work *Pop-Rock Music: Aesthetic Cosmopolitanism in Late Modernity*, discusses the notion of 'aesthetic cosmopolitanism' as a key concept to think about the global cultural condition of late modernity. According to the author, aesthetic cosmopolitanism should be analyzed as the combined effect of two dynamics:

> One consists of the power that emanates from the functioning of certain art forms, stylistic trends and aesthetic idioms as signifiers of modernity and contemporariness. The other consists of forces within national societies who work to absorb, implement, indigenize and legitimise such forms, trends, and idioms into the fabric of contemporary ethnic or national uniqueness.
> (Regev, 2013, p. 9)

Although one of my inspirations for this discussion is Regev's work, I guess his general model still addresses global and local cultures as two homogeneous entities: the 'first/global' world, which dictates the pace of cultural changes; and the local/indigenous/ethnic groups that 'adjust their aesthetic sensibilities' to those patterns of (global) cultural value,' in order to participate as equals in the 'cultural frontiers of modernity.' In other words, the local groups 'react' – in creative, ironic, or resistant ways – to the 'global order.'

The author calls this process (quoting Meyer's work) expressive isomorphism: 'the process through which national uniqueness is standardised so that expressive cultures of different nations, or of prominent social sectors within them, comes to consist of similar – although not identical – expressive forms, stylistic elements, and aesthetic idioms' (Regev, 2013, p. 11). It is not my intention to deny that the gap between centre and periphery implies separations of a geographical, social, and symbolic nature. However, I reckon that the *Batalha do Passinho* case refers to a musical universe that, using digital communication tools, particularly pervades and stretches these cultural borders and, consequently, the notions of local-global, live-virtual, and favela-world are addressed here in a relational sense instead of as dual positions. In this sense, I agree with Appadurai when he affirms – in his book *Modernity at Large* – that

> the new global cultural economy has to be seen as a complex, overlapping, disjunctive order that cannot any longer be understood in terms of existing centre-periphery models (even those that might account for multiple centres and peripheries). The complexity of the current global economy has to do with certain fundamental disjunctures between economy, culture and politics that we have only begun to theorise.
> (1996, pp. 32–33)

Therefore, I would like to keep open the possibility of further exploring the idea of 'peripheral cosmopolitanism' – in a context where 'periphery' is understood as a way to ponder, intertwine, and negotiate spaces, themes, sonorities, and audiences, even when flowing through 'high visibility' spaces which are neither excluding nor in opposition to the centre (Vianna, 2003). As observed by Trotta and Trotta (2013, p. 162): 'From and by the idea of periphery it emerges a wide range of cultural products associated with a set of ideas and processes about the popular which thematizes and elaborates meanings toward this both physical and symbolical place.'

Connectivity and mediation are though keywords to address a complex process that is not particular to Brazil but is also happening all over the world. From Mumbai to Latin America, including Africa and other countries, I am sure we will find hundreds of examples that reinforce the idea of 'peripheral cosmopolitanism.'

Conclusions

> The appropriation process is fundamentally political: it is a battle for power over the configuration of a technological system and therefore the definition of who can use it, at what cost, under what conditions, for what purpose, and with what consequences. This confrontation, we argue, is deeply creative and fuels a powerful innovation engine.
>
> (Bar, Pisani, and Weber, 2007)

First, the aim of this chapter is to highlight the political battle involving the use of technology demonstrated here by the *Passinho* Dance-Off. This way, we state that the articulation between mobile phones and YouTube has created a social-technical network that reconfigured the daily space of funk territories, turning them into informational territories. The cultural practices of the youngsters originating from the funk scene who dance to choreographies created by themselves are made visible through the social-technical network, which also contributes to their protagonist role in the contemporary cultural scenario.

In this scenario, technological mediations play a central role. Far from being a posteriori elements that register the dance style born in the streets, mobile phones and YouTube are the main actors in the social-technical network that consolidates the *passinho* as an event through multiple mediations.

Moreover, it is also an example of a *mediatic chain*, that is, the circulation of actors through different networks: from streets to social media, from these to the official contest sponsored by Rio de Janeiro's mayor's office involving Borel, Andaraí, and Salgueiro favelas, and then to mainstream media shows, reaching an event of global mediatic visibility, the Rio 2016 Olympics, ending up circulating through a broad cultural and commercial circuit that returns to the streets and networks, continuously.

Finally, we suggest that through this visibility, the actors in this network transform the notion of 'aesthetic cosmopolitanism' into 'peripheric cosmopolitanism' – in a context where 'periphery' is taken as a mediation category that activates a set of values connected to the popular sphere, and whose meanings are in dispute and being negotiated. As we can see in the final scene of Domingos's documentary, when the dancers are in Rio's international airport, leaving the city for London for the Paralympic Games in 2012. They are happy, playing with each other at the airport. At this moment, they don't deny that they come from the favelas, but they affirm that they want to be 'connected to the world.'

Passinho is, therefore, an outstanding example for further discussion on the senses of the global south concept in the context of urban cultures and its consequences in the digital environment from the articulation among media, music, and communication technology.

Notes

1 It is important to note that *funk carioca* – or simply 'funk' in Brazil – is a dance music style different from what 'funk' means in the rest of the world, because Brazilian funk has its origins in Miami Bass. Also, in Brazil there is a specific name for the parties where people go to dance *funk carioca*, which is the so-called '*baile funk*.' Finally, the word *carioca* is a gentile for people born in Rio de Janeiro, and it is also used to mark the birthplace of Brazilian funk music.
2 The founders of the contest are Julio Ludemir and Rafael Mike Soares. See more information on this project at www.uppsocial.org/2013/03/esta-dada-a-largada-para-a-batalha-do-passinho-2013/ (accessed 28 February 2017). In 2013, the event gained even more visibility by winning sponsors such as Coca-Cola, raising new questions about the negotiations between the actors that go beyond the scope of this chapter.
3 See the official trailer at www.youtube.com/watch?v=1RfiTXqv98U. Accessed 28 February 2017.
4 See www.youtube.com/watch?v=gZ1XmMWqZP8.
5 For further discussion on other forms of computer-mediated performance, see Pereira de Sá and Holzbach (2010).
6 For more information, see Acesso à internet e à televisão e posse de telefone móvel celular para uso pessoal. IBGE, 2014. Available at http://biblioteca.ibge.gov.br/index.php/biblioteca-catalogo?view=detalhes&id=295753 (accessed 4April 2016).
7 In: site Alexa, quoted by Mizukami et al. (2014, p. 15).
8 In: http://wearesocial.net/tag/statistics/ (accessed 4 April 2016).
9 See, for example, Vakão and Sabará's video *Passinho do menor da favela*. In www.youtube.com/watch?v=PGXd4kIOQ1s (accessed 28 February 2017).
10 www.youtube.com/watch?v=pOJ0GyTlc6M (accessed 28 February 2017).

References

Adams, P. (2009). *Geographies of media and communication: A critical introduction*. Oxford: Wiley-Blackwell.
Andrade, L.A., and Pereira de Sá, S. (2012). This is not a song! Games, computação ubíqua e os novos canais para circulação musical. In Andrade, L.A., and Falcão, T. (Eds.), *Realidade Sintética: jogos eletrônicos, comunicação e experiência social* (pp. 73–94). São Paulo: Scortecci Editor.
Bar, F., Pisani, F., and Weber, M. (2007). Mobile technology appropriation in a distant mirror: Baroque infiltration, creolization and cannibalism. *Paper presented at the Seminario sobre Desarrollo Económico, Desarrollo Social y Comunicaciones Móviles en América Latin*, of Fundación Telefônica, Buenos Aires.

Brotas, D. (2013). Música e Mídia locativa: apropriações do lugar através de conexões musicais geolocalizadas. *Paper presented at the 12th annual Encontro Anual da Compós, GT Cibercultura meeting of anais da Compós*, Salvador.
Burguess, J., and Green, J. O. (2009). *Youtube – Online video and participatory culture*. Cambridge, UK; Malden, MA: Polity Press.
Castells, M. (1999). A Era da Informação. Economia, sociedade e cultura. [The Age of Information: Economy, society and culture]. *Paz e Terra*, 3, 411–439.
Couldry, N., and McCarthy, A. (2004). *Media space: place, space and culture in a media age*. London: Routledge.
Domingos, E. (2013). *A Batalha do Passinho* [Passinho Dance-Off]. Rio de Janeiro: Osmose Films.
Galloway, A. (2003). Resonances and everyday life: ubiquitous computing and the city. Draft, in: Purse Lips Squarejaw. Accessed 29 July 2010. Retrieved from www.purselipsqaurejaw.org/mobile/cult_studies_draft.html
Haesbaert, R. (2002). *Territórios alternativos* [Alternative Territories]. São Paulo: Contexto.
Haesbaert, R. (2004). *O mito da desterritorialização: do fim dos territórios a multiterritorialidade*. [The myth of deterritorialization: from the 'end of territories' to the multiterritoriality]. Rio de Janeiro: Bertrand Brasil.
Herschmann, M. (2013). Cenas, Circuitos e Territorialidades Sônico-Musicais (mimeo.). *Paper presented at the 36th meeting of Brasileiro de Ciências da Comunicação*, Manaus.
Instituto Brasileiro de Geografia e Estatística (Brazilian Institute of Geography and Statistics. (2016). Acesso à internet e à televisão e posse de telefone móvel celular para uso pessoal: 2014. Rio de Janeiro: IBGE. Retrieved from: https://biblioteca.ibge.gov.br/visualizacao/livros/liv95753.pdf
Jenkins, H. (2008). *Cultura da Convergência*. São Paulo: Aleph.
Latour, B. (2005). *Reassembling the Social: An introduction to actor-network-theory*. Oxford: Oxford University Press.
Lemos, A. (2007). Cidade e Mobilidade. Telefones celulares, funções pós-massivas e territórios informacionais [City Mobility: Mobile Phones, postmassive functions and informational territories]. *Revista Matrizes*, 1, 121–137. Retrieved from www.revistas.univerciencia.org/index.php/MATRIZes/article/download/3993/3749
Lemos, A. (2010). Você está aqui! Mídia locativa e teorias 'Materialidade da Comunicação' e 'Ator-Rede'. *ANAIS do XIX Encontro da Compós*. Retrieved from www.metodista.br/revistas/revistasims/index.php/CSO/article/download/2221/2309
Mitchell, W. J. (1995). *City of Bits*. Cambridge, MA: MIT Press.
Mizukami, P. et al. (eds) (2014). *Mapeamento da Mídia Digital no Brasil. Um relatório da Open Society Foundation*. Escola de Direito do Rio de Janeiro, Fundação Getúlio Vargas, Centro de Tecnologia e Sociedade.
Pereira De Sá, S., and Holzbach, A. (2010). #u2youtube e a performance mediada por computador. [#U2youtube and computer-mediated performance]. *Revista Galáxia*, 10, 146–160. Retrieved from http://revistas.pucsp.br/index.php/galaxia/article/viewFile/3429/3294

Regev, M. (2013). *Pop rock music. Aesthetic cosmopolitanism in late modernity.* Cambridge, UK; Malden, MA: Polity Press.
Russell, B. (1999). Headmap manifesto. August 2012. Retrieved from www.headmap.org/headmap.pdf
Santaella, L. (2008a). A estética política das mídias locativas [The Political Aesthetics of Locative Media]. *Revista Nomadas.* April, 128–137. Retrieved from www.scielo.org.co/pdf/noma/n28/n28a13.pdf
Santaella, L. (2008b). A ecologia pluralista das mídias locativas [The Pluralistic Ecology of Locative Media]. *Revista FAMECOS,* 15, 20–24. https://doi.org/10.15448/1980-3729.2008.37.4795
Santos, M. (1978). *Por uma geografia nova* [For a New Geography]. São Paulo: Hucitec-Edusp.
Sterling, B. (2005). *Shaping things.* Cambridge, MA: MIT Press.
Trotta, F., and Trotta, F. (2013). Entre o Borralho e o Divino: a emergência musical da "periferia" [Between "Borralho"and "Divino": the musical emergency of periphery]. *Revista Galáxia,* 26, 161–173. Retrieved from https://revistas.pucsp.br/index.php/galaxia/article/view/14698
Vianna, H. (2003). De olho nos ritmos em trânsito. *Revista ECO-PÓS. Rio de Janeiro, Ed. E-Papers,* 6(2), 135–146.
Virilio, P. (1995). *O Espaço Crítico* [The Critical Space) Rio de Janeiro: Editora, 34.
Weiser, M. (1991). O computador do século XXI [The computer for the 21st Century]. *Scientific American.* September. Retrieved from www.lri.fr/~mbl/Stanford/CS477/papers/Weiser-SciAm.pdf
Weiser, M. (1994). The world is not a desktop. *Interactions.* January. Retrieved from www.ubiq.com/hypertext/weiser/ACMInteractions2.html
Wertheim, M. (2001). *Uma história do espaço: de Dante à Internet* [History of the Dante Space to the Internet]. Rio de Janeiro: Jorge Zahar Publishers.
Zeffiro, A. (2012). A location of one's own: A genealogy of locative media. *Convergence: The International Journal of Research into New Media Technologies.* August, 249–266.

Movie: A Batalha do Passinho (2013). Dir. Emilio Domingos. Osmose Movies.

6

CUIR VISUALITIES, SURVIVAL IMAGINARIES

Rían Lozano de la Pola

This chapter[1] attempts to locate the appropriate tensions and questions to propose a visual criticism grounded in Latin America, in its paradoxes and political struggles, in its uncomfortable positions and alliances, centring specifically on the possibilities of producing a feminist and *cuir*[2] gaze and perspective. In doing so I intend to respond the following questions: What theoretical tools do we have to work out/decipher/analyze the epistemological possibilities which are generated by feminist and *cuir* visualities produced from the South and its peripheries? How can a *cuir* and decolonial grammar of Latin American visuality be proposed? How can we enact other ways of looking, and how can *other* bodies be made to appear?

Starting from these questions, I would like to propose a visual culture critical analysis from a specific place grounded in one of these 'Souths' and its contradictions: Mexico, a complex place in Latin America, which in some way is part of the North and the South at the same time. But I would like to analyse also from a specific perspective – that is, from feminist, decolonial, and *cuir* positions. Although, in the following pages, I will explain more thoroughly what I mean when I use the term *cuir*, let us say for now that it is a concept – an 'incorrectly said' term – which encompasses Latin American practices of resignification of US queer movements and theory. And although below I will further analyze the so-called decolonial perspective's contributions, I think it is appropriate to explain that I use this term because the text is written in English. If, instead, this were a Spanish publication, I would resort to the use of the denomination '*descolonial*' to avoid, following the recommendations of authors such as Silvia Cusicanqui, succumbing to Anglicisms, which – in this context – overshadow processes of *descolonial* struggles produced in Latin America and 'cover up and reformulate effective practices of colonization and subalternization' (Rivera Cusicanqui, 2010, p. 7), in this case within academic practice.

Indeed, it might be worth specifying, in these first paragraphs, that I'm not thinking of Latin America as if it were a pure, essential, and romanticized place, or a geographically and politically homogenous space. Quite the opposite: I understand Latin America to be a political place of enunciation, a position which is very determined in relation to the production of knowledge (Mignolo, 2007), and a place which shares a history related to colonialism and the resulting social-political, economic, and cultural processes. In Eugenio Valdés Figueroa (2005) words, Latin American and its culture is an alternative order, a *desorden* (dis-order), a mess, which suggests the 'reformulation of that which is Latin American, understanding it as a sociocultural relationship in an inbetween space, instead of a stable and single identity inside of a clearly delimited space.'

This chapter is divided into two sections. In the first section, I will provide an introduction to the field of visual studies, giving special attention to the development of decolonial proposals which have been produced in Latin America and which, in reality, operate as the theoretical and methodological frame where my work can be located. In the second section, I will address the production of that which I refer to as '*cuir* visualities' accompanied by the visual work of some independent Mexican publications. However, this chapter will focus more on sketching a path for understanding the politics of this kind of Mexican independent visual production rather than analyzing,[3] in detail, the visual examples reproduced in the following pages.

Visual culture studies in/from Latin America: decolonial perspectives

Visual culture studies, as an 'academic discipline,'[4] came about at the beginning of the nineties, in the context of the US and the UK academy. The proposal, which broadened art history's contributions and was nourished by cultural studies' development, seeks to analyze the huge power that vision and the 'visual world' currently exercise in both the creation of meaning and the establishment and repetition of aesthetic values, gender, class and racial stereotypes, and power relations. That is to say that visual culture studies critically analyzes the role that representations and the world of visual culture have had throughout history in the construction and modelling of bodies and subjectivities, as well as in the legitimation of binary and unequal power relations established between the subject and object of representation: man-woman, white–nonwhite, North-South, West-East, art-craft, and so on. Visual culture studies, as Irit Rogoff indicates (2002, p. 24), are much more than the study of images, and despite not underestimating the centrality of vision in the production of meaning, it 'opens the doors to a vast world of intertextuality where images, sounds, and spatial arrangements are read through each other.' It is specifically this intertextual character which permits the work with visual practices so unorthodox (for art history and aesthetics, at least) as those which appear on the pages of independent publications, related to the conformation of identity processes and political struggles. This questioning and widening of the field of knowledge, which directly refers to more traditional disciplines like art history and theory, has also been accompanied by a methodological change:

> An extension of its tactical and analytical resources [. . .] of the forms of doing practices themselves, which are more and more contaminated, mixed, and indistinguishable, not just from other supports, styles, disciplines or mediations, but even other uses of social practice, politics, construction of daily life, processes of identity agency, etc.
>
> (Brea, 2005, p. 10)

Despite the appearance of visual culture studies, in both academic and editorial environments, as it is fairly recent within them, the strategy and critical perspective that they use is actually inherited directly from critical studies – like feminist ones, among others – started decades before in a trajectory driven by the School of Frankfurt. Also, the fact that this work environment has been institutionalized under the name visual studies in the US academy doesn't mean that a specific genealogy and development in diverse Latin American practices doesn't exist. Following the path taken by scholars like Esther Garbara or Hugo Achugar, and without losing sight of the geopolitical configuration of this area of study, I consider that the practice of visual studies in Latin America can be a useful tool both to think about the politics of knowledge in this global south and to set *other* conversations in motion between Souths, but also to have an impact, at the same time in the (global) north's narratives. In the words of Esther Garbara:

> Focusing on the site of production of [Latin American] visual culture [. . .] does not limit the scope of their knowledge projects; instead, it can ultimately acknowledge and amplify their impact on the sites of production of hegemonic discourses.
>
> (Gabara, 2010)

From the studies of visual culture in Latin America, I am especially interested in contemporary contributions which have connected the work in this extended field of visuality, with the contributions of so-called decolonial theory. In this sense, some intellectuals like Joaquín Barriendos and Christian León have insisted on the importance of considering 'vision' as another fundamental element in the idea of coloniality – a concept conceptualized by Aníbal Quijano and developed by the modernity/coloniality group, by the end of the 20th century and the beginning of the 21st. Intellectuals taking part in this project, like Aníbal Quijano, Walter Mignolo, María Lugones, Zulma Palmero, Ramón Grosfoguel, and Nelson Maldonado Torres, among others, have developed a repertoire of critical categories for the analysis of contemporary societies and the colonial backdrop, which provides the foundation for Western modernity discourse. Among its fundamental contributions two particularly stand out. On the one hand, there is the linkage the group theorized between the terms *modernity* and *colonialism*, being two inseparable and correlative experiences developed from the 15th century with Latin American occupation and genocide. On the other hand, there is the difference that they made between *colonialism*, understood as the military occupation, the exploitation, and the juridical annexation of a territory by a foreign power; and *coloniality*, understood as the cultural logic of colonialism which persists in Latin America (and of course other societies, including ancient 'metropolis') despite the fact that the historical colonial process, as such, has ended.

> We understand the center of the coloniality of power not just as the system of control of the colonies and ex-colonies (that is, of the non-European and non-U.S. world) but also that which remains current and the base of the global order.
> (Mignolo, 2009, p. 8)

Drawing especially from Quijano's contributions, and as a Latin American alternative to postcolonial approaches (taking into account the specificities of the type of colonialism developed in the Americas), the group formed a triple critique of this idea of coloniality focusing on three central categories: the coloniality of power, the coloniality of knowledge, and the coloniality of being.

Furthermore, currently the definitions of the fourth and fifth categories are being worked on as other elements constitutive of modernity: the coloniality of seeing and the coloniality of gender. It is this broadening of the idea of coloniality and its relationship with feminist and gender studies and, in a more specific way, in the intersection between the coloniality of seeing and the coloniality of gender, in which I locate the analysis of '*cuir* visualities,' which the second section of this chapter focuses on.

Through the analysis of those practices, I aim to highlight and question the mechanisms by means of which the cultural grid of modernity has produced the invisibilization and the stigmatized visibilization (de Pedro and Rosauro, 2015, p. 21) of certain social groups and certain bodies: *indios*, transsexuals, *locas*, political dissenters, the poor, women, the sick, and so on. Because, as Joaquín Barriendos points out, the 'coloniality of seeing' is also constitutive of modernity and, as a consequence, it operates as a standard of domination.

The inter-epistemic dialog which decolonial theory refers to should also be, in my view, a visual inter-epistemic dialog, since not all cultures give the same value to that which is seen, to that which is not seen, to what's available to be seen, to that which is hidden or unperceived; after all there are different ontologies of presence and absence [...] All of this requires a complete learning of unlearning certain inertias that we cling to [...] in the coloniality of the gaze [...] we need to denaturalize the ways in which the gaze operates; we need to reveal the racialization, the inferiorization, and the visual discrimination of difference.

(León, 2009)

Therefore, taking the paths made by the tradition of Latin American critical thought in its questioning of Eurocentric epistemologies and visual paradigms, this proposal of visual studies within and from the South face a double challenge.[5] On the one hand, this means unveiling, or making visible, the place of enunciation of the hegemonic gaze and understanding its mechanisms of production of epistemic racism through visuality and its universalist claims. On the other hand, it means presenting the production of other, non-hegemonic visualities and their proposals of creating a form of visual culture with 'decolonial agency', as proposed by Diego Falcon (2015), a researcher at la Universidad de San Francisco de Quito, as a response to the strategies of the coloniality of seeing. And this is because, as Christian Léon, a professor at FLACSO, Ecuador, points out (2011), thinking about visual studies in Latin America demands thinking about

> the diversity of histories and the structural heterogeneity which configure visuality on a modern-world system level [...] It is for this reason that one of the primary tasks of Latin American Visual Studies is to generate the intellectual conditions for their enunciation to have a place, for the opening of an *other* visuality, for the visualization of an *other* enunciation.

Cuir visualities: *Hysteria! Revista* and *Maricarmen*

As I indicated at the beginning of this text, this interest in working on the contemporary formation of *cuir* visualities is located at the intersection between the decolonial perspective, feminist and gender studies, and the critical theories of visuality. Beginning with the idea that images, like words, do things,[6] I am interested in analyzing the configuring of dissenting subjectivities, which are related to feminist and *cuir* approaches, through visual interventions.

This proposal is accompanied by some images from two independent Mexican publications: *Hysteria! Revista* and *Maricarmen*. As I specified in the first pages, I will not provide a deep analysis of those images. On the contrary, I will work *with* them in order to illustrate my general argument. *Hysteria! Revista* is a digital magazine 'of art and sexuality,' which is defined by its editors (Ivelin Meza and Liseth Gamboa) as 'a work of communicative and participative art.' It serves as a discursive and visual mediator within the Mexican transfeminist and *cuir* community. Currently, the magazine has 20 issues, available on their site: http://hysteria.mx. As for *Maricarmen*,[7] it is an independent zine published in Puebla by Tadeo Cervantes and Mr. Popper, which arose 'from the necessity to carry out a critique from the problematics which cross through and are implicated in politics of the body.' With a *cuir* perspective, its authors reflect on sexual diversity and feminisms, from their own bodies. These two publications, which both appeared in 2013, share elements which can help identify this field of *cuir* visualities. One reason for this is that their (printed or digital) pages spread texts and images from collaborators, who in one way or another make up a large part of queer/*cuir* activist activity in Mexico City through their publications, collaborations, issue launch events, 'parties,' and so on. Moreover, both are part of the same generational community, made up of people who are quite young (in their mid-twenties and early thirties) and who are very conscious of the generational gap and the different demands which exist between them and longer-existing LGBT groups in Mexico, formed in the 1970s.[8]

They are activists and militants in feminist and queer/*cuir* groups in Mexico City and they have connections to public universities: the editors are graduate and undergraduate students at UNAM (Universidad Nacional Autónoma de México), and many collaborators are also students and, in some cases, professors/investigators, related to visual arts, philosophy, pedagogy, architecture and design, and feminist and queer studies. This is a fundamental point not just to understand the theoretical baggage or education of the actors in this context but also to get an idea of the general consumer of these images and magazines. In addition, they are friends; they are convinced that affects are powerful political tools. So together they shape spaces where the playful, the fun, and pleasure coexist with forms of radical public critiques and processes of resistance.

In their publications, texts and images explicitly intervene in the need to reflect on specificities of that which is queer (strange, *torcido*, abnormal) in a context like the Mexican one, which is constituted – as was previously explained – by historical conditions of colonialism and coloniality. In this way, the representations of bodies that populate the pages of *Maricarmen* are not just sexually diverse or dissident; they are also brown, trans*,[9] fat, and precarious; they approach popular and working-class Mexican imaginary and make use of a humour that we could consider to be specific to this context. In this way, this *cuir*ness goes beyond an abstraction from academic theory, turning towards this South, indicating a new possibility of enunciation. In the same way, the themed issues of *Hysteria! Revista* are situated in the centre contemporary debates about sexuality, feminisms, and identity politics, but they also do it from this specific place. In the third issue, for example, titled *Akelarre* (and which was accompanied by the gathering/conference *Akelarre Cuir* in the MUAC [University Museum of Contemporary Art] in UNAM in January of 2014), the editors proclaimed their interest in

> practicing the possibility of creating alliances and complicities between distinct capabilities: trans, gay, hetero, non-hegemonic bio men/women, solidary women, those who fit in many of these categories and those who prefer not to get into any of them. A ritual space where we make and do politics, love, friendship, and complicity: parties, orgies, protests, stuffing ourselves full of food, workshops, arte: the proposal is to dissent through together pleasure, laughter, shouting.[10]

The cover is a drawing by Álex Aceves Bernal (Figure 6.1), a graduate student of the Faculty of Arts and Design of the UNAM and head of the artistic direction of *Hysteria! Revista*. As we can appreciate, the coven crow is conformed by different racial, hypersexualized bodies. Making a reinterpretation of Goya's *El Aquelarre*, the big goat has been replaced by a masked hairy figure, whose arms are tied with a bondage string. In Aceves's drawing, the witches are no longer offering babies to the goat-devil, but a big 'lube' bottle: a lubricant for the new, pleasant sacrifice. Or, in issue #9, 'Carnitas,' dedicated to the analysis and visibilization of 'fat bodies' with the objective of 'decolonizing' the normative (slender, white) type of body, the guest editor Alejandra Rodríguez (La Bala Rodríguez) explains that

> to speak of a fat body isn't just to speak of kilos and meat, because behind the normative discourse of slender figures and beauty

Figure 6.1 Hysteria! *Revista de sexualidad y cultura*, 'Akelarre' #3
Source: Cover by Álex Aceves, 2014.

standards is a very efficient mechanism which constructs self-depreciation, clearly tied to racism, classism and exclusion.[11]

Almendra Castillo/Rurru Mipanocha is the author of this cover (Figure 6.2). She also studied at UNAM and is a frequent collaborator of *Hysteria! Revista* and others independent publications in Mexico City. Her work is well known for mixing iconographic elements of pre-Columbian cultures (especially Mesoamerican) with other critical feminist/queer gestures, exposing sex and sexuality in a very explicit way. It is important to note that in the Mesoamerican worldview (as well as in other pre-Columbian cultures, and – saving the distances – in queer theoretical approaches), gender and sexual duality were not conceived as a static division. On the contrary, and as we can see in Mipanocha's illustration, masculine and feminine were both part of the same principle of creation and regeneration. Dealing with the type of generated images and the texts and editorial reflections which accompany them, it is worth asking what differences exist between that which is *cuir* (and therefore Latin American) and that which is queer (and therefore related to the United States)? And, what relationship does all of this have with independent visual production?

Queer theory,[12] as it is known, came about in the 1990s in the context of gay and lesbian communities in the United States, and today it is a theoretical and activist model which is fundamental to the struggles related to sexual dissidence all over the world. With one of its columns being performativity, maintained especially by Judith Butler – and her revision of Austin's theory of speech acts (1962) and the idea of iterability introduced by Derrida (2003) – queer theory allows us to think about gender in terms of 'gender acts,' which is to say that it permits us to analyze the specific bodily acts through which gender is constituted. This at the same time leads us to think about possibilities of cultural transformation using these same acts (Butler, 1988). From the standpoint of cultural production and visual studies, there have been many people responsible for analyzing the role that visual representations and artistic productions have had in the establishment of gender normativity and the colonial gaze. There have also been many artists and activists who, since the 1960s, have taken it upon themselves to present cultural space and artistic spheres as a preferred space to *twist* these same norms: from my point of view, this is the role that *Hysteria! Revista* and *Maricarmen* (among other cultural producers) are currently playing in Mexico. By presented racialized, fat, hypersexualized, crip queer bodies, independent publications are conforming, through the production of images, to an alternative critical visual culture that makes visible those historically invisible bodies.

Figure 6.2 Hysteria! *Revista de sexualidad y cultura*, 'Carnitas' #9
Source: Cover by Almendra Castillo aka Rurru Mipanocha, 2014.

But the use of the term 'queer' in Spanish loses much of its semantic weight, and above all, the fundamental strategy through which the community reclaims the insult while transforming it into something politically subversive.[13] In this sense – and from the graphic work of publications like the ones I'm referring to here, from artistic practices of groups like Invasorix, the performance work of authors like Lukas Avendaño or Felipe Osornio/Leche de Virgen Trimegisto, just to cite a few examples – we are using the term *cuir* to denominate certain Latin American practices of the resignification of US queer movements and theory (Davis and Lopez, 2010, p. 8), specifically in the arts and independent cultural practice. It is, quoting Sayak Valencia (2015), a geopolitical inflexion towards the South and from the periphery, which can also be read as a counterpoint to colonial epistemology and Anglo-American historiography. *Cuir* is the spelling which phonetically transcribes the Spanish (mis)pronunciation of the English word 'queer.' In this way, that first strategy of reclaiming the English insult through the appearance of queer theories and activisms in the United States 'goes through another *torcedura*'[14] and transformation to be taken to another (Latin American or Spanish-speaking) place. This alternative word in an English context would lose its strategic power.

If, as Butler explains (1990), the word was reclaimed so that its use, as a degrading linguistic practice, had been transformed in an act of visibility and recognition politics, *cuir* in contrast works to show another linguistic defect, related this time to the geopolitical origin of these damned subjects, and, in this case, also 'incorrectly said':[15] those who speak incorrectly in the South.

In this situated process of resignification, performative gender theories developed by the great US authors (Judith Butler, Eve Kosofsky Sedgwick, and Jack-Judith Halberstam) can be seen to be intervened inasmuch by goals and interests of Chicana feminisms, decolonial feminisms, *feminismos comunitarios*, and transfeminism, as by experiences of *indios*, the poor, *mestizos*, trans*, and all of these 'other bodies' that make up the Americas.

> Cuir is a move of agency from the South that provides us with tools to rethink distinct aspects that cut through us, as racialized, precarious, strange, etc., subjects. It distances itself from the queer from the North, since it doesn't use the same logics (universities which delegate part of their budgets to queer talks, Queer Studies departments, queer occupies etc.). It allows us to also create genealogies of ancestors who don't appear in the North's histories – Lemebel, Perlongher, the maricas (faggots), lenchas (dykes), putas (whores), unknown queens who existed before and during the Colony, etc.
>
> (Tadeo Cervantes, [16])

CUIR VISUALITIES, SURVIVAL IMAGINARIES

In this sense, we could say that queer theory is intervened in by the interest and also the need to analyze the historical role that constructions of gender and sexuality played in the colonial enterprise. Without overlooking transnational debates and junctions, *cuir*ing theory and cultural practices is what interests me. It can help to trace a Latin American genealogy and to locate the discussion of queer in a local/regional epistemology (Viteri et al., 2011, p. 47). Just as what I explained with the description of Latin America, here regional refers more to an epistemic and political positioning than to essentialist derivatives or purely geographical marks. But, just as importantly, what these visual examples show is that saying *cuir* doesn't stop being a graphic and phonetic operation of a 'bad' translation of a term of Anglo-Saxon origin – a mistranslation which also seems to operate in these modes of representation, extracted in this case from *Maricarmen* issues: a Mexican grandmother upset because of the revelation that 'queer is not an identity'[17]; a young and brown indigenous or *mestiza* girl, who is a '*loca*' (a queen) and a '*bruja*' (a witch); a drag queen yelling her anger ('Yes, I'm in a rage, but I have that right'[18]).

Saying *cuir*, through words and images, has the implication of not completely fulfilling the original US meaning of 'queer' because, paraphrasing María Amelia Viteri (2008), 'here, queer doesn't cut it.' It doesn't cut it because we don't know how to pronounce it correctly, and because it also doesn't cut it in presenting a whole history of colonial violence, repression, and political violence; dictatorships; and dirty state wars, which, in this part of the world (and probably in the so-called global south), cuts through histories of 'sexual diversity' and mechanisms of the construction of the gender binary.

Saying *cuir* in Mexico today also allows us to focus on all of these bodies which have experienced violence, have been disappeared, and have been rendered invisible by the state and its apparatuses: for being dissidents, for being brown, for being poor, for being queer. Saying *cuir* in Mexico today is to name thousands of murdered and disappeared victims of feminicides and transfeminicides.

Furthermore, saying *cuir* here, now, means to be aware of the powerful possibilities of using humour as a subversive strategy. As we know, and following Gin Müller's argument (2015, p. 37):

> not everyone in the world laughs in the same way, not at all; especially where there are many who have so little to laugh about. And there are so many who don't laugh at all about the 'joke' of the so-called 'other'.

Figure 6.3 '¡Ay hijitx!' *Maricarmen* zine. 'Activx busca pasivx. No obvixs' #2
Source: Nicolás Marín (Mr. Popper), 2014.

In any case, we could agree that this kind of practices bring together different ways of laughing at question related to unequal, racist, sexist, and classist power relationship and its colonial roots. In Müller's words:

> Queer humour focuses in solidarity on those that want to collectively laugh at hegemonic systems and see penetrating laughter as starting point for agency. The anger about discrimination and exclusion doesn't remain limited to the role of victim; queer humour is a sensual expression of physical excitation that reveals that unbearable paradox of social racism, sexism, and discriminatory processes, makes them visible, and a bit more level.
> (Müller, 2015, p. 37)

CUIR VISUALITIES, SURVIVAL IMAGINARIES

Figure 6.4 'Soy una loca.' *Maricarmen* zine. 'Activx busca pasivx.' No obvixs' #2
Source: Nicolás Marín (Mr. Popper), 2014.

Finally, we cannot forget that saying queer 'incorrectly' means diverting a type of discourse that, although it's already 'twisted,' continues to be foreign, white, *gringo*, and even 'cool' in a place like Mexico. In this way, 'incorrectly' also means a type of resistance to the one-way circulation of interpretive paradigms and theories produced in the US and European academy, which are distributed and (correctly) pronounced at a global level.

Figure 6.5 'Sí, tengo mucha rabia.' *Maricarmen* zine. 'Activx busca pasivx. No obvixs' #2

Source: Nicolás Marín (Mr. Popper), 2014.

Conclusion

Through the presentation of this type of independent visual production, I suggest thinking of visuality as part of this same modern-colonial project (with all its adjectives: capitalist, classist, racist, sexist, homophobic, transphobic) and challenge us to think of the *cuir* – or rather the *visualidades*

CUIR VISUALITIES, SURVIVAL IMAGINARIES

cuir – as a type of decolonial agency or in Silvia Rivera Cusicanqui's words, a type of 'decolonial practice,' *una práctica descolonial*. From the inspiration of Gloría Anzaldúa and Ema Pérez, two of our great theorists and Chicana poets, we are convinced that *cuir* and decolonial imagination and *cuir*-decolonial imaginaries are, in our context, a question of survival.

Notes

1 This chapter is a result of my research project 'Visual studies and *cuir* visualities in Latin America,' developed at the Instituto de Investigaciones Estéticas, Universidad Nacional Autónoma de México (Mexico City).
2 I use the term *cuir* to refer to Latin American practices of resignification of US queer movements and queer theory. In the words of the International Cuir, 'The queer/cuir variation registers the geopolitical turning towards the South and from the periphery, countering colonial epistemology and U.S. history.' Quote from the text of the project presentation 'La internacional cuir. Transfeminismo, micropolíticas sexuales y vídeo-guerrilla,' which took place in the Museo Nacional Centro de Arte Reina Sofía in Madrid (Spain) in November of 2011. It is available online at www.museoreinasofia.es/actividades/internacional-cuir-transfeminismo-micropoliticas-sexuales-video-guerrilla [consulted 12/09/2016].
3 I will engage a deeper analysis of the images themselves in a next step of this research project.
4 Matthew Rampley (2005, p. 57) suggested that perhaps, more than a differential field of study, visual studies should be considered a series of strategic interventions within existing disciplines. In other words, instead of fighting for the recognition of a new master discourse, it should be seen as an alteration in the boundaries between existing disciplines, in which various conceptual and discursive configurations are mobilized as a response to specific historical and contemporary chaos. Of course, this introduces visual studies as parasites of other fields of study, but it also emphasizes their foundational logic, that of not being art history, of not being cultural studies, of not being history of film or photography, and so on. It also frees them from the ossification which threatens to put an end to established disciplines. (Translated from the publication in Spanish)
5 According to Walter Mignolo (2009, p. 12), the idea of decolonial dissidence in art is a process that operates in two directions: 'one, the decoloniality of art and aesthetics showing its imperial regionalism; and the other, creating decolonial aesthetics and cognitive processes of decoloniality of the self and knowledge.'
6 The performative work of language was formulated by the British philosopher John L. Austin in his well-known book, *How to Do Things with Words*, first published in 1962.
7 It is important to note that Maricarmen is a woman's name in Spanish, but *marica* also means 'faggot.' The use of sense of humour and irony is also another shared features of those *cuir* experiences.
8 In any case, it is quite interesting to understand how this generation interacts with the previous one through understanding and recognizing identity

politics which were started in the 1970s. In this sense, issue #12 of the magazine *Hysteria! Revista*, titled 'Rosa Marica' (Pink Fag) and compiled by the guest editor Benjamin Martinez, explains in the editor's introduction: 'This time, *Hysteria!*, gives space to that which is Lesbian and Gay, without abandoning sex and gender dissidence. Certainly it's true that *cuir* transfeminism partially rejects canonical lesbian and gay conceptions; however, we can't ignore what these positions can tell us, as pioneers in the fight for sexual and identitary diversity.' For more, see http://hysteria.mx/editorial-12-rosa-marica/.

9 Here I am using the denomination employed by César Othón Hernández Romero in the thesis *Filiaciones Bastardas: respuestas queer/cuir y trans* ante imaginarios culturales hegemónicos en México y sus relaciones con el norte*, 2015, p. 14: '[trans*] is a contraction of the word transgender. By transgender, I refer to an umbrella term which gathers various phenomenons from gender diversity, like transexuality, *travestismo*, some aspects of intersexuality, as well as expressions of "atypical gender" in cultures in different parts of the world (like *loca*s and *vestidas* in the case of Latin America) [. . .] the word trans* includes, of course, gender transition, but also phenomenons of movement between nations, between races, between generations of people, between species, and many other crossing relationships that can move or travel.' Available at http://132.248.9.195/ptd2015/diciembre/304783304/Index.html.

10 http://hysteria.mx/editorial-3-akelarre/.

11 http://hysteria.mx/editorial-9-carnitas/.

12 According to Paola Arboleda Ríos (2011, p. 112), drawing from the Licia Fiol-Matta's argument in the book *A Queer Mother for the Nation. The State and Gabriela Mistral* (2002), 'the fluidity and the indetermination of the term queer allows it to be used in the different, but perhaps complementary, ways. In the first place, as an adjective, it is a general term which designates the coalition of marginal (self)identifications (homosexual, transexual, transgender, bisexual, etc.). For the second use, queer defines the field of study and combination of theories which are framed within critical sexuality studies. Finally, as a verb, Fiol-Matta asserts that "queering gives the researcher more agency to critique sexuality's uses and to make much broader the spectrum of people and practices accountable for homophobia, racism and sexism"' (Fiol-Matta, 2002, p. xxxviii).

13 In the words of Brad Epps, 'the circulation of the term queer in Spanish-speaking contexts doesn't reflect its linguistic weight, since it is only verifiable in the U.S. context where the word had a history: the pejorative and homophobic meaning which was later reclaimed and subverted in the form of political affirmation' (2008, p. 899).

14 *Torcedura* in Spanish has a meaning similar to 'twist' and a variation, *torcido*, also has connotations of perversion. While referring to genealogical debates about these terms, Sayak Valencia (2015, p. 20) signals that by going into etymological depths it can be supposed that queer (first registered in the Scottish language in 1500 to refer to 'that which is weird, peculiar, and eccentric') in reality comes from the Latin word *torquere*: bent, which in fact in Spanish, *torcido* – twisted, crooked, and deviant – is much closer to the Latin form. This would therefore, as Valencia says, lead to tracing a different genealogy which would do away with the exclusivity, the

US copyright, which has caused many debated and rejections in the Latin American context.
15 In Spanish, the terms 'damned' (*malditos*) and 'incorrectly said' (*maldichos*) have a very similar spelling and etymology. This play on words disappears in the English translation.
16 T. Cervantes, private correspondence, 18 March 2015.
17 This image is a very known meme in Mexico, representing Carmen Salinas, a famous soap opera actress well-known by her roles as selfless Mexican mothers.
18 While writing this text, I've received word that another trans woman (Alessana Méndez Flores) has been murdered in Mexico City. Transphobic violence has grown in recent years, causing Mexico to be the country with the second most transphobic hate crimes in the world, after Brazil.

References

Achugar, H. (2000). 'Nuestro Norte es el Sur'. A propósito de representaciones y localizaciones. In Moraña, M. (Ed.), *Nuevas perspectivas desde/sobre América Latina: el desafío de los estudios culturales* [New perspectives since, on Latin America: the challenge of cultural studies]. Santiago: Cuarto Propio.

Arboleda, P. (2011). 'Ser o estar "queer" en Latinoamérica? El devenir emancipador en Lemebel, Perlongher y Arenas '. *Íconos*. N° 39. FLACSO Ecuador (pp. 111–121).

Austin, J. (1962). *How to do things with words*. Oxford: Oxford University Press.

Brea, J. L. (2005). Estética, Historia del Arte, Estudios Visuales [Aesthetics, Art History, Visual Studies]. *Estudios Visuales*, 3, 8–25. Retrieved from www.estudiosvisuales.net/revista/pdf/num3/brea_estetica.pdf

Butler, J. (1988). Performative acts and gender constitution: An essay on phenomenology and feminist theory. *Theatre Journal*, 40, 519–531. https://doi.org/10.2307/3207893.

Butler, J. (1990). *Gender trouble: Feminism and the subversion of identity*. New York: Routledge.

Davis, F., and López, M. A. (2010). Micropolíticas Cuir. Transmariconizando el sur. *Ramón, 99: Revista de artes visuales*, 8–9 April. Retrieved from www.academia.edu/20313838/Ramón_99_Micropolíticas_Cuir_Transmariconizando_el_Sur

De Pedro, A., and Rosauro, E. (Eds.). (2015). *Cómo ver cómo: Textos sobre cultura visual latinoamericana* [How to see how. Texts on Latin American visual culture]. México: Editorial Foc.

Derrida, J. (1972). *Marge de la philosophie* [Margins of Philosophy]. Paris: Les éditions de Minuit.

Derrida, J. (2003). Firma, acontecimiento y context [Signature, Event, Context]. In *Márgenes de la filosofía* [Margins of Philosophy] (pp. 347–372). Madrid: Cátedra.

Falconí Trávez, D. (2015). Los hieleros del Chimborazo y Baltazar Ushca, el tiempo congelado: narraciones fílmicas y literarias del indigenismo ecuatoriano. Un análisis intertextual y decolonial de la subalternización nativa.

Extravío. *Revista electrónica de literatura comparada*, 8, 38–57. Retrieved from www.uv.es/extravio
Fiol-Matta, L. (2001). *A Queer Mother for the Nation. The state and Gabriela Mistral*. University of Minessota Press.
Gabara, E. (2010). Gestures, practices and projects. [Latin] American re-visions of visual culture and performance studies. *e-misférica*, 7(1), Retrieved from http://hemisphericinstitute.org/hemi/en/e-misferica-71/gabara
León, C. (2009). Diálogos sobre la colonialidad del ver. Entrevista con Joaquín Barriendos. Retrieved from http://latronkal.blogspot.mx/2010/05/dialogos-sobre-la-colonialidad-del-ver.html
León, C. (2011). "Cultura visual, tecnología de la imagen y colonialidad. Hacia una crítica decolonial de la visualidad desde América Latina". http://www.centroecuatorianodeartecontemporaneo.org/proyectos/investigacion/estudios-imagen-2/jornada-estudios/christian-leon/leon
Mignolo, W. (2009). Prefacio. In Palermo, Z. (Ed.), *Arte y Estética en la encrucijada descolonial* [Art and Aesthetics in the Decolonial CrossRoads] (pp. 11–20). Buenos Aires: Ediciones del Signo.
Mignolo, W. (2007). *La idea de América Latina: La herida colonial y la opción decolonial* [The Idea of Latin America: Right, The Left, and The Decolonial Option]. Barcelona: Gedisa.
Müller, G. (2015). Penetrating laughter: Queer humour as a performative resistance strategy. In Large, T. (Ed.), *Joke Book* (pp. 34–37). Berlin: nGbK.
Rampley, M. (2005). La amenaza fantasma: ¿la cultura visual como fin de la historia del arte? In Brea, J. L. (Ed.), *Estudios visuales. La epistemología de la visualidad en la era de la globalización* [Visual Studies. The Epistemology of Visuality in the Era of Globalization] (pp. 39–57). Madrid: Akal.
Rivera Cusicanqui, S. (2010). *Ch'ixinakax utxiwa: una reflexión sobre prácticas y discursos descolonizadores* [Ch'ixinakax utxiwa: a reflection on practices and decolonizing discourse]. Buenos Aires: Tinta Limón.
Rogoff, I. (2002). Studying visual culture. In Mirzoeff, N. (Ed.), *The Visual Culture Reader* (pp. 14–27). New York: Routledge.
Valdés Figueroa, E. (2005). Lo latinoamericano y el arte. La política del lugar en la era del tsunami. In *Las horas. Artes visuales de América Latina Contemporánea* [The hours: visual arts of contemporary Latin America]. Zurich: Catálogo de exposición Daros-Latinamerica.
Valencia, S. (2015). Del queer al cuir: ostranénie geopolítica y epistémica desde el Sur glocal. In: Lanuza and Carrasco (comps.) *Queer & Cuir. Políticas de lo irreal*. Queretaro: Fontamara/Universidad Autónoma de Querétaro.
Viteri, M. A. M., et al. (2011). Cómo se piensa lo 'queer' en América Latina? [How is the 'Queer' thought of in Latin America]. *Íconos. Revista de Ciencias Sociales*, 39, 47–60. https://doi.org/10.17141/iconos.39.2011.742
Viteri, M. A. M. (2008). Queer no me da: traduciendo fronteras sexuales y raciales en San Salvador y Washington D.C. In Araujo, K. and Prieto, M. (Eds), *Estudios sobre sexualidades en América Latina* [Studies on sexualities in Latin America] (pp. 91–108). Quito: FLACSO – Sede Ecuador.

7

RISKING IMAGES

The political and subjective production of images in Brazil's 2013 mass protests

Roberto Robalinho

> Mr. hear my heart, feel my pulse. Mr. can you see my white hair. . . . To live – is it not? – it's very dangerous. Because you don't know yet. Because learning to live is what living really is.
>
> (Rosa, 2001, p. 601)[1]

For a body, a subject, death is the greatest risk, a unique and irreducible passage that defines our humanity. To be man or woman is to have this fragile existence, the risk of not being anymore. To live, to be in this world, is to assume a risk, and death is the dramatic and rendered moment of this existence in risk. Riobaldo, narrator of Rosa's novel warns us throughout the book that 'To live – is not? It is, dangerous' (Rosa, 2001, p. 601).[2] For him, narrator of his story, life is a great carnal and subjective risk. There are many risks in his trajectory: death, love, war, the possibility of losing his soul and becoming something else. He tells his story from the unstable perspective of being, from this risk of being. This creates a narrative problem: how can one frame the trajectory of this shifting being, this being in risk, on the limited space of narration? For Riobaldo, telling his story is also weaving a geography of *sertão*,[3] his homeland. It is necessary to invent another mode of narration, one that is overtaken by the dangers of living and the risk of being. Narrating is, at the same time, risking yourself opening your being to the world and protecting yourself from the effects of this gesture.

Riobaldo's narrative dilemma is a starting point to think about the relation between images of political and subjective production in Brazil's 2013 mass street protests. The focus of this chapter is to understand the *risk of being* as a form of political and subjective production made possible by image agency. *Risk* is not an abstract space but is political, aesthetical, subjective, corporal, and negotiated as narrative by images. To frame political and subjective production as *risk*, creates a challenge to the analysis, especially an analysis of the production of images where this dangerous space appears. How can we look at these images and what they generate of political risk without undermining conflicts and keeping the streets flames alive?

In February 2014, there were new protests against the increase in public transport fares in Rio de Janeiro's Central train station. On this day, a cameraman from a major Brazilian TV channel was hit on the head by a mortar launched by the crowd. The image of his head on fire on hegemonic media became a symbol of protesters' excessive violence, of how dangerous the protests were. The cameraman died a week later from his head wound, turning media discourse even more aggressive.

In December 2014, the 59th edition of Brazil's most important journalist award, *Prêmio Esso*, in its 59th edition announced that the winner in its photojournalist category was Domingos Peixoto from Globo's newspaper: 'for capturing the moment, Santiago Andrade, cinematographer for *Bandeirantes* TV channel, is hit by a rocket launched by participants of violent protests in Rio's centre.' The text highlights the hard truth when a

Figure 7.1 Photo by Domingos Peixoto, winner of *Esso*'s photojournalist prize 2014

Source: Retrieved from www.premioesso.com.br/site/noticias/release_2014_05.aspx

body is hit and falls down; Peixoto's four photographs render the moment that results in Santiago's death.

The political use of this photograph incarnates the greatest risk of being, the risk of death. This is a body that tumbles down and dies but also a narrative network that comes from an image to kill all protests. There is a double death, of the man with the camera and of the multitude's political actions. These photographs of *Prêmio Esso* 2014 juxtaposed with activist and anonymous images captured from the same protest where Santiago was killed is the focus of this chapter. This image web will help readers think about the agencies between image and political production, especially this place of corporal and subjective production in risk. A search for a form of looking at these images that maintains this place of risk creates the horizon for this work, an analytical approach that maintains this risk of being. To look at these images is to be with June 2013's political production.

Breaking an economy of image

First, we should briefly understand the context behind the protests in Brazil. In 2013, all seemed to be going well. We had a long-term left-wing government, a series of wealth-distribution policies that took us away from the UN hunger map, employment was on the rise, minimum wage was on the rise, and analysts said we even had a new middle class that arose from poverty. Huge world events occurred in our country as well: the 2014 World Cup and the 2016 Olympic Games. Still, in June 2013, the streets of Brazil were overtaken by large numbers of protestors. Every important city across Brazil had thousands of people protesting every week. In one night in Rio nearly a million were on the streets. The spark that ignited the multitude was urban mobility and the increase in bus fare. Of course, images of extreme police violence on social networks and on the news also fed this fire. Soon, other desires erupted and a cry could be heard: it is necessary to invent other cities and other forms of being in the city.

If we take a closer look at Brazil's major cities, we see a series of previous conflicts, especially involving housing removals and renovations for the mega sporting events. We could see for some time many political actors resisting these violent policies. A process similar to the Arabic Spring that was consequence from a build up of many different actions throughout the Arabic world. However, it was the dramatic gesture of a Tunisian setting fire to his own body, an unberable image, that took people to the streets.

Images had an important role during the protests in Brazil. Not just serving as evidence of State Violence, but the experience of the protest itself was mediated by images, in a sense that it was difficult to draw a line separating images from the experience of the event. As if both existed simultaneously, one creating the other, images became an important agent in the relation between the event, the experience of the event, and its subjective political production. You could be on the streets, breathing tear gas and shedding blood, or these bodies at risk could affect you in your own home as you watch the protest on your computer. There can be many different protests, and between all of these forms of experience and of being, there is a series of singular images being produced. The event produces images that produce the event.

To help frame this idea of risk and liminality we can look at Schechner's performance theory (2005), where performers, stage, bodies, spectators, and props invent a space where transformation can happen. Through an aesthetic expression, fissures and social reality crisis can be reflectively exposed and lived by performers and spectators. In many ways, protesters in the streets use their bodies, and the images of their bodies, to fracture Brazilian political social reality. However, we must make a distinction: Schechner's analysis is still under the paradigm of representation and of how accessing these representations is a way of understanding how a community of performers and spectators are thinking of themselves and their community, whereas in our case, representation itself is a problem and the idea of risk, of perpetual transformation, is a way political and subjective production has found to escape representation.

The multitude on the streets through their bodies, subjects, and images in risk engender a liminal territory of political action, especially if we think territory as a space of agency (Deleuze and Guattari, 2005), where subjectivities are forged or are in process of being constituted. Also, it is not a static and determined space:

> The territory is in fact an act that affects milieus and rhythms, that 'territorializes' them. The territory is the product of a territorialisation of milieus and rhythms. [. . .] There is a territory precisely when milieu components cease to be directional, becoming dimensional instead, when they cease to be functional to become expressive.
>
> (Deleuze and Guattari, 2005, p. 315)

The challenge is to look at expressions that come from the streets, the political gestures that break out, producing territory through image agency. Which brings problems to the analysis, once we cannot simply describe a territory, or as Alvarez and Passos state: 'How can we access the 'rhythmic characters' and the 'melodic landscapes' aware that our own description is also part of our own-world' (2009, p. 69).[4] To talk about a territory is to share and produce it. This chapter will tackle this problem.

In *Prêmio Esso*'s photographs, the body of a cameraman falls down – a double death of the body and of image itself. Mainstream press embodies even more in this death that cannot be detached from its image. The heavy corpse comes to justify the end of protests that had become too 'violent.' The use of these photos by the press, and the prize, constructs the tragic and totalizing unit of death, ending all sense and possibilities produced by protesters. In this image strategy there is a simplification of the event, as if all political experience could be expressed in that spark that explodes in Santiago's head. This aesthetic provokes a distance such as Chouliaraki identifies on the mediation of images of suffering:

> This means that image tends to bring forth the formal properties of suffering as a spectacle on the screen (the blood, the flesh, the tears) and take away the content of the suffering as a painful reality for somebody out there in the world.
> (Chouliaraki, 2006, p. 50)

There is an evident aesthetic dimension to politics as Rancière points out in his work. Politics happens according to a distribution of the sensible that is staged and disputed (Rancière, 2011). To think politics is to think of aesthetics and sensible and visibility regimes that organizes this relation. The use of the photographs shares an ethical regime of image (Rancière, 2009), in which more than representing the image reveals a truth and exposes a human fragility, qualifying the context of the death as 'violent protest.' It is not just a synthesis. It is a framing of the image that organizes the senses of the event – the death of the cinematographer, the event, the image, services a moralist view of the world from the hypertrophy of the photographic instant (Barthes, 2010). Not only death is reduced but also all that is connected to it or all experiences that irradiate from the tragic event.

However, there is a political production in how image mediates the event, which creates a territory where desires arise and new subjects, bodies, and city are constituted. These bodies, subjects, and their acts on the streets, although very carnal, exist not only in their materiality but also through their aesthetical existence as image on multiple screens. There is a liminal relation between image and political action, where the boundaries between one and the other are faded. It is a double liminal territory since its subjectivity is in danger but also it exists in contiguous risk between streets and images.

In this context, to end the protest's political senses through the image of a body that tumbles down is also an attempt to end this liminal space. Against subjects at risk is the stillness of this body. Against the faint border between image and political action is the irreducible and totalizing death of the static image. If political production happens in the risk of transformation, of the flows that are invented on the streets, nothing is more contrary to this movement than the stillness of death and of the image as a mirror of this death. You empty the potency of subjects, bodies, and actions and at the same time, you empty the image's agency of these bodies, subjects, and actions. That is why, maybe, this really is a double death, of a body and of the image.

We should look carefully at the four photographs. All photos have the same distance in relation to the object, even when the body hits the ground. The only movement is a zoom out so that at any moment, from the first photo on, we see the fragile body and the flame. There is a constant emptiness around the cinematographer and on the background, as if this death had no origin but the event itself. If there is a political use of this image, diminishing meanings, the framing also desires an end, stability, through the absence of any turbulence that could disrupt our focus on the body that falls to the ground.

Nevertheless, this isn't the only image produced on that same day, and we could compose this tragic event with other images and investigate other political and subjective senses that may arise. There is a fact that helps us to think about this problem. After Santiago's death, there was an investigation to discover who fired the fatal rocket. In the same way that this death happened as an image, so did the investigation: through a series of disputes on social networks with different and diverse images, a search for the responsibility for this death was established. Images became a battlefield for a series of analysis, narratives, and experiences. The event was lived also through its images. There wasn't any image capable of elucidating what really happened; there wasn't a pure image, as there isn't a pure event. The event multiplied, depending on which image or perspective you would endorse.

For activists, the role of the police was important in this death, and for police and major media channels, it was the opposite. Both knew the power of image and its ability to drain the potency of the crowd's protest. It is important to highlight that this is also a dispute over a body. Although there is an image of a body going down, there isn't a precise image of the moment someone launched the rocket. We have the vision of the dead body, but what provoked his fall remains invisible – a play between image and body and what is visible and invisible. This game organizes networks and the dissemination of images. The texts, descriptions, and comments online concentrate on what is and is not visible in the images. Image by itself is not enough; you need to build a politics of the visible on social networks that controls and directs the gaze.

This process reveals the importance of image in June 2013's political production. Image dispute is also a power dispute: 'those who are the masters of the visible are the masters of the world organising and controlling the gaze' (Mondzain, 2002, p. 3). In the game of image where a gaze is forged, not only there is a production and circulation of image but also a true management of image. The power of image is not necessarily on the image itself but in the management of making visibilities and invisibilities that establish a politics of the gaze. This process is very close to what Mondzain (2005) calls an economy of image. The author concentrates on how a Western Christian statute is constructed through a byzantine discussion on icon, idol, and image. How can the holy trinity become image or an icon? How can we materialize that which is immaterial? According to Mondzain, 'incarnation that gave flesh and blood to images, while also giving them the power to lead to the invisibility of its divine model' (2002, p. 7). Through these questionings related to image, the economy becomes the management of these ambivalent relations of the body of image, those who dominates the economy also dominates the power of image:

> The visible world, the one that is given to us to see: is it liberty or enslavement? In order to be able to envisage a world radically founded on visibility, and starting from the conviction that whatever constitutes its essence and meaning is itself invisible, it proved essential to establish a system of thought that set the visible an invisible in relation to each other.
> (Mondzain, 2005, p. 3)

These protests were in many ways framed by visual disputes composed of an economy of image. For example, the dispute over the role of black blocs during the protests: were they just vandals or the front line of resistance? The same would apply to police, if they were pacifying streets or just estate violence. These image management processes engendered political gestures, subjects, and space. The conflict on the streets became a conflict of image and of image management. It is in this contiguous territory between streets and screens where the political production surfaced. However, is resistance to an economy of image the production of an alternative counter economy, or there is more to how the nature of the relation between images and protests may also disrupt an idea of an economy of image?

Breaking the spectacle

Although a counter *economy of image* is as important as a resistance strategy, as a form of creating alternative narratives, there is political production present in this management process close to a liminal relation between image and street protests – of the bodies in the streets that produce images that produces bodies. A production that radicalizes abolishing distances between bodies, once the protest passes, exists contiguously between street and screens. This faint boundary is where a territory is negotiated and politics happens. From an analytical perspective, it is hard to establish limits that organize and regulate locating where politics and bodies inhabit, whether in the multitude or the screens. We could expand this perspective to see how the multitude on the street is also the one that watches the images. The multitude becomes all that are on the streets and in front of the screens united by this transversal visual border.

This politics is effective by its spectacular nature, not only because it is framed and disputed by multiple lenses and media but also because of this simultaneous existence in the carnality of protests on the street and its spectacular immateriality on screen. In many ways we are close to Debord's (1994) concept of the spectacle mediating all spheres of social life, and society is expressed and constituted through the spectacle. In a way that our historical time is defined by the absence of a borderline between the spectacle and all dimension of social life,

> The spectacle cannot be set in abstraction opposition to concrete social activity, for the dichotomy between reality and image will survive on either side of any such distinction. [. . .] Each side therefore has its share of objective reality. And every concept, as it takes its place on one side or the other, has no foundation apart from its transformation into its opposite: reality erupts within the spectacle, and the spectacle is real. This reciprocal alienation is the essence and underpinning of society as it exists.
> (Debord, 1994, p. 10)

According to Debord, we live an extreme modernity 'dominated by categories of seeing' (1994, p. 14), where life and its irradiation becomes 'speculative,' and happens no more in what life has to offer but in what it can show or allows to see. Wars, love, politics, work, arts – everything exists through the spectacle logic. It is in this spectral relation, between who performs and who watches, where we realize social reality. Our own subjectivity functions in the logic of spectacle. Sibilia identifies this specular subjectivity through the exposure of intimacy in blogs in the internet (2008) or by processes of constant *reprogrammation* of the body (2011). In contemporary modes of life, in the spectacle society, processes of subjectivation need to be visible, performed on public space, and configured on subject's own bodies. I am who I can show, exhibit, and expose on public space.

In this sense, to protest on the streets is a form of a self-spectacular performance. Political action is action to be seen by another and therefore has a spectacular and performative nature. However, if we agree with Debord that contemporary life and sociability are possessed by the spectacle, and the boundaries between one and the other are suspended, we cannot equal these lives and these performances. If we are implicated in a *spectacle society* where political and subjective processes are constituted through their spectacular nature, we have to think about this image of politics or this political process that needs image to exist. How can images bring about a resistance to the *spectacle logic*? What relation with image the multitude invents negotiated between bodies on the streets and on screens turns protests disruptive and insurgent?

One of the cries in the crowds on the street was: 'you don't represent me.' They also clearly attacked our political institutions such as the Congress, assemblies, parties, and politicians. The bottom line was that they didn't represent who was on the streets. Political representation, a tool of social intervention, didn't correspond to protesters' desires. It is an evident political problem where we should ask, how is politics possible outside representation? How can we render democratic processes that question the limits of representative democracy? However, the bodies in June's protests didn't necessarily have an answer to their desires. Instead, they had practices that renewed every time they took to the streets. If representation is questioned, you can't have assemblies and leaders that lead protests or determine a route. The crisis of representation embodies also aesthetic problems. What is the form of this new political production critical to representation?

Images produced by activists, collectives, and anonymous people exhibited simultaneously or soon after protests are not just part of a *spectacular* experience but also an invention of a new political action. If representation is in dispute, this dispute is also present on images. More than representing, images produce the protests together with bodies. They bring about political gesture from the multitude in the moment they are occurring. Image management happens together with the protest and the corporal performance on the streets. Protests and images are not just spectacular; they are multiple and simultaneous, since the event is composed by many different gazes.

The protest occurs in this negotiated territory of an agency between multiple images and the streets, abolishing the spectator's classic space. There is a break in the separation between spectacle and spectator, shattering an idea of representation. The investigation of Santiago's death is a good example of how the event senses are disputed through images creating dissense and multiple meanings. When Debord (1994) presents his *spectacle society* as an intensification of a modern experience, he refers to an intensification of the separation of representation. These images shift this logic breaking this space of separation to produce new subjects and politics, therefore producing a resistance to the *spectacle* and to an *economy of image*.

Instead of describing and organizing the world, the June 2013 protest images suggest a production of a world. This gesture is close to contemporary documentary practices as noticed by Comolli in *The Risk of Real*[5] (2004). Politics and subjects that are made by risk, in the turbulent territory of image, produce worlds, cities, and new unexpected existences. Image from inside Rio's Central Station during the protests where Santiago was hurt are very different from *Esso*'s prize photographs.[6] The shots, up to five minutes long, seem to focus randomly on the bodies protesting or passengers that are by chance in the station. There is no division between protesters and passers-by. They are part of the same action. And it is the action that moves the image, at first following the crowd shouting 'jump across, 'cause today is free,'[7] and later concentrating on police confrontation. The handheld camera is in constant motion, most of the time at eye level, incorporating the cameraman's point of view, who also narrates and comments what he sees. In many videos we're not certain if the person recording is a protester or passenger. And this same camera, by chance, encounters someone who interacts with it: police who try to stop the recording and even the confrontation that makes the camera move once again. What we see is fragmented, lacking pieces of action, with no narration but the presentation of the video on the YouTube page. There is no unity, only the encounter of bodies and cameras with the contingency of the protest. The two movements that attract these images come from the protest: first, protesters seizing the ticket gate when youths manage to express their desire for a free life; second, the confrontation when police decide to clear the ticket gate and take protesters outside.

In these movements, subjects are made and unmade, political actions and gestures are produced, bodies are violently repressed by the power of the estate. There is no stability and even less visual organization. There is no translation of what happened. There is experience, and we are taken by its turbulence. The risk of images is inscribed in these bodies that put themselves at risk so that, in these fragments of action, tears, noise, and cries expose not only their desires but also the city's fractures. Against representation and an *economy of image* that organizes, ordains, and infiltrates our spectacular lives, these images disorganize, disrupt, and resist the world of spectacle inventing new worlds. The battle of the bodies is also of its images.

Transcrossing

In June 2013, there wasn't a specific image that ignited the streets. The unbearable thing that provoked the multitude wasn't isolated in an image but in a politics of image. It was the intersection of images, subjects, and politics in risk that created a territory where a cry could be heard – we must change our lives in the cities. How can we look at this agency and maintain a liminal perspective?

Pignarre and Stengers (2005) develop the concept of *capitalist sorcery* from an analysis of the book *Webs of Power: Notes from the Global Uprising* by American activist Starhawk (2002). Their goal was to think about forms and techniques of resistance to contemporary capitalism. It's strange to put capitalism and sorcery together. The authors arrived at Starhawk because they discovered she was central in the organization of the 1999 Seattle World Trade Organization (WTO) protests and she was also a witch. Their suggestion is that witchcraft practices challenge a Western modern tradition, exposing what they call *unknowns of modernity* (Pignarre and Stengers, 2011, p. 49). The rational practice of politics joins with the liminal world of witchcraft as an epistemic perspective. It is not just a practice but also a way to question the world. The epistemic, pragmatic, and liminal nature of witchcraft as political practice is what interests us.

What if, like Pignarre and Stengers (2011), we think capitalism as *systems of sorcery*? What if instead of blinded by ideology we were captured by a spell, which like every good spell is not evident, visible, but inside our soul, body, and daily lives? Instead of having the curtains of ideology pulled as a first step to resistance, we must assume our vulnerability to sorcery to be able to fight against it. When you think about capitalism from the perspective of sorcery, the risk of being captured never ends and it is necessary to protect oneself; it is necessary to invent counter-spells to avoid capture. Living is very dangerous. To deal with sorcery is to walk a risky and liminal path:

> To dare to place capitalism in the lineage of systems of sorcery is not to take an ethnological risk but a pragmatic one. Because if capitalism enters into such a lineage, it is in a very particular fashion, that of a system of sorcery without sorcerers (thinking if themselves as such), a system operating in a world which judges that sorcery is only a simple 'belief,' a superstition that therefore doesn't necessitate any adequate means of protection.
> (Pignarre and Stengers, 2011, p. 40)

The terrain of witchcraft is very dangerous, as is the terrain of images. There is always a risk. To comprehend this risk as a perspective of being and action, as is the case with the production of images in the protests of June 2013 in Brazil, is to share this sorcery perspective. As previously mentioned, there is a liminal relation between images and June 2013, where protests create images that create protests. There isn't a clear separation line between the event and its images. This disorganizes, disrupts, and breaks all that regulates and separates lives in the cities, exposing the *unknowns of modernity*. To act through the framework of sorcery is to reclaim the proximity between mankind and nature that modernity and capitalism separated. To look at these burning images of June 2013 is an epistemic challenge in confrontation with modernity and a work frame within sorcery. If the gesture that produces these images belongs to this liminal space, our perspective should share the same doubt, the same *unknowns of modernity* claimed by sorcery.

Let us go back to Riobaldo's dilemma in Rosa's novel (2001) and follow his heartbeat – living is dangerous. In the end of his story he is trapped with his men in a shootout. Diadorim, a bandit from Riobaldo's group, leads the reinforcements that manage to free him, but he is shot dead in the process. Riobaldo has a secret passion for Diadorim throughout the book. It is now late afternoon – the magic hour. Diadorim's body is laid out on a table to be washed. An old lady undresses him, and to Riobaldo's surprise, a woman – not a man – lies dead on the table: 'pain can no more than surprise'[8] (Rosa, 2001, p. 615).

The risk of being is so great that in a second the body of Diadorim became a woman. If we extend the idea of narrative to life, as Rosa does through Riobaldo's tale, we can see how he resolves the dangers of living without reducing the potency of risk. This is very close to our epistemic question of how to look at the flames from June 2013 without killing them. Riobaldo ends the book by saying, '*Nonada*, there is no devil, there is only human, men. Transcrossing'[9] (Rosa, 2001, p. 624). The key to this mode of narration is the idea of *transcrossing*, of being while crossing or of being while narrating since it's this gesture that enables him to cross his homeland. Riobaldo and the *sertão* exist through this *transcrossing* narrative. If we look at the case of Santiago's death, we can see how images shaped what happened. There was a visual battle that was also an epistemic battle, and the event itself assumed many forms. Images not only disputed political senses; they also transformed the event. So, we could say, that to narrate Santiago's death is to assume this risk of transformation related to the multiple images disputing what happened. When we look at Santiago's death from a *transcrossing* perspective we assume this risk of transformation; we assume that to narrate through images is to give existence and political potency. Politics is made in this *transcrossing*, which in Riobaldo's case enables Diadorim to be man and woman, and in these images allows subjects and cities to be transformed.

We should look at the flames of these images as a *transcrossing* territory of political and subjective production. Instead of just describing we should co-inhabit this space, in a sense of learning from the streets with its gestures. Looking at and analyzing these practices cannot also be a way of practicing them, or at least a way we can assume the risk of being with them and produce our own *transcrossing*, right?

Notes

1 Translated from: 'O senhor escute meu coração, pegue meu pulso. O senhor avista meus cabelos brancos . . . Viver – não é? – é muito perigoso. Porque ainda não se sabe. Porque aprender-a-viver é que é o viver, mesmo' (Rosa, 2001, p. 601).
2 Translated from: 'Viver – não é? É muito perigoso' (Rosa, 2001, p. 601).
3 Backlands.
4 Free translation from: 'Como acessar os 'personagens rítmicos' e as 'paisagens melódicas,' cientes de que nossa descrição também faz parte de um mundo-próprio' (Alvarez and Passos, 2009, p. 69).
5 Free translation from *Sous le risque du réel* (Comolli, 2004).
6 These images can be seen at www.youtube.com/watch?v=bE8Ck_W3Nmg; www.youtube.com/watch?v=MvJRJmSyV8I; www.youtube.com/watch?v=hGVkipmZnQo; www.youtube.com/watch?v=7-tYfnCnmHo; www.youtube.com/watch?v=Dnqz8kQo31k.
7 Protesters seized ticket gates at the station and let people pass without paying, shouting 'jump 'cause today is free,' roughly translated from the Portuguese: 'pula que é de graça.'
8 Free translation from: 'a dôr, não pode mais do que a surpresa' (Rosa, 2001, p. 615).
9 Free translation from: 'Nonada, o diabo não há, o que existe é homem humano. Travessia' (Rosa, 2001, p. 624).

References

Alvarez, J. and Passos, E. (2009). Cartografar é habitar um território existencial. In Passos, E., Kastrup, V. and Escóssia, L. (Eds.). *Pistas do método cartográfico*. Porto Alegre: Editora Sulina.
Barthes, R. (2010). *Camera lucida: Reflections on photography* (Reprint Ed.). New York, NY: Hill & Wang.
Chouliaraki, L. (2006). *The spectatorship of suffering*. London: Sage.
Comolli, J.L. (2004). *Voir e povoir: l'innonce perdue, cinéma, télévision, fiction, documentaire* [View and power: The lost innocence: cinema, television, fiction, documentary]. Paris: Verdier.
Debord, Guy. (1994). *Society of the spectacle*. New York, NY: Zone Books.

Deleuze, G. and Guattari, F. (2005). *A thousand plateaus: Capitalism and schizophrenia*. (B. Massumi, Trans.). Minneapolis, MN: University of Minnesota Press.
Mondzain, J.M. (2002). *Can an image kill?* (S. Shafto, Trans.) Retrieved from https://bibliodarq.files.wordpress.com/2013/11/3-c-mondzain-m-j-can-images-kill.pdf
Mondzain, J.M. (2005). *Image, icon, economy: The Byzantine origins of the contemporary imaginary*. Redwood, CA: Stanford University Press.
Rancière, J. (2009). *The future of images*. London: Verso.
Rancière, J. (2011). *The emancipated spectator*. London: Verso.
Rosa, J.G. (2001). *Grande Sertão: Veredas*. Rio de Janeiro: Editora nova Fronteira.
Pignarre, P., and Stengers, I. (2011). *Capitalist sorcery: Breaking the spell*. London: Palgrave Macmillan, 2011.
Schechner, Richard. (2005). *Performance theory*. Routledge, New York, NY and London.
Starhawk. (2002). *Webs of power: Notes on the global uprising*. Gabriola Island: New Society Publishers.
Sibilia, P. (2008). *O show do eu: a intimidade como espetáculo* [The show of the self: intimacy as spectacle]. Rio de Janeiro: Nova Fronteira.
Sibilia, P. (2011). *O sonho da reprogramação corporal: biotecnologias, ciências da vida e produção de subjetividade na sociedade contemporânea* In Neutzling, I. and Ruiz, C.M.M.B. (Eds.). *O (des)governo biopolítico da vida humana* [The Biopolitical (Dis)government of Human Life] (pp. 123–145). São Leopoldo: Unisinos & Casa Leiria.

8
JOURNALISM CULTURES IN EGYPT AND LEBANON

Role perception, professional practices, and ethical considerations

Zahera Harb

This chapter explores journalism cultures in post-Arab uprising contexts (post-2011). It begins with the assumption that changing socio-political contexts may not only have been a factor in the increase in the number of media organizations in the region but may also be influencing journalistic practices and norms. The chapter uses semi-structured interviews and personal observations to explore journalism practices, roles, and approaches in two Arab countries: Egypt and Lebanon. It assesses norms and tendencies that may have shaped journalism cultures. It aims at identifying similarities and differences in Arab journalism practices and values and questions whether we can speak of a universal journalism culture in the Arab world or several.

A number of studies have examined journalism in the Arab world, but most of these have been either country focused (Duffy, 2013, 2014; Sakr, 2007, 2013; Mellor, 2005), broadly designed (for example Pintak, 2011, 2014; Mellor, 2007), or restricted to address the political economy and media systems with little attention to journalists' practices, values, and principles (see Gunter and Dickinson, 2013; Lahlali, 2011; Rugh, 2004; Sakr, 2001, 2007). This chapter seeks to address the deficit, focusing on practices, norms, and codes while also paying attention to the relationship between the cultural and the political as well as the political and economic.

The chapter draws on the study by Hanitzsch et al. (2011) to explore journalism practices in two Arab countries, using journalism culture as an analytical concept and object of inquiry. Such a conceptual approach provides 'a more intuitive way of looking at the diversity of journalistic practices and orientations' (Hanitzsch et al. 2011, p. 273) because it produces 'a particular set of ideas and practices by which journalists legitimate their role in society and render their work meaningful' (Hanitzsch, 2007, p. 369). The chapter will examine these practices and ideas under the following three themes: social responsibility, ethics of journalism practice, and level of professionalism.

The countries this chapter aims to explore are Lebanon (plural and diverse model, but still bound by confessional system and ideologies) and Egypt (a country of media freedom contradictions post–Arab uprisings with general tendencies among journalists to express loyalty to those in power. The largest in the Arab world in terms of population and area). As mentioned earlier, this study adopts interviews and observations as research approach to study journalism culture/s in two media savvy centres in the global south: Egypt and Lebanon. The select journalists chosen will be those confined within organizational structures, which means those working in media organizations who are salaried workers and are bound by organizational norms.

Journalism culture as a tool of inquiry

The concept of journalism culture integrates diverse scholarly discourses, most notably discussions of professionalism, objectivism, professional role perceptions, and ethical standards (Hanitzsch et al., 2011, p. 274). According to Hanitzsch et al., the concept is (as culture itself is) a process of continuous change, renegotiation, and redefinition (2011, p. 274). Hanitzsch (2007) proposes studying journalism culture through exploring culture as a set of ideas (values, attitudes, and beliefs), practices (of cultural production), and artefacts (cultural products, texts). Journalism culture, as Hanitzsch (2007, p. 369) put it,

> becomes manifest in the way journalists think and act; it can be defined as a particular set of ideas and practices by which journalists, consciously and unconsciously, legitimate their role in society and render their work meaningful for themselves and others.

This chapter investigates through thematic interview analysis journalism cultures in Lebanon and Egypt at three levels: journalism and journalists' role perception, professional practices and performances, and ethical considerations. It follows loosely Hanitzsch's (2007) three levels of analysis in the chain of news production. According to him, journalism cultures are articulated at three 'basic levels' of analysis:

> At the cognitive level, they shape the foundational structure on the basis of which the perception and interpretation of news and

JOURNALISM CULTURES IN EGYPT AND LEBANON

news work take place [...] At the evaluative level, they drive the professional worldviews of journalists (e.g. role perceptions) as well as occupational ideologies (e.g., 'objective Journalism,' 'investigative Journalism') [...] At the performative level, they materialise in the way Journalists do their work (e.g., methods of reporting, use of news formats). Journalistic practices are shaped by cognitive and evaluative structures, and journalists – mostly unconsciously – perpetuate these deep structures though professional performance.

(Ibid., p. 369)

Hanitzsch also identifies 'three essential constituents: institutional roles, epistemologies, and ethical ideologies' (p. 371). He divides these further into 'seven principal dimensions: interventionism, power distance, market orientation, objectivism, empiricism, relativism and idealism' (Ibid.). Not all these dimensions will be applicable to this chapter, but it is good to present them and use the framework as a contextual tool for the three main areas this study is concerned with: role perception/social responsibility, ethics of journalism practice, and level of professionalism. Thomas Hanitzsch and Claudia Mellado's (2011) study on 'what shapes the news around the world' confirms that political and economic factors are 'clearly the most important denominators of cross-national differences in the journalists' perceptions of influences' (p. 404). The study asserts that 'the way political and economic influences are perceived by journalists is highly dependent on the national context' (p. 416). This chapter considers the political and economic factors in exploring journalism cultures and how they are shaped in both Lebanon and Egypt.

Egypt and Lebanon: the journalism scenes

William Rugh, in his book *The Arab Mass Media* (2004), divided the Arab media into four categories:

1 The mobilizing media, which is characterized by the almost total subordination of the media system to the political system;
2 The loyalist media system, which is privately owned, but follows the line of governments, as those regimes can still control their resources (like paper or transmission rights) and persecute journalists through legal systems;
3 The diverse media system, where the press is described as free; and
4 The transitional system, where the media begin to move from the mobilized and loyalist systems to being diverse (Rugh, 2004, pp. 252–253).

Rugh situated Egypt within the transitional media and Lebanon within the diverse media systems. Rugh's categorizations need to be re-visited as a whole, which is not in the scope of this chapter, but when it comes to Egypt and Lebanon the categorizations no longer apply. As this chapter will indicate, Egypt is within the framework of polarized loyalist press as introduced by Hallin and Mancini (2004). As one interviewee put it, 'we don't have independent media, but independent journalists' (M, interview with author, 2016). In case of Lebanon, on the other hand, Rugh's categorization is not fully representative because, as I argued elsewhere, 'while the Lebanese media system is diverse and free from government and state control, it is not free from political and economic affiliation' (Harb, 2013, p. 39). One of the Lebanese journalists interviewed for this chapter summarized the case of Lebanese press, emphasizing that in Lebanon 'we have freedom of speech, but we don't have free press' (N, interview with author, 2016).

Egypt witnessed an influx of newly established TV channels after January 2011. Among them were channels financed and supported by the Muslim Brotherhood. There had been a time where we started seeing a shift in moving away from the one homogenized message in support of the government and the country's leaders in both print and broadcast media (Diab, *Guardian* 2011). That didn't last long. Following the 30 June revolt and the military force's steady movements to control the political scene in Egypt, the media at large were used as a mobilizing tool in the hands of the army led by Abed Al Fatah al Sissi. Journalism notions of fairness and balance in covering events vanished. The country's media was divided into two extreme media clusters: one in support of the brotherhood (*Ikhwan* in Arabic), including *Aljazeera Misr (Stands for Egypt* in Arabic) and the other in support of the military. Hate speech against 'the other' on both sides became dominant until the military-led authorities closed down channels affiliated with the Muslim Brotherhood and other Salafi-affiliated religious channels.

The message became one across the board; the terminology became one. Slogans like 'The people want to execute the Muslim Brotherhood followers' became a celebratory message. There have been several attempts to balance the scene in Egypt including a satire program produced and presented by who came to be known as the 'Jon Stewart of the Arab world'; Bassem Youssef, a current affairs program produced and presented by Reem Majed; and one produced and presented by Yousri Fouda. Within two years, the increase of private satellite TV stations in Egypt stopped being a celebratory move towards media diversity; instead, print and broadcast media ended up at large singing from the same hymn sheet, that of military rule.

JOURNALISM CULTURES IN EGYPT AND LEBANON

The three programs mentioned above were put off air for presenting what was assumed to be critical voices against the political and military elite.

Hallin and Mancini (2004) argue that political parallelism between media organizations and political organization generates a low level of professionalism in journalism. They maintain that a high degree of professionalism in journalism means that journalism is differentiated as an institution and form of practice from other institutions and forms of practice – including politics (Ibid.: 38). This lack of autonomy tends to be a dominant feature among a majority of Egyptian journalists; journalists became tied to the political actor whom they support. To borrow Hallin and Mancini's term, the media in Egypt became 'instrumentalized' (Ibid.: 37). Journalists in Egypt (mainly broadcasters) identify themselves with particular points of view, which meant not serving the public (even though they claim they are), contradicting their own standards of practice as specified in the Code of the Profession ratified in 1986 which, as this chapter will demonstrate later, none of the journalists interviewed for this chapter uses as a reference in their daily work.

During Mubarak there was no claim of independent media. Egyptian airwaves are now dominated with hours and hours of one-man or one-woman shows, talking heads claiming they possess the truth, the wisdom, and that their audiences should be grateful they are sharing it with them. As prominent broadcast journalist Reem Majed put it in a paper presented at a conference in Berlin, 'the media is playing the lapdog role rather than the watchdog role, keeping an un-informed populace, that can be easily confused, deceived and directed' (Majed, 2015).

Fabrications and counter fabrication, hatred and counter hatred is what dominates the Egyptian media scene these days and it seems it is going to be the ruling scene for some time to come with Abed Al Fatah el Sissi telling the Egyptian people in an exclusive interview with Egyptian OnTV and cbc channels on May 5 2014 before he took power, 'the state should contribute in "correcting" people's ethics through using mechanisms such as the media, the family and religious institutions' (Darweesh, *Ahramonline*, 2014).

Lebanon, on the other hand, is characterized by the *interwoven* relationship between the media and the political elite. This polarized media system went through different phases and engendered different media models after Lebanon gained its independence in 1943. The civil war (1975–1990) witnessed an influx of illegal TV and radio stations which were later regulated in post–civil war Lebanon. The regulation mirrored the confessional political system. Even though the law specified that no political party or politician should own a dominant majority in any of the newly licensed

TV stations, the practice came to echo the socio-political structure of the Lebanese society (Dajani, 1992).

This makes it closer to what Hallin and Mancini (2004) identified as the 'Polarized Pluralist Model,' which applies in Mediterranean countries of southern Europe and is characterized by a politically polarized media, closely associated with political parties and a plurality of media, representing the diversity of political interests. According to Hallin and Mancini, the media of the Mediterranean countries in many ways seem close to 'Curran's (1991) model of 'radical democratic' public sphere,' in which the media function as a 'battleground between contending social forces' (Hallin and Mancini, 2004, p. 140). The media in Lebanon follow closely these function patterns. Within the pluralist polarized media module, there seems to be a tendency towards low levels of professionalism (Harb, 2013).

This lack of autonomy tends to be a dominant feature among Lebanese journalists became tied to the political actors with which they are affiliated. Here also, as in Egypt, the media became 'instrumentalized' (Hallin and Mancini, 2004). The media is being controlled by outside actors, parties, politicians, social groups or movements, or economic actors seeking political influence (Ibid.: 37). Most journalists in Lebanon in the years that followed the assassination of former prime minister of Lebanon Rafic Hariri in 2005 (see Harb, 2013, for more context on post-2005 media scene in Lebanon) identified themselves with particular political points of view, which meant contradicting the Lebanese Code of the Profession ratified in 1974 and adopted by the Press Federation in Lebanon, and which again, as in the Egyptian case, none of the journalists interviewed for this chapter uses as a reference in their daily work.

Lebanon's broadcasting scene has always been well-developed, lively, and diverse, reflecting the country's pluralism and political divisions. Lebanese media feature diverse opinions, aggressive question-and-answer television shows with government officials and politicians, and lively criticism of authorities and policies (see Boulos, 1995; Dajani, 1992). However, political affiliation, thus self-censorship, remains a problem. Authorities, owners, and editors are quick to clamp down on journalists who cross both unstated and stated boundaries on sensitive topics. There always existed an *interwoven* relationship between the media and Lebanese politicians. Politicians had a strong appetite for owning and even running media organizations. Many prominent politicians own shares in private broadcasters and publications (Harb, 2013).

In his book *Disoriented Media in a Fragmented Society: the Lebanese Experience* (1992), Professor Nabil Dajani of the American University of Beirut argued that the Lebanese press was characterized by a general tendency to oppose the national government. However, 'this did not mean that it played the "watchdog" role safeguarding public interest.' Its opposition to the government, the analysis revealed, was usually a result of its support for, or bondage to, another authority that was 'politically and/or militarily active on the Lebanese scene' (Ibid.: 127). In addition, the fact that the Lebanese media supported a particular authority did not necessarily mean that it would continue in its support for this authority. The country went through a long period of civil war, 'during which new political authorities appeared, and several others changed positions' (Ibid.: 127).

This situation did not change much in post–civil war Lebanon. Despite the fact that newspapers readership is not as widespread in Lebanon or the Arab world, as Dajani (1992) suggests, some journalists and writers are viewed as 'opinion leaders,' while their ideas and writings are used as starting points during several political or social debates. In Lebanon, being a journalist and a political activist at the same time are functions that complement, not contradict, each other. There are several journalists who pursued political careers after working in journalism for several years. Journalism has turned out to be a route to becoming members of parliament or cabinet ministers. In the case of Egypt and Lebanon, journalism seem to fit with the Staab (1990) functional model, where journalists are seen as political actors 'due to the expected effects of news, they select certain events for publishing that might possibly cause the anticipated effects in reality' (Staab, 1990, p. 428).

Expert interviews as method

Fourteen in-depth interviews were conducted for this study. For Wimmer and Dominick (1997), this kind of interviewing is unique because it 'generally uses small samples [. . .] provides detailed background about the reasons why respondents give specific answers [and] obtains elaborate data concerning respondents' opinions, values, motivations, recollection experiences, and feelings' (p. 100).

For this study, semi-structured and structured interviews were used. As a form of structured and semi-structured interview, the 'expert' interview was applied, since my interviewees were of less interest to me as people than in their capacity as experts in the field of journalism. It is said that 'If concrete statements about an issue are the aim of the data collection, a semi-structured interview is the more economical way' (Flick, 1998: 95). By this it can be seen that such an interview basis accords with the aims of this chapter.

Seven journalists from Lebanon and seven from Egypt were interviewed. They are spread across print, broadcast, and online mediums. Their expertise ranges from very senior to senior and midcareer journalists. Twelve of them were asked a set of fixed open-ended questions, and two (the more senior, one in each country) were asked contextual questions relating to the current and future state of journalism in Egypt and Lebanon. Interviews were conducted via email, Skype, and face-to-face. Some of the email interviews were complemented by face-to-face interviews. The two interviews with more senior journalists were deemed necessary after conducting the first 12 structured interviews. There was a need for at least one voice from each country to conceptualize what came across as dominant features in the journalists' responses. The small number of the journalists interviewed (14) should not affect the validity of the method since the in-depth interview is the appropriate method to gather detailed information from a small sample of respondents, as stated by many researchers (Wimmer and Dominick, 1997; Seale, 1998; Flick, 1998; Flick, 2009). The selection of these journalists was not random. In Egypt these are, en masse, journalists who have been critical of what has become of Egyptian journalism and have voiced their opinions publicly. In Lebanon, I worked with some of them as a journalist; others were selected as newcomers to the profession and had made their way up the popularity scale mainly on social media. Journalists selected were defined as those who had at least some 'editorial responsibility' for the content they produce.

They have all granted the researcher consent to be quoted and named, but to free this research from any risk of potential harm that might come to these journalists in the future, mainly in Egypt, for sharing their views here, I have decided to anonymize interviewees' names and affiliations and will be quoting them using random first letters. As one Egyptian interviewee put it, 'journalists live in a state of fear . . . Big Brother is watching' (M, interview with author, 2016). There are up to 35 Egyptian journalists in detention right now for 'publishing offences' (S, interview with author, 2016). The latest clampdown on journalists took place in November 2016, when an 'Egyptian court sentenced the head of the country's journalists union and two further board members to two years in prison while additionally handing each of them fines of around $650 for harbouring two wanted journalists' (*The New Arab*, 2016a).

Role perception: journalists as educators versus journalists as advocators

El Issawi and Cammaerts (2016) studied how Egyptian journalists perceive their role in what they called 'democratic transitions.' They interviewed more than 50 journalists as part of a bigger study. Most of the journalists interviewed expressed 'their difficulty in drawing a line between their personal political positioning and their professional role' (p. 559). Their analysis showed that the radical/oppositional role against the Muslim Brotherhood government suited those interviewed better than the normative facilitative role 'after which most Egyptian journalists re-assumed their traditional collaborative role in the service of the ruling (military) regime' (p. 562). However, those interviewed for this chapter have identified the importance of the normative facilitative role that journalism should play. They recognized the need for journalism to inform the public on all issues that matter to them. Also, they all agreed on the importance of journalism in fulfilling people's rights to know and to be heard. Journalism role perceptions varied from informing the public factually and accurately, to being the voice of the people, to monitoring power and holding it to account, to educating and enlightening the public. Saying that, the advocate and adversarial roles aiming for social and political change were not an issue among Egyptian journalists interviewed, as was the case with the Lebanese journalists.

All Egyptian journalists interviewed for this chapter emphasized the importance of reporting factually and informing the public. Some felt that it is their role to educate and enlighten the public, which resonates with Egyptian President Abed el Fatah el Sissi's understanding of the role of the media, mentioned earlier, as a tool to help 'correcting people's ethics.' Journalist D states: 'My role as a journalist is to report events impartially and expose corruption in Society. To educate and enlighten the public with factual reporting of events' (D, interview with author, 2016). 'To be the voice of the people, to Investigate corruption and misconduct by powerful people in Society' (A, interview with author, 2016), was another theme that emerged.

Seeking the truth was one aspect that was contested by some of the interviewees, as Journalist M put it:

> I don't think finding truth is journalism role. I believe that truth is like a puzzle, and the facts are like the tiny pieces of the puzzle, and I believe the role of journalism in any society should be the tiny pieces that can help the society making its own puzzle. A journalist is the 'digger' in pursuit of these tiny pieces of the big puzzle.
>
> (M, interview with author, 2016)

Journalists as opinion leaders is another theme that was disclosed. Journalist E believes that

> Journalists need to search for all information so they can themselves form an opinion than pass it to the public. They need to

collect info from different sources, so their work could be identified as balanced and fair and not bias or propagandist.

(E, interview with author, 2016)

These journalists are fully aware of the ideals of journalism's role and see them as universal, like informing the public on issues that matter to them and that an informed society is more capable of governing itself. However, many of them are also aware that it is difficult to practice this role in Egypt at the time being. Equally important is the role journalism plays in independently monitoring power. 'A reporter should be conscious of the power and the value of generating news.' However, as Journalist W says, it is hard to achieve that since 'there is no free press in Egypt' (W, interview with author, 2016).

The Lebanese journalists interviewed for this chapter identified the role of journalism in slightly different terms with common tendency towards emphasizing the importance of its role to inform the public and create informed public opinion to achieve common public good. Role perception varied from being an advocator and campaigner for human rights and bringing change to society, to being a medium to transfer information fairly and impartially, to apply meaning and analysis to information, to educating the public and holding power to account. However, the role of journalism differed when it came to identifying the role of journalists, where being an educator and advocator for change and building public opinion became more dominant. Journalist K does not believe in journalism as a message, 'especially when it comes to revealing important cases like in corruption cases and human rights abuses. Journalists' role is to create informed public opinion and enhance public knowledge about an issue to establish public debate about it' (K, interview with author, 2016).

Journalist L, who is one of Lebanon's prominent journalists covering human rights issues, strongly believe in journalism's role to

> Engage in campaigns to advocate social change and try to give the readers and audiences what they need not what they want. Journalists should highlight public's concerns and endorse change for better societies. Journalists should be biased towards their publics and not towards politicians and those in power.
>
> (L, interview with author, 2016)

Having the journalists advocating for the common good was also expressed by Journalist F, who is a print political journalist. F believes that with social media informing the public, journalists' role is to add contexts, background, and analysis to stories, which help audiences and readers to form an opinion on one issue or another, without it becoming 'propaganda.' 'My goal would always be to fight corruption and those in power's attempts to get away with it' (F, interview with author, 2016). Nevertheless, Journalist O expressed his doubts in achieving role definition, saying:

> Journalism role is different depending on what the journalist is allowed to do in different political and social contexts. The main principal is not to use or abuse my role as journalist to achieve personal benefits. The role of journalists in society is not to be a tool in the hands of those in power.
>
> (O, interview with author, 2016)

Universal professional values hailed, but hard to implement

Egyptian journalists interviewed for this chapter identify fully with what they call universal values of objectivity, impartiality, neutrality, fairness, and balance in the coverage. They say they try to achieve some of these when practicing journalism, but they don't always succeed. They see these notions as the notions of professionalism that distinguish what they do from other professions. Journalist D, despite recognizing these notions as features of the profession, points to the fact that 'Egyptian journalism lacks these notions these days' (D, interview with author, 2016). Others have agreed. When they were asked what notions they apply and fulfil in their work among those listed, there was an agreement on accuracy and credibility. Many have asserted that these two notions have gone missing from much of Egyptian journalism these days, especially broadcast ones.

One of the journalists interviewed has been put out of work because of her questioning the political status quo. Journalist M says: 'we are terrorised to stop asking questions. They want to forbid us not from just the act of asking, but from the act of thinking that leads to the question' (M, interview with author, 2016). Another one resigned because a senior journalist was fiddling with the accuracy of his reporting. A third one said:

> My current job title is deputy editor in chief, but I don't exercise any editorial authority. In practise, I'm a 'senior journalist' [...] I try to apply these principles. Some stories are rendered 'unpublishable' by editors because of political considerations and where impartiality is not tolerated.
>
> (W, interview with author, 2016)

However, Journalist W draws the attention that on the other hand,

> some stories do not serve their purpose if reported and written entirely neutrally (like doing injustice to victims of war, occupation, violence, genocide etc.), by giving voice to the culprit and weaving their defensive argument in the story.
>
> (W, interview with author, 2016)

Most of the journalists interviewed here have received international journalism training, hence identifying with the principles mentioned earlier, or have the language skills to read and follow international media which, in their words, has informed their way of practicing journalism. These journalists are abiding by their social responsibility role but are either stopped by their superiors or by the authorities through direct prosecution as happened with Hosam Bahgat, the investigative journalist from *Mada Masr* online news website (M, interview with author). Journalist B was clear in stating that any story that has to do with the Egyptian army and the military is a red line, not to be crossed (interview with author 2016). Self-censorship is highly practiced according to Journalist B. Journalist W complements this picture by confirming that Egyptian journalists 'operate now in a climate of fear' (W, interview with author, 2016).

Egyptian journalists do not share common ideology, as all journalists interviewed here asserted. Journalism body is divided into two categories: those interviewed here, who aspire to report independently, accurately, and credibly and try to abide by the social responsibility model of the press, and those who are fully acting as political actors, propagating to those in power and, as Journalist M put it, 'constructing the notion that Big Brother is a faultless and God-like leader' (M, interview with author, 2016).

In the midst of the gloomy situation that these journalists find themselves in (an environment where journalism values and principles are neglected), Journalist E sees a good sign in that 'journalists are trying to search and assess local issues from an international perspective, and this didn't use to happen before' (E, interview with author, 2016). Journalist B, a senior editor, sees hope in the new generation of journalists that he has been involved in training. He believes that they have the knowledge to differentiate between good and bad journalism (B, interview with author 2016).

Lebanese journalists interviewed for this chapter, as their Egyptian colleagues, believe in the notions of objectivity, impartiality, neutrality, balance, and fairness as universal. Lebanese journalists interviewed observe these principles as a clear indication for professionalism. These notions were agreed as being the emblem of professionalism. They aspire to apply it, but the two principles that mattered most were honesty and accuracy. There is a sense of social responsibility that came across all journalists interviewed, a sense of obligation to play a role in achieving social justice and equal rights to all. These were mostly evident in Journalist F's and Journalist L's interviews.

> Honesty, accuracy, don't fall under source manipulation and try to achieve as much objectivity as possible. The source of these principals is my own belief in my right to live in a better and fairer society, where people don't need to beg for their basic needs and civic rights. I gained these from my own conscience, readings and my cultural social and family background.
>
> (F, interview with author, 2016)

> Objectivity, accurate reporting from the field, be ethical and work on improving and developing my skills at all times. Readers and their issues are my priority. To be accurate and credible. Some of it comes from what I learned at university, some from the organisation I work for and some from my own readings and working and talking to people. Of course, there is the background of morality, I as a journalist was raised to follow.
>
> (L, interview with author, 2016)

However, O, who is of a younger generation than F and L and believes in true and credible reporting, does not believe in objectivity. For him, journalists cannot be separated from their society.

> My main principle is truth and not to hide or masquerade truth and cause harm to society. Journalism's responsibility is to protect the public from any harm. The only principal and value for me is to be responsible for what I publish, be professional and accurate in the information and news I report. I don't believe in objectivity.
>
> (O, interview with author, 2016)

Being an activist and campaigner and working for what the journalists believe is the common good are mostly shared by the journalists. They, similar to the Egyptian journalists, believe that journalism in Lebanon and the Arab world is these days very low on professionalism.

> It should be universal but sadly they are not applied universally. Very big reputed organisation in different part of the world and the Arab world in specific these principles are not applied. We see

lots of propaganda and biased reporting. Neutrality has vanished or almost vanished. Wars are being fought on the media front.
(L, interview with author, 2016)

Asserting that these principles should be universal and that every journalist should work hard aspiring to achieve them, Journalist K 'tries to be accurate and abide by objectivity and balance,' for her 'clarity in writing news is important.' She believes that 'every person has the right to information and the right to freedom of speech without fear of persecution and harm' (K, interview with author, 2016).

The fear factor that has been dominating the Egyptian journalism scene applies to Lebanon too, but fear in the Lebanese context is fuelled by different motives. The fear factor that shadows Lebanese journalism these days is economic in nature. Journalists are afraid of losing their jobs because of current market trends, especially in the print sector where many newspapers are struggling, and the number of journalists that have been put on the redundancy list is increasing. Journalist R says that she is living in fear of losing her job now that she has a daughter. She says 'now I have to think of providing for my daughter and offer her good education and better life' (R, interview with author, 2016).

Besides, newspapers are facing the ghost of closing down for financial reasons. *Assafir* is one of those papers struggling financially, which led to its publisher declaring the closing down of the paper because of financial difficulties (*The New Arab*, 2016c). The paper did not close at that time, due to what was reported as 'last-minute funding' (*The New Arab*, 2016b). However, few months later I witnessed first-hand the rollout of *Assafir*'s last issue on 31 December 2016. The newspaper *terminated* its operations, after 42 years in the business, due to financial and funding woes. Similarly, *Annahar*, established in 1933, has ended 2016 with major cuts in budget and staff, laying off more than 60 people according to the Lebanese media (Karam, *Arab News*, 2017).

Prominent journalist and writer Wasef Awada explained that newspapers in Lebanon had never depended on circulation for revenue. Awada, who is a board member of the Lebanese journalists' syndicate in Lebanon, stated that the Lebanese media has never been independent of the political scene: 'it has always been a mirror of the political division in the country and it has always supported itself financially from outside political sources be it internal or external state funding' (Awada, interview with author, 2016).

Professional means ethical

Ethics follow closely the discussion of professionalism. Almost all journalists in Egypt and Lebanon relate between level of professionalism and

JOURNALISM CULTURES IN EGYPT AND LEBANON

ethics. Being honest (the number-one principal for most of them) is seen as being ethical. Ethics is learned through university journalism education and training or by reading ethical codes from around the world or by editorial standards set by the organization they work for. None of the journalists interviewed from either Lebanon or Egypt mentioned the code of ethics adopted by their respective journalists' unions and syndicates a long time ago. In the case of Lebanon, it resonates with a previous study I conducted at the beginning of the millennium, when the majority of journalists surveyed didn't know an ethical code existed (Harb, 2013). In both countries there is high emphasis on one's own conscience to decide what is ethical and what is not.

In Egypt, Journalist E put it clearly: 'I follow my conscience in trying to apply these norms. I read other international code of principles and those are my source of what I view as professional' (E, interview with author, 2016). Journalist E, however, does not believe in balance as a principle but believes in 'practicing or managing my bias in a professional and objective way' (E, interview with author, 2016).

Journalist M offers a clear example of how thinking ethically means thinking professionally:

> Professionalism, independence, objectivity, transparency, integrity, accuracy, diversity, accountability, respect of the personal freedom and privacy of individuals, respect of the inviolability of the human body, harm limitation principle, respect of the law, no absolute reality, relativity, raising questions rather than giving exemplar answers, respect of the norms and the ethics of dealing with victims and survivors, respect of all human rights and after all having recourse to my professional and human conscience. These are the professional and ethical norms and values of journalism as a profession, I learned and experienced them throughout the different phases of my formation and my career as a journalist.
>
> (M, interview with author, 2016)

Lebanese journalists interviewed are aware that values and principles of the profession are being undermined and breached by several institutions. However, they are also asserting that being ethical means being professional. Journalist L lists what being unethical means, mirroring what is currently practiced by many Lebanese journalists:

> Not falling for the temptations of being unethical for the sake of achieving personal benefits is essential for keeping your moral and ethical obligation in this profession. Objectivity and credibility are

important factors to keep your reputation as an ethical and professional journalist.

(L, interview with author, 2016)

Journalist K highlighted another aspect of the scene that currently dominates Lebanese journalism practices. She lists what it means to be ethical for her as a journalist: 'to avoid sensationalism, respect individual privacy and not to intrude and invade people's privacy. Additionally, to avoid including my own view or opinion when presenting information to the public' (K, interview with author, 2016). As mentioned earlier in the chapter, the journalists interviewed here from both Egypt and Lebanon are representative of a certain calibre of journalists that are trying hard to abide by what they see as professional and ethical practices, based on their education, training, experience, and ability to access international news platforms from around the world.

Discussion

Even with this selective sample of journalists who defends professional and ethical norms, there did not seem to be a contradiction between advocating for objectivity and impartiality and being an advocate for human rights, social change, and bringing reform into the political system. This mirrors to a certain extent what Pintak and Ginges (2009) reported in their work, *Inside the Arab News Room*. They concluded that 'Arab journalists thus see no contradiction between objectivity and overt support for political and social reforms or balancing reporting and respect' (p. 173). However, what this study has shown is that journalists believe that those notions are universal, but understanding what do they stand for is contextual; hence they are practiced differently. This contextual understanding of such notions differs also between journalists in Lebanon and Egypt. In Lebanon journalists interviewed saw themselves as 'advocators,' 'missionaries' (Hanitzsch, 2007: 373), and actors of change for the common good, with journalists taking a more active and assertive role in their reporting, while journalists in Egypt interviewed focused on finding and reporting the 'truth' accurately and factually as their main objective in order to achieve an informed society that will hold people in power to account.

The journalists were explicitly asked if they believed these notions they abide by are Western notions or universal ones, and it was clearly stated they are universal or, in very few cases, both. The answer to that recognition is the fact that Lebanese students study Western philosophies and cultures and, as Jad Melki (2009) explains, relates to the variety of academic

JOURNALISM CULTURES IN EGYPT AND LEBANON

traditions practiced in Lebanese universities campuses. Most Lebanese and Egyptian journalists interviewed have gone through training with international news organizations either inside Lebanon and Egypt or outside. Besides, the universality of access to stories and information has introduced the journalists with models of practice they appreciated. When it comes to understanding professional standards and ethics, territoriality becomes negligible and globalization makes it easier for journalists in both nations to adhere to what they identify as universal values of journalism. However, as the interviews have revealed, territoriality does exist when assessing dominant practices versus roles within national borders.

Arguably, for some in both Lebanon and Egypt, forming an opinion and reflecting on that opinion in the stories journalists produce were not put in contradiction with notions like balance and impartiality, hence taking us back to contextualizing of how the norms are understood and practiced. In Egypt, online media has been seen as an alternative space to the traditional format, which relates to what De Angelis (2015) identify as 'Renegotiation of the boundaries of the journalistic profession' (p. 107). Nevertheless, the dominant influencer is still traditional media formats, mainly TV. De Angelis's notion of 'new opinion journalist' had an impact between 2012 and 2015 but has been phased out now according to Journalist E (interview with author, 2016).

According to Hanitzsch (2007), 'A shared occupational ideology is believed to serve as the "cultural cement" that holds journalists together as a profession and that, therefore forms the foundation of journalism identity' (p. 370). Journalists interviewed unanimously said that journalists in both countries don't share a common occupational identity. It comes clear that at least one of the interviewees didn't share a common ideology with their peers. It is also evident that journalists interviewed don't share the same values as those peers that are dominating the mainstream media scenes in both countries. If we take the power distance role (Hanitzsch, 2007) as an example, journalists interviewed position themselves at the high end within 'the adversary pole of the continuum,' which 'captures a kind of journalism that openly challenges the powers that be' (p. 373). The other end of the pole is where the mainstream is mostly situated. According to (Hanitzsch, 2007):

> This kind of journalism is bluntly loyal: taking on a 'propagandist role' practicing 'agitator journalism' being defensive of authorities, routinely engaging in self-censorship, and serving as a mouthpiece of the Government or the party.
>
> (p. 374)

It is a hybrid identity where some journalists are struggling to maintain what they believe is universal professional roles and those carrying the 'loyal' banner where they 'pay disproportionately high attention to the authorities and rarely question the official sources as authoritative, credible and trustworthy.'
(p. 374)

The loyalist position seems to be more commonly adopted and dominant in Egypt than in Lebanon. However, this mix of professional ideologies exists in both countries. These professional ideologies, which according to Hanitzsch 'can be understood as crystallizations of distinctive arrays of journalism-related values, orientations, and predispositions that articulate themselves as dominant professional culture' (2007, p. 370) is not distinctive and is a mixture of different ideologies that emerge based on political, cultural, social and intellectual differences. Media in Lebanon is politically and ideologically bound with certain political groups, hence the 'participant' role model is associated with several and different political powers within the country. In Egypt the political power is assigned within the state; the regime and the 'loyal' role becomes associated with the regime and its military apparatus.

Hanitzsch says 'Journalism culture is a fast-changing object of inquiry' (2007, p. 371), and that is true in both Lebanon and Egypt.

Lebanese journalists interviewed fit mostly within the 'interventionist' role, which is 'socially committed, and motivated' while the Egyptian journalists interviewed seem generally to be advocating 'truth' and factual reporting with tendency to be detached in matters of politics and holding those in power to account when detachment could be applicable.

Market-driven fear seems more evident within the Lebanese journalism scene, while fear in Egypt is generated by the state and its military apparatus.

In relation to ethics and ethical ideologies, hybrid and mixed ideologies are also evident here. Some base their ethical consideration on personal and moral philosophies, some on what they studied and read, some on editorial and ethical guidelines set by their institutions, and others on a mixture of all. However, journalists interviewed speak that practices in the mainstream are less idealistic and more outcome-oriented, which translates to 'harm will sometimes be necessary to produce good.' These according to (Hanitzsch, 2007, p. 379) are low on oriented ethical considerations.

Journalism cultures in Lebanon and Egypt share some common journalism values and differ on others. The sample interviewed here is representative of a segment of the journalism communities in both Lebanon and Egypt. It highlights the hybridity of roles and professional norms and understanding of them. These norms, albeit being seen as universal, have been localized to fit with different understanding of what journalism's role is in societies that are witnessing rapid political change. This segment of the journalism communities in both Lebanon and Egypt believed in the idea of 'universal journalist' following a set of 'universal values,' discussed here, despite the fact these values are of Anglo-American origin. What matters to them is seeking an identity that differs from what the mainstream media content in both Egypt and Lebanon advocate. The main configuration they believe in amounts to 'to be professional is to be ethical.' Accuracy and integrity are at the top of their list.

References

Boulos, J.-C. (1995), *Television History and Stories*. Lebanon: FMA.
Dajani, N. (1992), *Disoriented Media in a Fragmented Society: The Lebanese Experience*. Beirut: American University of Beirut Press.
Dajani, N. (2001), The changing scene of Lebanese Television. *TBS Electronic Journal*, 7 (Fall/Winter). Accessed: 9 January 2005. Retrieved from www.tbsjournal.com/Archives/Fall01/dajani.html
Darweesh, P. (2014), Abdel-Fattah El-Sisi gives first ever TV interview, *Ahramonline*. Retrieved from http://english.ahram.org.eg/NewsPrint/100549.aspx
de Angelis, E. (2015), The new opinion journalism in Egypt: Hybrid professional culture and distributed control. *Afriche e Orienti*, 1–2, 103–120. Retrieved from www.academia.edu/download/50002970/New_Opinion_Journalism_in_Egypt.pdf
Diab, O. (2011), New Egypt, new media, *The Guardian*, 10 March 2011. Retrieved from www.theguardian.com/commentisfree/2011/mar/10/egypt-media-newspapers-mubarak-propaganda
Duffy, M. J. (2013), 'Cultures of Journalism' in Arabic- and English-language Newspapers within the United Arab Emirates. *Journal of Middle East Media*, 9, 24–45. Retrieved from http://jmem.gsu.edu/files/2014/09/JMEM-2013_ENG_Duffy.pdf
Duffy, M. J. (2014), Arab media regulations: Identifying restraints on freedom of the press in the laws of six Arabian Peninsula Countries. *Berkeley Journal of Middle Eastern & Islamic Law*, 6, 1–31. https://doi.org/10.15779/Z384S3C
El Issawi, F. and Cammaerts, B. (2016), Shifting journalistic roles in democratic transitions: Lessons from Egypt. *Journalism*, 17, 549–566. https://doi.org/10.1177/1464884915576732
Flick, U. (1998), *An Introduction to Qualitative Research*. London: Sage.
Flick, U. (2009), *An Introduction to Qualitative Research* (4th ed.). London: Sage.
Gunter, B. and Dickinson, R. (2013), *News Media in the Arab World, A study of 10 Arab and Muslim Countries*. London: Bloomsbury Academia.

Hallin, Daniel and Mancini, P. (2004), *Comparing Media Systems: Three Models of Media and Politics*. Cambridge: Cambridge University Press.

Hanitzsch, T. (2007), Deconstructing journalism culture: Toward a universal theory. *Communication Theory*, 17, 367–385. https://doi.org/10.1111/j.1468-2885.2007.00303.x

Hanitzsch, T., Hanusch, F., Mellado, C., Anikina, M., Berganza, R., Cangoz, I, . . . and Wang Yuen, E. K. (2011), Mapping journalism cultures across nations. *Journalism Studies*, 12, 273–293. https://doi.org/10.1080/1461670X.2010.512502

Hanitzsch, T. and Mellado, C. (2011), What shapes the news around the world? How journalists in eighteen countries perceive influences on their work. *International Journal of Press/Politics*, 16, 404–426. https://doi.org/10.1177/1940161211407334

Harb, Z. (2013), Mediating internal conflict in Lebanon and its ethical boundaries. In Matar, D. and Harb, Z. (Eds.). *Narrating conflict in the Middle East: Discourse, Image and Communication Practices in Lebanon and Palestine* (pp. 1–16). London: I. B. Tauris.

Jad, M. (2009), Journalism and media studies in Lebanon. *Journalism Studies*, 10, 672–690. https://doi.org/10.1080/14616700902920174

Karam, J. (2017), As lights go out at As-Safir, dark times ahead for Lebanese press. Retrieved from www.arabnews.com/node/1033221/media#.

Lahlali, E. M. (2011), *Contemporary Arab Broadcast Media*. Edinburgh: Edinburgh University Press.

Majed, R. (2015), Paper presented at Freie Universität conference, Berlin.

Mellor, N. (2005), *The Making of Arab News*. London: Rowman & Littlefield publishers.

Mellor, N. (2007), *Modern Arab Journalism Problems and Prospects*. Edinburgh: Edinburgh University Press.

The New Arab (2016a), Egyptian press union chief sentenced to two-year jail stint. Retrieved from www.alaraby.co.uk/english/news/2016/11/19/egyptian-press-union-chief-sentenced-to-two-year-jail-stint

The New Arab (2016b), Last minute Funding saves iconic Lebanese Newspaper fromclosure. Retrievedfromwww.alaraby.co.uk/english/news/2016/3/28/last-minute-funding-saves-iconic-lebanese-newspaper-from-closure

The New Arab (2016c), Lebanese newspaper to close after decades in print. Retrieved from www.alaraby.co.uk/english/news/2016/3/24/lebanese-newspaper-to-close-after-four-decades-in-print

Pintak, L. (2011), *The New Arab Journalist, Mission and Identity in a Time of Turmoil*. London: I. B. Tauris.

Pintak, L. (2014), Islam, identity and professional values: A study of journalists in three Muslim-majority regions. *Journalism*, 15, 482–503. https://doi.org/10.1177/1464884913490269

Pintak, L. and Ginges, J. (2009), Inside the Arab Newsroom. *Journalism Studies*, 10, 157–177. https://doi.org/10.1080/14616700802337800

Rugh, W. (2004), *Arab Mass Media*. London: Praeger.

JOURNALISM CULTURES IN EGYPT AND LEBANON

Sakr, N. (2001), *Satellite Realms: Transnational Television, Globalization & the Middle East*. London: I.B. Tauris.
Sakr, N. (2007), *Arab Television Today*. London: I.B. Tauris.
Sakr, N. (2013), *Transformations in Egyptian Journalism*. London: I.B. Tauris.
Seale, C. (1998), *Researching Society and Culture*. London: Sage.
Staab, J.F. (1990), The role of news factors in news selection: A theoretical reconsideration. *European Journal of Communication*, 5, 423–443. https://doi.org/10.1177/0267323190005004003
Wimmer, R. and Dominick, J.R. (1997), *Mass Media Research: An Introduction* (7th ed.). Boston, MA: Wadsworth.

9

CONCRETE POETRY IN BRAZIL AND GERMANY
The avant-garde reviews history through new media

Luca Romani

The present study tentatively re-conceptualizes the notion of the avant-garde in the literary context, based on a reflection on the relationship of the Second Avant-Gardes with narratives regarding the past and memory. In fact, while some features can be said to pertain to all avant-garde movements, the concern with the past and the challenge to represent/reconstruct it as truthfully as possible seem to be distinguishing elements of the Second Avant-Gardes. If it is so, the very concept of avant-garde needs to be re-considered in its complexity, seen as something more articulated than a merely forward-oriented entity devoted to the destruction of what remained behind it temporally. My hypothesis is that the particular concern of the Second Avant-Gardes with past and memory – which actually questions the 'traditional' definition of avant-garde – roots in the transformed historical conditions in which they were immersed, that is, in the drastic reconfiguration of the relationships between South and North taking place in the post-WWII world. Europe was in a profound crisis, while the global 'peripheries,' and especially Latin American ex-colonies, became aware of their responsibility for cultural re-construction after the disaster of war and Holocaust.[1] This process of re-'ordering' of the global cultural geography consisted in the establishment of a new balance between North and South, wherein the latter came to confront itself on *equal* terms with the North, and a South finally becoming 'global.'

The discourse is based on a specific case study that can be identified as the very first and most exemplary instance – at least in the literary context – of 'cross-cultural current': *concrete poetry*. Two culturally and socially divergent national entities contributed the most to its rise and growth, namely Brazil and Germany. These were also the two realities which established the most intense and fruitful exchange within the worldwide web of concrete poetry, coming in many cases to very similar aesthetic proposals. However, in the present chapter I will focus on their sharing of the concern with past and memory; I will consider, on the one side, Haroldo de Campos's literary criticism and, on the other side, some excerpts of Franz Mon's radio poem (Hörspiel) *Das gras wies wächst* (1969). Since the material analyzed in the two cases is of clearly different natures, the chapter may appear to be an 'unbalanced treatment'; but this is less a methodological choice of mine than a constraint imposed by the available corpus, namely the absence of Brazilian concrete poems dealing with Brazil's national past. However, this divergence should not distract the reader from the actual focus of this study: the concern with memory and representations of the past that Brazilian and German concrete poets shared and the significance that this element has in a possible reformulation of the very concept of avant-garde.

Concrete poetry and media

Although critics never came to a single unified univocal definition of the concrete aesthetics,[2] concrete poetry can be described in general terms as a kind of poetic expression that highlights the *materiality* of the word to the extreme, both in its auditory and its visual/typographical dimensions. A particular characteristic is '[the] concentration upon the physical material from which the poem or text is made' (Solt, 1968, p. 9). Concrete poetry is thus in contrast with the conception of the word as a mere vehicle of established meaning, transforming it in something present and concretely perceivable, visible, and tangible which can hit and affect the human body. The *signifier* gains as much (or more) importance as the *signified*; that is, the phonetic and typographic features of the word are put on the same level as its semantics. Moreover, concrete poetry is characterized by the complete abolition of the verse and the linear syntax in general, so that the recipient's attention is deflected from the narration regarding some object or concept *external* to the poem itself and is directed on the meta-discourse of the text.

Both mentioned features (materiality and non-linearity) are deeply tied with and influenced by the revolution in communication that occurred during the post-WWII. The stress on the 'physical materiality' of the word was based on the utilization of new typographic and audiovisual technologies and devices that permitted making the word a 'complete organism, with psycho-physical-chemical proprieties, touch antenna circulation heart: alive' (Campos, Campos, and Pignatari, 2006, p. 71). The non-linearity responded to the communicative conditions of modern mass media, namely immediateness. In this sense, Décio Pignatari affirmed explicitly that 'since the Gutenberg era and the hegemony of the written word are coming to an end, it is necessary to adapt poetry to the rising era of electricity and electronics, an era of communicational instantaneity' (Pignatari, 1971, p. 66).[3] A linear-discursive device like verse cannot keep up with the impressive acceleration of information and communication processes. It was necessary to establish a poetic language that dialogues with mass media by synthesizing and compressing information.[4] The concrete poem was thus 'totally contemporary' (Campos, Campos, and Pignatari, 2006, p. 211),[5] since it followed the changing communicational needs of the post-WWII society and reacted to the development of new media, up to the point that it could be considered as a *new medium* itself, as much as television, radio, and cinema.[6] In the present chapter I focus on the different *media* used by two concrete poets for addressing the challenge of re-presenting/re-thinking their respective national past. The term *media* is to be taken in its widest sense, namely in connection to the original Latin root 'medium': any means that transmits some kind of information, also including experimental poetry, translation and literary criticism.

Short history of the term 'avant-garde'

Starting from the beginning of the 20th century, the French term 'avant-garde' has been used to identify artistic or intellectual movements with strong tendencies to develop experimental and unconventional forms of art. The term originated from the military, and its literal translation in English is 'fore-guard' or 'advance guard.' In that context, it referred to a numerically restricted unit which preceded the bulk of the army in its advance by means of rapid and high-risk incursions within the enemy's territory. Quite interestingly, most of these definitional aspects remained the same when the term was transferred to the artistic sphere. A relatively restricted number of authors developed groundbreaking concepts of art, preceding the majority of intellectuals and artists and thus risking academic disdain and public derision. The avant-garde authors took this risk not only consciously but even proudly, as they returned the same (or even greater) disdain and derision to conformist scholars and moralistic public.

Moreover, the avant-garde had an 'enemy' who it attacked primarily through acts of 'preventive war': namely the publication of quite (verbally) violent manifestos. The idea of 'battle' was one of the essential elements that characterized the artistic activity of several avant-garde movements. As Gonzalo Aguilar rightly stated, 'the efficiency of a Dada act or of some futurist performances lies [. . .] in their violent insertion in the social context' (Aguilar, 2005, p. 36).[7] The elements of *elitism* and strong opposition to official canons actually characterized each and every avant-garde movement, from the 'historical' ones up to those that emerged immediately after WWII, and they seem to be the sole features fully shared by movements that were extremely distant from one another both in terms of aesthetic and political points of view (for instance, Futurism and Surrealism). The *non-conciliation*, intended as general contrast with any kind of official institution and with a generally conservative public, has always been a unifying element for all avant-garde movements. In practice, the concept of the 'avant-garde' is defined essentially in *relational* terms. While the features described above pertain to both the *historical* and the Second Avant-Gardes, the latter acquired a character that was completely lacking in the avant-garde currents arisen before WWII: the interest for the reflection on past and memory.

Brazil: the *Noigandres* group

The Campos brothers and Décio Pignatari founded the *Noigandres* group in São Paulo in 1952. While poetic production was initially the main activity of the three poets, critical essays and translations became more and more important after the 'end of the concretism,'[8] with the goal of clarifying the complex poetry developed by the group as well as the poets' thoughts regarding many different issues. The considerations by Haroldo de Campos on the history of Brazilian literature aimed at redefining its evolution, and thus required a more general reflection on the history of Brazilian culture. This is the topic that I am going to explore below.

In his book *Brazilian Concrete Poetry: The Avant-Gardes in the Modernist Crossway* (2005),[9] Gonzalo Aguilar highlighted that Antonio Candido, one of the most influential literary critics in Brazil, approached the history of literature by searching for its *decisive moments*, which created a pattern of *continuity*.[10] This resulted in a diachronic perspective of the history of literature, namely in the conception of a linear evolution from a given point in the past up to the present, a chronologically ordered list of authors and movements that contributed to the gradual development of concepts and forms, always in the name of *continuity*. It is extremely significant that Candido considered Gonçalves de Magalhães trip to Europe in 1833 as a 'providential' moment for Brazilian culture.[11] In fact, the idea of an aesthetic continuity with respect to this cultural touchstone seems to necessarily implicate the characterization of Brazilian literature as a subordinate, Euro-dependent entity, a 'tropical' declination of the European canon. This conception was a sort of unassailable law within the Brazilian intellectual and academic spheres for long time. Many Brazilian literary critics assigned a merely 'exotic' role of Brazilian literature within the international context, recognizing it as 'a secondary bough of a secondary tree [. . .] a bough of Portuguese literature' (Campos, 1976, p. 14).[12] Thus, they 'negated purely and simply any integration of Brazilian literature on a level of international experience by reason of a vainglorious *tropicalism* (as cited in Franchetti, 2012, p. 44).[13]

This voluntarily submissive attitude, a kind of inferiority complex,[14] also had its effects on the quality of Brazilian literary criticism in general. The more or less marked adaptation to the imported canon seemed to be the main reference for establishing the greatness of an author. For Haroldo de Campos, the Brazilian literary historians 'subscribe[d] with reverence to the inherited partitions of "greater" and "minor" authors [. . .] allowing themselves only a moderate margin of divergence in relation to the established canon' (Campos, 1976, p. 14).[15] The authors who for any reason differed from that canon were discounted or even excluded from the official mainline of Brazilian literature, generally being written off as unimportant but tolerable exceptions that somehow 'confirmed the rule.'[16] The juxtaposition proposed by Silvio Romero[17] in this sense between the history of literature and the grammatical system is extremely significant. In both cases, 'the paradigms of the regular declinations and conjugations are given, and this is enough. The indication of the irregular phenomena completes the theory and *the whole is accomplished*' (as cited in Aguilar, 2005, pp. 346–347, emphasis added).[18] Décio Pignatari described this situation by sadly recognizing:

> When the sector is that of literature, and the country, Brazil; and when the poet-inventor dares audacious and surprising thinking, by proposing general projects of creation and culture, it is almost sure that he is going to be isolated, as a foreign body or an exotic enclave that the organism tries to ignore in order to endure.
> (Pignatari, 1971, p. 142).[19]

A radically opposite approach was developed by the *Noigandres* group and particularly by Haroldo de Campos, who emphasized the necessity of overcoming the merely diachronic vision of art history, aesthetically indifferent and which he considered a banal collection of chronological data.[20] As an alternative, Haroldo proposed a 'retrospective-synchronic view' proceeding from the present to the past without respecting a chronologically linear path but rather 'jumping' from one point to another in the search for the *moments of rupture* within the universal history of art: namely those 'exceptional' personalities who constructed radically new languages or new categories of thought and perception. In this synchronic perspective, the *aesthetic* and not the *chronological* actuality of a work of art is considered. In other words, the value of an artist is given by his/her degree of original creativity and invention and not by his/her compliance with the dominating aesthetic patterns at a specific moment in the linear flow of art history.

CONCRETE POETRY IN BRAZIL AND GERMANY

The American poet Ezra Pound expressed this concept in a radical affirmation that

> all ages are contemporary [. . .], the real time is independent from the apparent one, and many dead people are contemporary of our grandsons, while it seems that many of our contemporaries met in Abraham's breast or in some more adequate receptacle.
> (as cited in Campos, 1969, p. 208)

Of course, this approach does not imply the total cancellation of the discourse on the historical context of an author or movement. The relationship between diachronic and synchronic visions cannot be one of reciprocal exclusion but rather it is dialectic. Anatol Rosenfeld claimed the necessity for integration between both approaches, declaring that 'a critic, however radically "synchronic" [. . .] also has to keep a "diachronic" horizon open, by indicating [. . .] the vision inherent to the epoch in which the work arose' (as cited in Campos, 1969, pp. 215–216).[21] What must be actually guaranteed is 'the ordering of knowledge in such a way that the following person (or generation) could, as rapidly as possible, find its living part, and lose the least amount of time with obsolete questions' (as cited in Campos, 2006, p. 18).

The three founders of the *Noigandres* group applied these ideas in two tightly intertwined spheres, namely literary criticism and translation. The latter, defined as 'a privileged form of critical reading' (Campos, 2006, p. 46),[22] was a peculiar *medium* for the realization of the retrospective-synchronic view. During the 1970s, Haroldo and Augusto de Campos translated the works of many foreign authors into Portuguese with neither temporal nor spatial constraints: Dante, the Provençal *Troubadours*, and the Japanese *haiku* were translated along with contemporary authors like Ezra Pound and Vladimir Mayakovski.[23] As for criticism on Brazilian literature, the *Noigandres* group searched for the *moments of rupture* that created a *discontinuity* in its apparently regular flow. They saved artists like Pedro Kilkerry and Joaquim de Sousa Andrade[24] from total oblivion by highlighting their non-conformation to the dominating European canon. The claim for intellectual autonomy is particularly strong in relation to the episode 'O inferno de Wall Street' from the poetry collection *O Guesa Errante* (1888), whose author had been disdainfully defined as a 'mad man' by Silvio Romero.[25] In Haroldo de Campos's words:

> Anticipating Ezra Pound, the Brazilian poet [. . .] by means of the montage technique with fragments extracted from reviews of the time, multi-lingual quotations, interventions of historical

and mythological characters and lexical and syntactic inventions, projects a brutal vision of the 'Financial Hell' [. . .] typical of the emergence of capitalism. Before Mallarmé, he allows himself to be influenced by the mosaic of a newspaper, by the graphic configuration of this section of his poem.

(Campos, 1976, p. 19)[26]

The critical revision of Brazil's literary past based on the synchronic-retrospective approach assumes a clearly postcolonialist character. The re-evaluation of Brazilian personalities who contributed to the evolution of literature on an international level implicates the questioning of the established hierarchy between central and peripheral cultures. The break with the idea of Brazil's incontrovertible cultural subordination to Europe and the claim for a native capability for original invention are expressed by the *Noigandres* poets through the concept of the 'anthropofagic act.' This formula, coined by Oswald de Andrade in his *Manifesto Antropofago* (1928),[27] indicates the critical incorporation and re-elaboration of the 'civilized' cultural canon, in order to elaborate new aesthetic products with *universal* validity. In some 'militant' essays by Haroldo de Campos,[28] he employs 'alimentary-cannibalistic' terms for clarifying the significance of the anthropophagic act:

> The Europeans have to learn how to live together with the new barbarians who, in another alternative context, are devouring them and making them flesh of their flesh and bone of their bone, have been long since re-elaborating them chemically through the impetuous and irrefutable metabolism of difference.
> (Campos, 2006, p. 250)[29]

The shared centre-periphery logic, according to which Latin American writers are inevitably 'ex-centric' and 'de-centred' subjects destined to be continuously nourished by the 'irradiating centre' of European civilization, are thus drastically rejected. The idea of a *global* 'interzone' emerges, where the intellectual energies of the 'barbarians' enter into contact with the 'civilized' cultures on a level of absolute equality, and where Brazil is recognized as a national subject 'in a dialogical and dialectic relationship with the universal.'[30] And if it is true that European writers must 'recognize and re-devour the differential marrow' provided by the 'voracious barbarians' of planetary civilization,[31] Brazilian literary critics and poets must also become aware of this radical change, so that they 'will be allowed, from now on, to claim, in a loud voice, what is due to [Brazilians], the contribution of original information that [they] must claim as [their] contribution to the evolution of the forms of universal literature' (Campos, 1976, pp. 15–16).[32] Finally, *Noigandres*'s critical re-evaluation of the history of Brazilian literature is clearly tinged by the awareness of colonialism and the hegemonic relationships between 'global north' and 'global south.' By means of the synchronic-retrospective criticism, the *Noigandres* poets show a postcolonial attitude that they rely on for proudly claiming their own leading position in the global contemporary poetic context. In fact, the synchronic-retrospective approach opposes the conception of Brazilian literature as a homogeneous and linear sequence of 'Euro-dependent' authors, since it allows for the rescue and valorization of rebellious *fragments* of the past that do not fit into the accomplished and uniform image that most Brazilian literary critics would claim accounts for the *whole* of Brazilian literature, a 'total image' (Didi-Huberman)[33] that was manipulated, because the discrepancies and discontinuities that made it 'dirty' were erased, leaving a limpid but certainly less truthful representation.

Germany: the *Konkrete Poesie*

In Germany, the poets of the *Konkrete Poesie* movement were facing the past of their country, though in completely different conditions. Post-WWII Germany was like no other place in the world. In the land of the executioners responsible for a tragic and destructive war and the authors of abominable crimes, the moral scourge was so severe that it was extremely hard to think about a 'normal' future. Yet it was necessary to go forward, somehow.

A first step was to overcome the immense cultural gap that had emerged between the end of the Weimar Republic and the end of WWII. Twelve years of cultural and intellectual emptiness had to be filled up as rapidly as possible through the rescue of 'another' German literature, one that was very different from that written by some pen pushers celebrating the Aryan race and imposed on students and scholars through the indoctrination and manipulation of thought implemented by the regime. In this sense, very important testimonies can be found in the essays by concrete poets like Franz Mon and Ernst Jandl, who as students personally experienced the utter lack of any literary movement – especially Dada and Expressionism, which would become the main poetic references in their subsequent creative activity.[34] In 1946, the publication of Carola Giedon-Welcker's *Anthologie der Abseitigen* showed the need to rethink literature and poetry in relation to the real, contemporary context. Her anthology included texts by revolutionary authors such as Hans Arp, Hugo Ball, Kurt Schwitters, Tristan Tzara, and other pioneers whose work was seen as 'an audacious advance in the new land of language' (Mon in Busch and Combrink, 2009, p. 404).[35] In the same year, a part of Joyce's *Finnegan's Wake* was also translated and published in the first issue of the *Fahre* review. Movements such as Dada, Surrealism, and Expressionism, until then censored by Goebbels's propaganda, began to re-emerge, showing the extreme allure of the aesthetic evolution that had occurred on an international scale during such a brief and dark period.

A second and much more awkward issue was how to address the dramatic occurrences of the preceding decade. The Adornian statement of 1949 about the 'barbarian act' of composing poetry after Auschwitz seemed to block all attempts to say anything in front of a reality that deserved only reflection and silence. How could a German poet express himself about the greatest tragedy in human history, in light of his awareness regarding the responsibility of his own people for abominable crimes in the name of the Aryan race? Wouldn't *non-representation* be the only possible way? This perspective was strongly opposed by many of the most important representatives of German *Konkrete Poesie*, who claimed the need to invent new ways of expression, to create a new language for talking about something generally described as 'irrepresentable.' For Heißenbüttel, Adorno's statement 'is a pathetic statement that risks bringing silence over the monstrous once again' (Heißenbüttel in Schöning, 1983, p. 269).[36] Ernst Jandl's statement in regard to the necessity for a 'new way' in poetry is also very significant:

> I fear that we cannot speak anymore about some things we spoke about in the poetry of the past. We cannot express them at all, unless a totally different way for speaking about them is found. And I think, one of these attempts is to go to the basis, almost to the foundation of language, and there, the suffering, the pathos is found and expressed, more convincingly, more profoundly, more concretely.
> (as cited in Schöning, 1983, p. 208)[37]

A peculiar product of German *Konkrete Poesie* through which a radically new poetic language was achieved was the *Neues Hörspiel* (New Radio Play). This hybrid literary product produced and broadcast by radio stations was a mix of drama, music, and experimental poetry. Microphones and recorders highlighted certain phonetic features of the articulated syllables/words and gave them peculiar rhythmic or melodic characteristics. Moreover, new devices that became available starting from the 1950s, like

CONCRETE POETRY IN BRAZIL AND GERMANY

stereophony and tape recorders, were employed significantly in realizing more complex 'soundscapes.'[38] The tape recorder created the possibility to intervene in the recording, not only by accelerating or slowing the sound of the voice on a linear axis but also (and most importantly) by cutting the recording at any point. In this way, it became possible to either definitively cut out any undesired feature (thus creating a sort of *distancing effect*) or to re-order the obtained fragments into new 'artificial' sequences. Thus the tape recorder was the starting point for the *montage-technique* that characterized a lot of experimental art starting from the beginning of the 20th century.[39] This technique was first developed in poetry. As for stereophony, it allowed for the superimposition and interplay of several voices within a sonic space, which could be experienced not only in its temporality but also in its profundity and its *multidimensionality*.

Several German concrete poets used this experimental form for attempting the hard task of representing the recent past of their country. Heißenbüttel's *Deutschland 1944* (1979)[40] consists of a collage of quotations from German personalities exclusively dating back to 1944. For Franz Mon, this *Hörspiel* represents 'the political situation of the Germans in the moment that the fragments of the nation began to burst in a slow explosion' (Mon, 1981, p. 55).[41] Other poets tried to address the hardest issue of the German recent past: the Holocaust. In Ludwig Harig's 'Ein Blumenstück' (1969), the reading of fairy tales and the singing voices of children playing in the middle of blooming flowers are acoustically combined with the insistently repeated name of Rudolf Höß, the last commander of the Auschwitz concentration camp. Total innocence and abominable guilt are put side by side, in the attempt to 'find the monstrous' by showing 'how suddenly the sentimental moves close to the monstrous' (Heißenbüttel in Schöning, 1983, p. 269).[42] Particularly significant is Franz Mon's *Das gras wies wächst* (1969).[43] An in-depth analysis of a few excerpts from this *Hörspiel* should suffice to show how the interaction between experimental poetry and new technical devices helped the German poets in their attempt to represent a theoretically 'irrepresentable' occurrence.

The *Hörspiel* opens up with a series of verbs with *ab-* as prefix (which conveys the idea of separation/interruption) followed by a list of names and then by a sequence of repeated *außerdem* ('moreover'). The three sequences are acoustically intertwined in a *montage* realized by means of the tape recorder. The image narrated by this initial section represents the Jewish people suddenly interrupting their activities for a Nazi head count immediately before leaving for a concentration camp. The adverb *außerdem* suggests the vexation, humiliation, and violence accompanying these events.

Some acoustic elements provide further clues for building a possible plot. The *ab-* is pronounced separately from the root of the following verbs in such a marked way that it efficiently expresses a vague premonition: what is being abandoned will never return. The list of names starts from the diphthong [ei] (pronounced /ai/), so that the name 'Eichmann'[44] gradually appears in the listener's mind. This acoustic similarity seems to suggest the proximity of victims to their executioners, their communal belonging to humankind. The whispered '*wo*' ('where') that immediately follows this first tripartite section is characterized by an uninterrupted crescendo, and thus seems to turn into an onomatopoeia of the steam engine of a departing train. This idea is also supported by the substitution of /v/ with /f/, as the latter phoneme clearly recalls the whistle or hiss of the steam pouring out. At a later stage,[45] the root '*eich*,' strictly connected with the word '*Eiche*' (oak tree), is repeated many times in connection with different suffixes. All words built with this root induce in the German-speaking listener an intimate connection with the name of Adolf Eichmann. The possible associations generated through the simple juxtaposition between this root and the following suffixes are quite complex. I am only suggesting some hypotheses.

The sequence '*eich-maul*,' if its two constitutive sections are considered, may give rise to the following impressions: '*maul*' is a pejorative denomination for 'face,' since it refers primarily to an animal's muzzle; and since a simple metonymy of '*eich*' would indicate the particularly hard wood of an oak, '*eich-maul*' evokes a 'stony-faced,' impassive, and cynical personality. If the animal-like connotation is added, the resulting figure would be similar to that of a 'cynical muzzle,' a suitable definition for Adolf Eichmann. The word '*eichmarks*' (calibration mark) and '*eichmaß*' (measurement) seem to refer to the extreme precision needed for managing a concentration camp. The exact calculation of all values was actually one of the main activities of the Nazis in the concentration camps: the systematic measurement of live and dead prisoners and (no less important) of their remains was essential for the functioning of the camp. This has always been seen as one of the most impressive, inhuman aspects of the Holocaust. Finally, '*eichlaub*' (oak fronds) and '*eichkatz*' (squirrel)[46] may refer to the environmental context around the camps, the German and Polish countryside that is later defined as '*eichplatz*,' both in the sense of the place of the oaks and Eichmann's place.[47] The constant presence of the latter figure is expressed through the superimposition between the voice that articulates all *eich* compounds and that repeating the word '*hier*' (here), as if in a tit for tat: *Eichmann? Hier!* The perfect symmetry between the phonemic sequence of '*eich*' (/aiç/) and of '*hier*' (/çia/), disposed as if in an inverted echo, is dramatically highlighted by means of stereophony.

CONCRETE POETRY IN BRAZIL AND GERMANY

The examples above illustrate the strict interaction between the experimental, non-discursive language of concrete aesthetics and the new technical devices that *supported* narrative non-linearity. The impact of this *Hörspiel* would have been impossible without elements like stereophony and tape recorder, which underline the spatiality of sound at the expense of its temporality and allow for the shaping of a complex, non-univocal acoustic image. The experimental *Hörspiel* is an unprecedentedly efficient expressive *medium* thanks to the non-clarity of the acoustic image created. In the foreword of *Das gras wies wächst*, Mon explicitly claimed that 'the listener of this *Hörspiel* doesn't listen to a story. There are dialogues, but not a coherent plot' (in Schöning, 1969).[48] Thus, every listener builds his own story, a representation that depends on his cultural background, his imagination and ability for association. In this way, infinite *possible* images, that certainly do not provide *all* truth on the absolute evil of the Holocaust, but help to approach it, are generated. *Das gras wies wächst* is a remarkable reply to the idea that the Holocaust is an 'impossible image' destined for non-representation, since it allows us to *approach* 'that which we don't understand but won't give up trying to understand' (Didi-Huberman, 2008, p. 162).[49]

In conclusion, different *media*, whether innovative literary criticism, experimental poetry, or new technical devices, allowed the main representatives of concrete poetry to reflect on the past in a way that never occurred on such a profound level in any *historical* avant-garde movement. I think that the global character of concrete poetry, namely the coexistence in a unique poetic movement of authors pertaining to both the 'global south' and the 'global north' and facing completely different cultural and sociohistorical contexts, has been a determining factor in the dramatic *complexification* of the reflection on the past achieved by its members. The Brazilian poets looked back at their national past with a postcolonial perspective, re-discovering and revitalizing some forgotten fragments of Brazilian 'barbarian' creativity and thus legitimizing the claim of the international value of their own aesthetic experience. The German poets, on the other hand, looked back at their most recent national past with a reaction to the widespread feeling of representational or communicational impossibility that characterized the whole artistic sphere in the post-WWII German-speaking countries. They saw the attempt to salvage that past from complete silence as a necessary step in returning dignity and respectability to Germany in front of all humankind. They understood that it would have been impossible to go forward without looking back.

A last element deserves to be mentioned. In spite of the dramatically different functions of their 'memories,' both German and Brazilian concrete poets shared a peculiar aspect in dealing with the past: their opposition to simplification, leading either to uniform and 'total' images or to completely non-existent, 'impossible' images. Highlighting of the significance of the *fragments* and their multiple *possible* relationships provided partial but irrevocable fragments of truth.

Notes

1 See Klengel (2011).
2 See Solt (1968), p. 7.
3 'Estamos chegando ao fim da Era Gutenberg, ao fim da hegemonia da palavra escrita, para entrarmos na era da Instantaneidade, que é a era da eletricidade e da eletrônica.'
4 See Pignatari (1971), pp. 16 and 157.
5 Here I quote the whole excerpt: 'A poesia brasileira é totalmente contemporânea, ao participar na própria formulação de um movimento poético de vanguarda em termos nacionais e internacionais, e não simplesmente em sentir-lhe as conseqüências com uma ou muitas décadas de atraso, como é o caso até mesmo do *Movimento do 22*.' ['Brazilian poetry is totally contemporary, by participating in the very grounding of a poetic avant-garde movement in national and international terms, and no more simply by feeling the consequence from one or many decades of delay, as was even the case of the *Movimento do 22*.']
6 See Campos, Campos, and Pignatari (2006), p. 67.
7 'A eficácia de um ato dadaísta ou de algumas performances futuristas está [. . .] em sua inserção violenta no contexto social.' This excerpt, as many others that will follow in the footnotes, was freely translated into English from Brazilian Portuguese by the author of this article.
8 The 'end of the concretism' is generally identified with the second half/end of the 1960s, when the revolutionary force of concrete aesthetics lost momentum. See for example Aguilar (2005), pp. 155–157.
9 '*Poesia concreta brasileira: as Vanguardas na Encruzilhada Modernista.*'
10 See Aguilar (2005), p. 336.
11 See Aguilar (2005), p. 348.
12 'Um ramo secundário de uma árvore secundária [. . .], esgalho da portuguesa.'
13 'Negando pura e simplesmente qualquer integração da literatura brasileira num plano de experiência internacional, por razões de tropicalismo porquemeufaunista [*sic*], como se lhe fosse destinado, sem remissão, o papel de literatura exótica ou de exceção.'
14 See Campos (1976), p. 15.
15 'Subscreve com temor reverencial as partilhas herdadas de autores "maiores" e "menores" [. . .], permitindo-se apenas uma discreta margem de divergência em relação ao cânon constituído.'
16 See the following excerpt: 'Espantoso sistema brasileiro! [. . .] Os movimentos mais radicais, as concepções mais revolucionárias são tranquilamente absorvidos pela gelatina verde-amarela, insossa insípida e insalubre' (Pignatari, 1971, p. 126). ['The Brazilian system is terrible! [. . .] The most radical movements, the most revolutionary conceptions are smoothly absorbed by the green-yellow jelly, unsalty, insipid and insalubrious.']

CONCRETE POETRY IN BRAZIL AND GERMANY

17 It must be highlighted that Silvio Romero was a steady reference for Brazilian criticism after the publication of his *History of Brazilian Literature* (1888), which was generally considered a 'perfect' canonical model in Brazil.
18 'Dão-se os paradigmas das declinações e conjugações regulares e tanto basta. A indicação dos fenômenos irregulares vem completar a teoria e *fica tudo acabado.*'
19 'Quando o setor é o da literatura, e o Pais, o Brasil; e quando o poeta-inventor se encoraja até a audaciosa e surpreendente veleidade de pensar, propondo projetos gerais de criação e cultura, é quase certo que venha a ser isolado, como um corpo estranho ou um enclave exótico, que o organismo procura ignorar para poder suportar.'
20 See also the following excerpt: 'Gosto de ler a tradição como partitura transtemporal, fazendo, a cada momento, "harmonizações" síncrono-diacrônicas, traduzindo, por assim dizer, o passado de cultura em presente de criação' (Campos, 2006, p. 258). ['I like to read the tradition as a transtemporal score, making at every moment some synchro-diachronic "harmonizations," translating so to speak the past of culture in a present of creation.']
21 'Uma crítica, por mais radicalmente "sincrônica" que seja [. . .], ainda assim tem de manter aberto o horizonte "diacrônico," pondo em referência [. . .] a visão inerente à época em que a obra surgiu.'
22 'A tradução é uma forma privilegiada de leitura critica.'
23 See for example the following publications: Campos (2003). *Invenção: de Arnaut e Reimbaut a Dante e Cavalcanti*. São Paulo, Arx; Campos, Campos, & Pignatari, (1960). *Cantares de Ezra Pound*. Rio de Janeiro, Serviço de Documentação MEC.
24 Augusto and Haroldo de Campos published books and essays on Joaquim de Sousândrade, such as *Re/visão de Sousândrade* (1964) São Paulo, Edições Invenção; *Sousandrade – poesia* (1966), Rio de Janeiro Agir. They also published a book on Pedro Kilkerry: *Re/visão de Kilkerry* (1971) São Paulo, Fundo Estadual da Cultura.
25 See Campos (1976), p. 18.
26 'Antecipando-se a Ezra Pound, o poeta brasileiro, através da técnica de montagem de fragmentos extraídos de jornais da época, de citações polilínguas, da intervenção de personagens históricos e mitológicos, de invenções vocabulares e sintáticas, projeta uma contundente visão do "inferno Financeiro" [. . .] característico da emergência do grande capitalismo. Antes de Mallarmé, ele se deixou influenciar pelo mosaico do jornal, para a configuração até gráfica dessa seção de seu poema.'
27 See Andrade (1991). Translated by Leslie Bary. 'Cannibalist Manifesto' (pp. 38–47) Latin American Literary Review. Pittsburgh: Dept. of Modern Languages, Carnegie-Mellon University. 19 (38).
28 See Campos (2006), p. 14.
29 'Os europeus [. . .] têm de aprender a conviver com os novos bárbaros que há muito, num contexto outro e alternativo, os estão devorando e fazendo deles carne de sua carne e osso de seu osso, que há muito os estão re-sintetizando quimicamente por um impetuoso e irrefragável metabolismo da diferença.'
30 See the following excerpt: 'Pensar o nacional em relacionamento dialógico e dialético com o universal. A "antropofagia" oswaldiana [. . .] é o pensamento

da devoração crítica do legado cultural universal, elaborado não a partir da perspectiva submissa e reconciliada do "bom selvagem" [...] mas segundo o ponto de vista desabusado do "mau selvagem," devorador de brancos, antropófago' (Campos, 2006, p. 234). ['To think of a nation in a dialogic and dialectic relationship with the universal. Oswaldian "anthropofagy" [...] is the thought of the critic devouring the cultural world heritage, not elaborated starting from the submissive and reconciled perspective of the "good savage" [...], but following the disenchanted point of view of the "bad savage," swallower of white people, the cannibal.']
31 See Campos (2006) p. 255.
32 'O crítico poderá agora [...] reivindicar alto e bom som aquilo que nos é devido, o contributo de informação original que temos a reclamar como coisa nossa na evolução de formas da literatura universal.'
33 See Didi-Huberman (2008).
34 See Mon, *Die Anfänge des experimentellen Schreibens in den fünfziger Jahren*. In Busch & Combrink (2009), p. 403.
35 'In einem kühnen Vordringen in sprachliches Neuland.'
36 'Das ist ein pathetisches Wort und hat in sich die Gefahr, neuerlich das Ungeheurliche zu verschweigen.'
37 'Ich fürchte, das man über gewisse Dinge, über die im Medium Dichtung in der Vergangenheit bereits gesprochen wurde, überhaupt nicht mehr sprechen, sie nicht mehr ausdrücken kann, wenn man nicht eine völlig andere Art, über diese Dinge zu sprechen, gefunden hat. Und ich meine, einer dieser Versuche geht eben auf diesem Weg nach unten, in die Niederungen der Sprache sozusagen, und dort ist das Leiden, das Pathos genauso vorzufinden und auszudrücken, überzeugender, ins Nähere gehend, konkreter.'
38 See Schafer (1977).
39 Duchamp's *readymades* or Eisenstein's films are perfect examples, as they approximate two or more essentially different elements in a space that is totally alien to both of them in a way that provokes strong associative effects and affects.
40 The printed score was published in 1967, while the *Hörspiel* production occurred only in 1979.
41 'Die politische Landschaft der Deutschen in dem Augenblick [...], da die Brocken der Nation in zeitlupehafter Explosion auseinanderzufliegen beginnen.'
42 'Dem Ungeheurlichen auf die Spur zu kommen [...]; wie das Gemütliche unversehens dem Ungeheurlichen benachbart ist.'
43 The title does not make sense in the original language. It is a *montage* and can be translated as follows: 'the grass showed grows' or 'the grass how it grows.'
44 Adolf Eichmann was the inventor of the extermination camps; his name is often present (or alluded to) throughout this *Hörspiel*.
45 The number pages are completely absent in the printed score; the references are made on the basis of specific points established by the author himself. The specific point I am referring to in this case is number 19 (with reference to Schöning's edition of 1969).
46 The exact word is actually *Eichkätzchen*.
47 In German, the strict connection of the squirrel with the oaks is expressed in the word itself, for the squirrel is the 'oak's little cat.'

48 'Der hörer des folgenden hörspiels erfährt keine geschichte. Es gibt zwar dialoge, aber keine zusammenhängende handlung.'
49 'Aquilo que não compreendemos, mas a cuja compreensão não queremos renunciar.'

References

Aguilar, G. (2005). *Poesia concreta brasileira: As Vanguardas na Encruzilhada Modernista* [Brazilian concrete poetry: The avant-gardes in the modernist crossway]. São Paulo: EdUsp.
Andrade, O. (1991). Translated by Leslie Bary. 'Cannibalist Manifesto' (pp. 38–47) Latin American Literary Review. Pittsburgh: Dept. of Modern Languages, Carnegie-Mellon University. 19 (38).
Campos, A. (2003). *Invenção: de Arnaut e Reimbaut a Dante e Cavalcanti.* [Invention: from Arnaut and Reimbaut to Dante and Cavalcanti]. São Paulo: Arx.
Campos, A. and Campos, H. (1964). *Re/visão de Sousândrade.* [Re/vision of Sousandrade]. São Paulo: Edições Invenção.
Campos, A. and Campos, H. (1966). *Sousandrade – poesia.* Rio de Janeiro: Agir.
Campos, A. and Campos, H. (1971). *Re/visão de Kilkerry.* [Re-vision of Kilkerry]. São Paulo: Fundo Estadual da Cultura.
Campos, A., Campos, H. and Pignatari, D. (2006). *Teoria da poesia concreta: textos críticos e manifestos 1950–1960.* [Theory of concrete poetry: critical texts and manifestos 1950–60]. (4th ed.). São Paulo: Brasiliense.
Campos, A., Campos, H. and Pignatari, D. (1960). *Cantares de Ezra Pound.* [Ezra Pound's Cantos]. Rio de Janeiro: Serviço de Documentação MEC.
Campos, H. (1969). *A arte no horizonte do provável: e outros ensaios.* [Art in the horizon of probable: and other essays]. São Paulo: Perspectiva.
Campos, H. (1976). *A operação do texto* [The operation of the text]. São Paulo: Perspectiva.
Campos, H. (2006). *Metalinguagem & outras metas: ensaios de teoria e crítica literária* [Metalanguage & other goals: essays of literary theory and critic]. (4th ed.). São Paulo: Perspectiva.
Didi-Huberman, G. (2008). *Images in spite of all.* Chicago, IL: The University of Chicago Press.
Franchetti, P. (2012). *Alguns aspectos da teoria da poesia concreta* (4th ed.) [Some aspects of the theory of concrete poetry]. Campinas: Unicamp.
Giedon-Welcker, C. (1965). *Anthologie der Abseitigen = poètes à l'écart.* [Odds' anthology = rejected poets]. Zurich: Verl Der Arche.
Harig, L. (1969). *Ein Blumenstück* [A piece of flower]. In Schöning, K. (Ed.). *Neues Hörspiel: Texte Partituren.* Frankfurt am Main: Suhrkamp.
Harig, L. (1979). *Ein Blumenstück* [LP]. Kassel: Produktion NDR/WDR. Audiothek der 'documenta 8'.
Klengel, S. (2011). *Die Rückeroberung der Kultur. Lateinamerikanische Intellektuelle und das Europa der Nachkriegsjahre (1945–52)* [The Reconquest of

Culture: Latin American Intellectuals and the Europe of the Post-War Years (1945–1952)]. Würzburg: Königshausen & Neumann.

Mon, F. (1969) *das gras wies wächst*. In Schöning, K. (Ed.). *Texte; partituren* [Texts; scores] Frankfurt am Main: Suhrkamp.

Mon, F. (1981). 'Eine Art von Erinnerung hatte sich erhalten'. Zu 'Deutschland 1944' von Helmut Heißenbüttel ['A way of memory was maintained'. About Helmut Heißenbüttel's Deutschland 1944]. *Text+Kritik*, 69/70, 55–59. Retrieved from https://etkmuenchen.de/search/Details.aspx?page=40&ISBN=9783883770734-.WNp53BKGOqA

Mon, F. (2009). *Die Poesie wird konkret. Die Anfänge des experimentellen Schreibens in den fünfziger Jahren* (pp. 403–422) [Poetry becomes concrete. The beginnings of experimental writing in the Fifties]. In Busch, B. and Combrink, T. (Eds.). *Doppelleben, Literarische Szenen aus Nachkriegsdeutschland* [Double lifes, literary scenes from Post-War Germany]. Göttingen: Materialien zur Ausstellung.

Pignatari, D. (1971). *Contracomunicação* [Contracommunication]. São Paulo: Perspectiva.

Romero, S. (1888). *Historia da literatura brasileira* [History of Brazilian literature]. Rio de Janeiro: H. Garnier.

Schafer, M. (1977). *The tuning of the world*. Toronto: McClelland and Stewart Limited.

Schöning, K. (1969). *Texte, Partituren*. Frankfurt am Main: Suhrkamp.

Schöning, K. (1970). *Neues Hörspiel: Essays, analysen, gespräche*. [New Radio Play: essays, analyses, conversations]. Frankfurt am Main: Suhrkamp.

Schöning, K. (1983). *Hörspielmacher: Autorenporträts und Essays*. [Radio play makers: Authors' portraits and essays]. Königstein: Athenäum.

Solt, M. E. (1968). *Concrete poetry: A world-view*. Bloomington, IN: Indiana University Press.

10

BETWEEN REMEMBERING AND FORGETTING

Memory, culture, and the nostalgia market in the Brazilian mediascape

Ana Paula Goulart Ribeiro

We live immersed in a culture of memory characterized by a general fear of forgetting. In this context, memory emerges as a duty or obsession in almost all aspects of social life. We are eager to consume memorialistic products: movies, series, books, objects. The past has a strong impact on individuals and is imposed as a duty: we must preserve it, we must redeem it, and we must never allow it to be lost. This has increasingly made it lucrative for the culture and entertainment industries.

There are diverse mnemonic practices that shape the culture of memory. We propose to study what we call the 'nostalgia market.' This peculiar market is characterized by the sale of objects and narratives that, in one way or another, refer to the past, whether as historical and cultural reference or only as an aesthetic model.

The nostalgia market is made up of varied niches. It is present in all kinds of consumption industries: architecture, clothing, decoration, toys, games, furniture, jewellery design, bars, and restaurants. In such cases, vintage (the originally old) and retro (those things that look old) are confused in the search for new forms of beautiful, in the context of what some believe to be the depletion of modern aesthetic models.

Nostalgia as an object of consumption seems to be everywhere, but it occupies a prominent place in the media. The cult of nostalgia for the past pervades society as a whole, including the most common personal practices (such as the desire to store and archive everything and the fear of forgetting); however, it is in the media that it gains greater visibility and social power. There is an intrinsic relationship among the cultures of memory, nostalgia, and media, and it is this argument that we will develop in this text, aiming to try to understand how nostalgia, through the media, builds social identities and subjectivation processes.

We are interested to observe a specific characteristic of the nostalgia media market: its global dimension, but also national and regional forms, especially in global south countries. Hollywood is the producer of an immense variety of movies and series with nostalgic appeal. And most of these audiovisual products are very successful in nations like Brazil. The popularization of streaming platforms – such as Netflix, Crackle, and Now – changed the habit of Brazilian audiences and significantly increased the consumption of North American and European audiovisual products, especially those of serial fiction.

Brazilian television – especially Rede Globo, the most important national television network – has also invested heavily in nostalgic products. Soap operas and fictional series have turned to the past in an increasingly significant way. The emotional appeal comes in various forms, either by the rescue of characters from the past and by the reconstitution of epochs (1930s, 1950s, 1960s), or by reference to lifestyles and consumption of 'the old times.'

What do we mean by nostalgia?

Not every reference to the past is nostalgic. But what distinguishes nostalgia from other uses of the past and other mnemonic practices? The term *nostalgia* was first used in the 17th century, literally meaning 'desire to return home.' Created in 1688 by the doctor Johannes Hofer, the term nostalgia was used as diagnosis for many soldiers and sailors away from their homelands during various wars of the 18th century. The symptoms were fever, insomnia, tachycardia, lack of appetite, and weakness. At that time, spatial mobility was rare, and the cadence of time was broken only by extraordinary events, such as wars and natural disasters. The departure from the homeland was an anomaly, and in many individuals it provoked a disruptive state, considered pathological.

But, in the early 19th century, the term nostalgia had gained widespread acceptance as an evil that could affect individuals of any profession, ethnic group, or nationality. When time began to accelerate for many, creating deep discontinuities in life, nostalgia was no longer a problem for only a few displaced people.[1] Awareness of the inexorable change – the transience of existence, as Freud would say (1989) – led many to want their lost places and time. The modernity valued the new and disdained tradition, but it also produced – as one of its seemingly contradictory effects – the desire to contain history and the refusal of the irreversibility of time.[2]

Nostalgia is understood, in this case, as a problematic relationship that individuals, groups, and societies establish with linear time and directed to progress, as configured by the Enlightenment tradition. Nostalgia would be a particular type of mnemonic practice, in which temporality is tensioned by a movement that tends to value the past. The past is thought of not as archaic but as an authentic place of return, whether of moral, political, or aesthetic values.

Because of this problematic relationship with modernity, nostalgia has traditionally been conceived – both in politics and in the arts – as a feeling to be avoided, either because it is viewed as uncritical and essentially conservative, or because it is understood as a romantic and naive search for a 'lost time.' It seems to us, however, that in contemporaneity the notion of nostalgia gained nuances that need to be better known.[3]

The nostalgic gesture can acquire varied and even opposite meanings in the media culture. The nostalgic products produce practices and narratives that – crossing national and linguistic boundaries – establish different, and sometimes even opposite, links to the past. They seem to create a tense and contradictory relationship between remembering and forgetting, as we will see.

To end these theoretical considerations, it is important to say that there is in the nostalgia market an essential economic dimension. The past – especially because of its emotional appeal – sells a lot. It mobilizes in such a way the economy of material and symbolic goods of several countries that it is even difficult to measure it. It has local and national characteristics but is also a transnational and globalized phenomenon. Nostalgia, which was once a disease, today helps to sell images from the past, generating much profit for the entertainment industry. But the economic strength of the nostalgia market does not interest us in itself. It is like a cultural phenomenon that the subject instigates us.

Historical themes and reruns

The close relationship between nostalgia and media culture can be observed in different contemporary audiovisual products. We could cite several examples of the appropriation of nostalgia by the global media entertainment industry. One would be the wave of cinematic blockbusters that have explored the historical theme, such as *Troy* (2004), *Alexander the Great* (2004), *Kingdom of Heaven* (2005), *Downfall* (2004), *300* (2006), *Marie Antoinette* (2006), *The Queen* (2006), *Elizabeth: The Golden Age* (2007), *The Young Victoria* (2009), *Lincoln* (2012), and many others.

Of course, this is not a new narrative of contemporary cinema. Hollywood epics like *Joan of Arc* (1948), *Cleopatra* (1963), and *El Cid* (1961) also had success in the past. Although there is continuity in this practice, it appears that historical themes have received more intensive and systematic investment in recent years. And this phenomenon is not restricted to movies. On television, series like *Rome* (2005), *The Tudors* (2007), *The Borgias* (2011), *Vikings* (2013), *The White Queen* (2013), *Marco Polo* (2014), *Narcos* (2015), and *The Crown* (2016) stand out.

There are channels dedicated entirely to history, such as the History Channel, and programs that follow the same logic. In Brazil, we have *Arquivo N*, which is broadcast by 24-hour cable news channel GloboNews. *Arquivo N* invites viewers to travel through time via in-depth reports on events and people that have left a mark on history. The show includes images from the archives of TV Globo and other stations, as well as sound bites from radio stations, headlines from old newspapers, and interviews with witnesses of relevant events.

It is also worth highlighting the success of *Canal Viva*, from cable broadcaster Globosat. Since its debut, the channel has devoted much of its programming to reruns of shows first broadcast by Rede Globo. Launched in May 2010, Viva is one of the most watched channels on Brazilian pay TV. It is interesting to note that the channel also reprises successful foreign series such as *Dallas* and *Twin Peaks* and also invests in its own productions. In May 2016, for example, it released a new version of *TV Mulher*. The original program debuted in 1980 and was the first targeting the modern woman and not housewives. The new show is presented by the same host, the journalist Marilia Gabriela.

Along the same lines of appealing to the emotional memory and nostalgia of viewers, there is *Vale a Pena Ver de Novo* (Worth Seeing Again), the evening programming on Rede Globo, which since 1980 has rerun successful soap operas from the station. Its long run – almost 40 years – demonstrates the good reception of this type of initiative.

Reruns are key to the programming of most pay TV stations. Some reprise relatively recent programs just to be able to fill their programming, while others invest in the nostalgic desire of the viewer. Thus, an entire generation that grew up in the 1970s can re-watch their childhood series, like *Batman*, *I Dream of Jeannie*, *Bewitched*, *Lost in Space*, *Land of Giants*, *Seinfeld*, and many others that have been successful in Brazil and abroad. To the delight of fans, these series are also often marketed on DVD.

The relationship of Brazilian teledramas with the past is not new. Since its beginnings in the mid-20th century, television fiction has explored historical themes and era reconstructions. However, recent productions that explore this dimension with a systematic emphasis draw attention, especially miniseries (television serials similar to soap operas, but shorter). The theme appears to be associated not only with the fictionality, but also with the so-called facts and real characters. In general, TV Globo produces two miniseries per year, and from 2003 to 2014, one of them has always been dedicated a historical or biographical theme.[4]

Era reconstructions

The market of nostalgia bets a lot on period reconstitutions. Films and telenovelas invest in historical themes. But there are also audiovisual works that do not refer to actual events and real characters, instead creating fictional universes set in a bygone time. Numerous could be the examples. A number of Western television shows have successfully capitalized on the reconstruction of past times, including *Stranger Things* (2016–), *Mad Men* (2007–2015), *Gotham* (2014–), and *Game of Thrones* (2011–), all with great success in Brazil.

We will, however, analyze only some Brazilian series. Our idea is to try to observe, even briefly, the different narrative strategies used to represent the past in each one of them. Many would be the possible examples, as much has been invested in this type of production in the country. It is worth remembering that not every reconstitution of the time is necessarily nostalgic. Nostalgia is in a certain specific use that is made of the past, which can – in turn – assume varied meanings. To give an idea of the different types and meanings of nostalgia, we will cite three fictional series exhibited by Rede Globo.

Queridos Amigos (2008) recounts the reunion of 12 friends in 1989 and takes stock of the utopias of Brazilian youth in the 1970s. The starting point could not be more nostalgic: the protagonist discovers that he has an incurable disease (and that he will die soon) and decides to reunite his best friends. The group met during the military dictatorship in Brazil and established a deep friendship. In this series, the consciousness of death – of finitude, therefore – is a starting point for the consecration of friendship and for the reunion of the characters with the values and ideals of their youth.

Os Dias Eram Assim (2017) begins in Rio de Janeiro in 1970. Renato Reis (Renato Góes) is a young doctor, ethical, idealistic, and passionate about work. He falls in love with Alice (Sophie Charlotte), a rich but questioning and libertarian girl. Her father is a wealthy contractor who finances a special group that pursues opponents of the dictatorship. He is behind the persecution of Renato's brother, involved in resistance to the dictatorship.

Caros Amigos and *Os Dias Eram Assim* construct very different views of the period of the Brazilian military dictatorship (1964–1985). In both, however, the subject is treated seriously, and it is possible to perceive nostalgia as a look that seeks to expresses what we can call 'desire for utopia.' The past is not mythified as best. In both series (more especially in the last one) there are crude and hard scenes in which the dictatorship's ills are exposed, such as scenes of torture. But in the past reconstructed was still possible to 'imagine a future.' We can say that the two series reconstitute a past that had a future. And it is exactly here that is the nostalgic dimension of the series.

The characters – mainly the protagonists – are moved by the belief or the hope of a possible transformation of the reality. No one is a nihilist: everyone has ideals, beliefs, and struggles for freedom, social equality, injustice, racism, sexual freedom, and gender equality.

Boogie Oogie (2015) tells the story of two women who were traded in the maternity ward in the 1950s and who, 20 years later, dispute the love of the same man. As well as *Caros Amigos* and *Os Dias Eram Assim*, the telenovela explores the life of past decades: its plot also takes place during the military dictatorship. But the approach is completely different. There is no politicization of the theme but only appeal to the aesthetic sensibility of the time. The emphasis is on the clothing, music, dance, and consumption habits of the 1970s generation.

Remakes and reboots

Another phenomenon also seen in this culture of memory and nostalgia is remakes of old soap operas, which is becoming more and more constant on Brazilian TV. Since the early 2000s, Rede Globo alone has produced the following remakes: *Cabocla* (1979/2004), *Sinhá Moça* (1986/2006), *Ciranda de Pedra* (1981/2008), *Paraíso* (1982/2009), *O Astro* (1977/2011) *O Bem-Amado* (1973/2011), *Gabriela* (1975/2012), *Guerra dos Sexos* (1983/2012), *Saramandaia* (1976/2013), and *Rebu* (1974–2014). In 2016, the station also aired *Haja Coração*, a retelling of *Sassaricando*[5] (1987).

It should be reminded that this phenomenon is not exclusive to the Brazilian television industry. Cinema, especially Hollywood, has also invested heavily in rehashes of old classics. There are numerous examples, but some of the biggest box office hits include: *King Kong* (1933/1976/2005), *Godzilla* (1954/1998/2014), *Ocean's Eleven* (1960/2001), *Carrie* (1976/2002/2013), and *Planet of the Apes* (1968/2001/2011).

Both remakes and reboots as well as reruns are examples of memory culture phenomenon because they are a reminder, a nostalgic look back to the older ones. But it is also a phenomenon of the 'new,' because the originals have never been seen by younger people, many of whom were not even born at the time these programs or films were first released.

We must, however, be careful with the qualification of 'new,' which was purposely used in quotes. Even for those who watch this stuff for the first time, this is not something unheard of. Everyone knows they are seeing remakes or reinterpretations of cultural products of the past. And that fact is even widely touted by producers. It is used as a distinguishing element for the productions and is highlighted in the launch campaigns. We must also consider another thing. There are significant changes in the consumption and enjoyment of these products. In the case of Brazilian soap operas, for example, viewers already have a notion of the story lines and characters and seek to find out more about the unfolding of the plot in advance. In addition, it enables comparative curiosity, which causes people to seek information about the plots, characters, and actors from the first versions. For this, audiences have numerous websites and blogs dedicated to the television fiction and its history. Rede Globo itself has a portal – Memória Globo[6] – where the viewer can find detailed information, photos, and videos from all its productions (entertainment, journalism, and sports) since it first began broadcasting in 1965.

Why this interest in a cultural product of a past that one doesn't know? Why are young people interested in stories consumed by their parents and grandparents? Is it possible, in this case, to be talking of a nostalgia for something that was not lived? If so, what feeds this feeling?

The publishing market

Another field that is sensitive to the culture of memory and nostalgia is the publishing market. Many books focusing on past narratives have been great successes. In Europe, this phenomenon has gained momentum with the development of France's so-called *Nouvelle Histoire*, especially since 1970. A book like *Montaillou* by Le Roy Ladurie (1975), for example, shortly after his release, went to the top of the best-seller list for nonfiction (Burke, 1997). And since then, the little known town of Montaillou has become a popular tourist destination.

The editorial strength of the *Nouvelle Histoire* is an example of the interest shown by the public for narratives of the past. But this phenomenon is far from exclusively French. Similar writings are produced in other European countries and on the American continent. It is interesting to note, however, that in Brazil the best-selling history books are not written by historians but by journalists. These publications generally have a non-academic profile and are targeted at an audience of non-specialists. These narratives – as well as some produced by some professional historians – make what Argentinean Beatriz Sarlo (2007) called 'commercial terms of history' or 'history of general circulation.'

In this sense, it is worth remembering the journalist Eduardo Bueno's books that became best-sellers in Brazil at the end of the 1990s – *A viagem do descobrimento* (The Journey of Discovery) (1998), *Náufragos, traficantes e degradados* (Castaways, Dealers, and Convicts) (1998), *Capitães do Brasil* (Captains of Brazil) (1999) – and, more recently, the successful works of Laurentino Gomes, such as *1808* (2007), *1822* (2010), and *1889* (2013). It is worth highlighting the trend of almanacs and guides that drive the Brazilian publishing market. Some examples include *Almanaque dos anos 80* (The Almanac of the '80s) (2004), *Almanaque dos anos 70* (The Almanac of the '70s) (2006), *Almanaque do fusca* (The Volkswagen Beetle Almanac) (2006), *Almanaque dos quadrinhos* (The Almanac of Comics) (2006), *Almanaque da TV* (The TV Almanac) (2007), and *Almanaque dos seriados* (The TV Series Almanac) (2008). There is also *Guia do Passado* (Guide of the Past), by Ronaldo Conde Aguiar, released in 2011. Another example is the relaunch, in book or facsimile form, of various publications from the past, such as the magazine *Pif-Paf*, the newspaper *O Pasquim*, and many others from 1970s.

We also cannot forget the emergence and incredible growth of history magazines targeting the general public. Fifteen years ago, there was not one publication of this kind in Brazil, and in the last 10 years, several have been launched. *Nossa História* (Our History), *História Viva* (Living History), *Revista de História da Biblioteca Nacional* (History of the National Library Magazine), *Aventuras na História* (Adventures in History), *Desvendando a História* (Unravelling History), *Descobrindo a História* (Discovering History), and *Leituras da História* (Readings from History) are just some of the better-known titles released in the last decade. Some of these publications are translations of foreign versions, but others feature their own essays written by Brazilian journalists and historians.

In relation to the publishing market, it is also important to highlight the role of biographies and autobiographies, which have been very successful in Brazil. In recent decades, these genres have reached record sales. This phenomenon, which has also occurred in many other countries, is a symptom of the culture of memory, but it is also related to the place that individual memories occupy in different social contexts of contemporaneity. There is appreciation, in various spheres, of the biography, of the life story, of the personal account, and, finally, of the role of the individual in history. It is the 'subjective turn' referred to by Beatriz Sarlo (2007).

Social networks, websites, and blogs

Without a doubt, life stories drive the publishing market. But they are also present in other social spheres. There is the explosion of biographical accounts and 'written about oneself' content on blogs, websites, and social networks. It is necessary in this case to consider various aspects. The first is related to the technological environment and to what we call 'the fantasy of archiving everything,' inspired by the reflections of Fausto Colombo (1991).

Digital technology and the web expanded the storage possibilities of information and images, significantly reducing problems relating to the occupation of physical space. This ability to keep digital files – which expands constantly – reinforces the desire and the idea of both institutions and individuals to save everything. Thus, the technology goes to the encounter of the mnemonic obsession of contemporaneity, infiltrating not only the process of collective culturing but also everyday life, ways of thinking, and the convictions of individuals and groups.

Recording and archiving our experiences seems indispensable. We photograph every moment of our travels and record every stage of our lives and our children's lives. Tablets and smartphones reinforce this urge to record as well as accelerate the flow of information and the files themselves, many of which are now shared instantly via social networks. Sometimes, we add filters to our pictures, trying to give them a vintage look. Applications like Instagram provide tools for this. One of them is called exactly 'nostalgia.'

The biographical boom is also related to the logic of exposure and the visibility to which individuals are subject in the highly mediatized societies (Berger, 2008). Narcissism and the desire for celebritization and distinction (Herschmann and Pereira, 2003) drive the use of photos and the recording of different moments of people's lives and allow the emergence of new forms of representation of oneself and others. Diaries with text, photographs, and videos are published on the web. There are a variety of styles and subject matters, but most follow the confessional model, exposing the very intimate in global windows.

It is these peculiar practices belonging to the autobiographical genre and the festivals of private life that Paula Sibilia (2008) calls 'the me show.' If before there was strict separation between public and private and a reverence for silent reading and writing in reclusion, there is now a shift of 'internalized' subjectivity towards new forms of self, more epidermal and flexible, oriented to the view of others.

But the internet does not only live off individualism. There are many sites that promote the sharing of common references and collective experiences. The countless pages of a nostalgic nature on social networks seem to indicate this. They are driven by the sharing of images and texts, and some promote face-to-face meetings, parties, and the sale of objects. The titles of these pages speak for themselves: *Bons Tempos* (Good Times), *Eu amo flashback* (I Love Flashback), *Quero voltar aos anos 80* (I Want to Go Back to the '80s), *De volta aos anos 80* (Back to the '80s), *Velharias – desenhos antigos* (Collectibles – Old Designs), *Música – a recordação eterna* (Music – The Eternal Recording), *Saudade FM – a rádio que faz recordar* (Saudade

FM – The Station That Makes You Remember), and *Projeto Autobahn – de volta aos anos 80* (Project Autobahn – Back to the '80s). On the latter, there is a post that rates the page as 'the best source to feed our musical, visual and cultural nostalgia in São Paulo.' The webpage *Coisa Velha* (Old Thing), which provides content related to business, cars, television shows, and old products in general, defines itself as 'a nostalgic social network.' It also has a blog and Snapchat and over one million followers on Facebook.

In addition to being virtual places for sharing files, memories, and product promotions, social networks also work as a space for the activation of sociabilities and the construction of nostalgic identities. Facebook has become – among other things – a meeting place for friends and acquaintances that have not seen each other for a long time. Using its search engine, you can find people you have lost contact with. And through just one person, it is possible to reconstruct an entire web of relationships lost in the past. As such, networks that go beyond kinship or immediate professional or family links are re-established. Contact is resumed and memories are shared: stories and old photos (from childhood, adolescence, or college).

Some final thoughts

After examining the phenomenon of nostalgia, we can come to a simple conclusion: there are people eager to collect, store, and consume memorialistic products, and the market has figured out not only how to channel this desire but also how to create new demands in this area. The past has a strong appeal to individuals and communities. This has increasingly made it a lucrative business for the culture and entertainment industries.

In a context of overvaluation of consumption, the nostalgia market benefits from an 'identity crisis,' characterized by the collapse of the outlook for the future and more fragile and provisional social and emotional bonds. Amid the dispersion and frailty of life, the past is valued because it allows you to assign more stable feelings to reality.

This means there is something important in nostalgia. In fact, we are talking about a specific way of experiencing time and space that says a lot about who we are, how we live, and how we signify ourselves and the world around us. The attachment to and appreciation of the past is not a new phenomenon, but the nostalgia boom of recent decades brings unique elements that are very significant to understanding our culture and our ways of dynamizing our identities. Why do we turn to the nostalgic pasts? What preterit experiences do we value, and what do we ignore? How do we produce forgetting? And how do we frame[7] our memories today?

The concept of nostalgia, in its old and even modern meaning, may not apply precisely to the phenomena we talked about here. Or maybe it only partially applies. Unbridled consumption of past stories and artefacts is a desire to bring back remnants of a previous time. And this is not new. But, nowadays, there seems to be something difference in this desire. First, the present is not always depreciated in relation to the past experience, viewed as best. Rather, the present seems to colonize our perception of the past (Hartog, 2013).

When we talk about nostalgia market (about products produced or only consumed in Brazil) is easy to say that the past often seems to run out in the immediacy of consumption. But the movement toward the past can also lead us to the densest experiences, which acquire different and even opposite meanings, as we have seen throughout this text. One can take a romantic and not problematic view, but it can also be done critically. The criticism in this case is not only of the past itself but also of what remains of it in the present.

Another issue is that nostalgic products sometimes return to a glorious past, of great achievements and personalities. But in others, they appeal to the memory of trivial, everyday, ordinary (like the old songs played on the radio, the films and series reshown on pay TV and *Ploc* parties[8]). In the second case, what is at stake is a nostalgia for the past that was lived and experienced by us in our childhood and youth.

This is a specific type of attachment to the past that Gary Cross (2015) calls 'consumed nostalgia' and which he identifies as a characteristic of fast capitalism. Images, sounds, smells, and tastes evoke personal memories and desires to revive sensations and emotions of the past, themselves linked to the forms of consumption of our formative years. This phenomenon tells us much about the experiences of today's adults. Our culture values youth and the potential of a child's future. This turns childhood and youth into the golden years that adults want to relive.

Anyway, the memory as an object of consumption can be problematic when it is not accompanied by some kind of reflection on the past experience, especially for its excesses. As paradoxical as it may seem, a lot of memories can mean no memory and thus forgetting. On the other hand, a characteristic of the nostalgia market that seems striking is that, in most cases, it is not the 'whole past' that we want to consume but its fragments – only some of its symbols and icons, many isolated and decontextualized. This happens with many cultural products mentioned in this text that use the past only as a reference, as production element of familiarity and identification with the consumer.

This brings us to another important aspect of the nostalgia market and memory culture as a whole. Our memories are deeply marked by the logic of our time, especially the speed. Today there is an overvaluation of memory, but at the same time, there are new understandings with relation to the past and unique ways of engaging our preterit experiences, which are very different from those of traditional societies and even at the beginning of modernity. We can say that if contemporary is mnemonic, it is in the same proportion amnesic.

The truth is that, in the times we live, remembering and forgetting articulate a logic that goes beyond the founding dialectics of all memory. There is a difficult and problematic relationship between memory and amnesia. These two dimensions coexist and establish complex and ambiguous connections between themselves in the different ways that the means of communication and entertainment industry use the past.

One question to consider is whether global cultural products, such as Hollywoodians, and those of other 'non-central territories,' such as Brazilians, drive nostalgia in similar or different ways. What is there the specific in our ways of remembering and forgetting? There is still much to investigate.

Notes

1 For more on the history of the term, see Davis (1979), Natali (2006), and Cross (2015).
2 Perhaps one of the most beautiful images of this feeling is Walter Benjamin's *Angel of History*. The angel has its eyes on to past, and under its feet, there is an accumulation of ruins upon ruins. He wanted to wake the dead and rebuild the destroyed, but he is pushed forward by a storm, which Benjamin (1985) calls progress.
3 The concept of nostalgia in its contemporary form is understood in very different ways. There is a first generation of authors, such as Fred Davis (1979) and Fredric Jameson (1991), and the authors who have developed research on the subject in the last years (Niemeyer, 2011); Holdsworth, 2011; Sprengler, 2011; Cross, 2015; Beail and Goren, 2015). Our studies are more in tune with the second generation of thinkers.
4 The aired miniseries were *A casa das sete mulheres* (2003), *Um só coração* (2004), *Mad Maria* (2005), *JK* (2006), *Amazônia, de Galvez a Chico Mendes* (2007), *Queridos amigos* (2008), *Maysa* (2009), *Dalva e Herivelto: uma canção de amor* (2010), *Chico Xavier* (2011), *Dercy de Verdade* (2012), *Gonzaga, de pai para filho* (2013), and *Serra Pelada, a saga do ouro* (2014).
5 In the 1990s, Globo had already aired other remakes: *Irmãos Coragem* (1970/1995), *Anjo Mau* (1976/1997), and *Pecado Capital* (1975/1998).
6 www.memoriaglobo.com.br.
7 On the dynamics of memory, which is given by framing work, forgetfulness, and silences in relation to the past, see Michael Pollak (1989, 1992).
8 Ploc was a brand of gum in the 1980s, and today the name is used to refer to parties that primarily play Brazilian music from that era.

References

Beail, Linda, and Goren, Lilly J. *Mad Men and politics: nostalgia and the remaking of modern America*. New York/London, Bloomsbury, 2015.

Benjamin, Walter. *Magia e técnica, arte e política: ensaios sobre literatura e história da cultura*. São Paulo, Brasiliense, 1985.

Berger, Christa. Lembrar, esquecer, narrar, expor, anistiar, cobrar. Política de memória e memória mediatizada. In Berger, Christa and Marocco, Beatriz (orgs.). *Ilha do Presídio: uma reportagem de ideias*. Porto Alegre, Libretos, 2008.

Burke, Peter. *A Escola dos Annales (1929–1989): a Revolução Francesa da historiografia*. São Paulo, Editora Unesp, 1997.

Candau, Jöel. *Memoire et identité*. Paris, PUF, 1998.

Colombo, Fausto. *Arquivos imperfeitos: memória social e cultura eletrônica*. São Paulo, Perspectiva, 1991.

Cross, Gary. *Consumed nostalgia: memory in the age of fast capitalism*. New York, Columbia University Press, 2015.

Davis, Fred. *Yearning for yesterday: a sociology of nostalgia*. New York, Free Press, 1979.

Freud, Sigmund. Sobre a Transitoriedade. *Jornal do Brasil*, 23/09/1989.

Hartog, François. *Regimes de historicidade: presentismo e experiência do tempo*. Belo Horizonte, Autêntica, 2013.

Herschmann, Micael and Pereira, Carlos Alberto Messeder (orgs.). *Mídia, memória e celebridades: estratégias narrativas em contexto de alta visibilidade*. Rio de Janeiro, E-Papers, 2003.

Holdsworth, Amy. *Television, memory and nostalgia*. Basingstoke, Palgrave Macmillan, 2011.

Jameson, Fredric. *Postmodernism or the cultural logic of capitalism*. Durham, NC, Duke University Press, 1991.

Le Roy Ladurie, Emmanuel. *Montaillou: village occitan de 1294 à 1324*. Paris, Gallimard, 1975.

Natali, Marcos Piason. *A política da nostalgia: um estudo das formas do passado*. São Paulo, Nankin, 2006.

Niemeyer, Katharina. *Media and Nostalgia: yearning for the past, present and future*. Basingstoke, Palgrave Macmillan, 2011.

Pollak, Michael. Memória, esquecimento, silêncio. *Estudos Históricos*, 2 (3), Rio de Janeiro, 1989.

———. Memória e identidade social. *Estudos Históricos*, 5 (10), Rio de Janeiro, 1992.

Sarlo, Beatriz. *Tempo passado: cultura da memória e guianda subjetiva*. São Paulo, Companhia das Letras, Belo Horizonte, Ed. UFMG, 2007.

Sprengler, Christine. *Screening Nostalgia: populuxe props and technicolor aesthetics in contemporary American film*. New York, Berghahn Books, 2011.

Sibilia, Paula. *O show do eu: a intimidade como espetáculo*. Rio de Janeiro, Nova Fronteira, 2008.

11

THE STRUGGLE OVER NARRATIVES

Palestine as metaphor for imagined spatialities

Dina Matar

This chapter starts from the premise that powerful epistemic and discursive entities have prevailed in the production of knowledge of the world divided between the global north and the global south (Resende, 2014). In such a configuration, any discussion of the global south, as an imagined spatiality often defined by its perceived differences from the global north, must also address how this imagination is interlinked with narrative, as image and discourse and, as such, ask how narrative plays a role in the emergence and persistence of particular epistemic formations that are also sustained by material and structural conditions of power and resistance. Nowhere is such a proposition more relevant to explore than in debates about the almost 70-year-old Palestine-Israel conflict which, this chapter proposes, offers us the possibility to interrogate the role of narrative in the construction (and subversion) of difference, otherness, and power relations and allows us to situate localized discursive and power struggles over historic Palestine within a series of global processes and practices that have shaped the way we map and imagine the world.

Drawing on this broad proposition, this chapter interrogates how mediated dominant narratives of the conflict between Israel and the Palestinians in mainstream media and public discourses in the global north and elsewhere have taken hold and persisted for almost 70 years. Specifically, it addresses how persistent and recurring visual and discursive narratives (in language and image) of Palestine and the Palestinians have served to support an implicit exceptionalism rooted in the claims of the Zionist movement and, thus, have constructed particular ways of seeing, or not seeing, Palestine, and certainly not from the viewpoint of its people, 'the narrated.' In situating the struggle over the right to narrate and the struggle over narrative with reference to the ongoing Palestinian-Israeli conflict at the centre of the discussion, the chapter elaborates on the assumption proposed at the outset, then moves on to address some examples of Palestinian self-narration and self-representation in film, documentary, photography, and digital media. While these self-narrations do not explicitly refer to the conflict, it proposes that it is in the act of telling that self-narration becomes inscribed as a political act, underlining its potential to disrupt dominant discursive and visual fields and to generate new ways of knowing and seeing the 'narrated,' or the spoken for.

By locating Palestine and its representation as central to the broader narratives and imagined geographies of the 'global south' and by implicitly implicating media in these processes, this chapter begins with a broad contextualization of the debates around the emergence of exceptionalist discourses around Palestine rooted in the historical dominance of the Israeli narrative before addressing some of the mediated processes and practices through which Palestine and the Palestinians have been talked about and visualized. The chapter then addresses the ways in which ordinary Palestinians on the margin are creating a broader range of narratives that challenge the status quo and that produce meaningful representations and knowledge about themselves as agents and actors in the construction of alternative spatialities and imaginaries. In conclusion, the chapter suggests that such narratives of everyday lives can question the taken-for-grantedness of powerful epistemic and discursive entities and challenge the constructed divisions between the global north and the global south.

Exceptionalism and Palestine

For decades and until very recently, much of the literature on Palestine/Israel has been dominated by an implicit exceptionalism rooted in the claims and narratives of the Zionist movement (Collins, 2011), serving to limit our understanding of and knowledge about Palestine and the Palestinians and their protracted conflict with Israel. Recent critical interdisciplinary scholarship (see, for example, Swedenberg and Stein, 2005; Khalili, 2010) has shown that this state of affairs is partly the outcome of structural inequalities and conditions imposed by the settler-colonial practices of Zionism since the creation of the Israeli state in 1948 and partly a result of the Zionist movement's narrative about itself. As some scholars have suggested, this narrative has been normalized and taken for granted in mainstream Western public and media discourses to the extent that it provides a restricted, if not biased, vision of the conflict. For example, Matar suggests that normalization is achieved through the 'establishment of patterned processes of thinking aimed at exacting disciplinary power that are then normalized in public and media discourses, making them sound natural and unproblematic' (Matar, 2016, p. 176), while Gil Z. Hochberg claims that a partitioned vision is evident in the inequalities inherent in the visual narratives, produced in film, photographs, and images of the conflict. As she notes, this vision

> isn't only an outcome of different national, ethnic, and historical epistemes produced as 'the visible,' but further relies on two distinct configurations or politics of the visual representation. Central to this regard is the question of the parameters placed on the legitimacy of displaying and circulating certain images in public.
> (Hochberg, 2015, p. 9)

Israel's settler-colonial project, as several studies have shown, incorporates a set of political, economic, and social structures and practices that form the basis of the current relationship between Israeli Jews and the Palestinians (Makdisi, 2010). Indeed, as Salamanca et al. write in their special issue on Israeli settler-colonial practices,

> from the earliest Palestinian accounts to the vast majority of contemporary research, the crimes committed against Palestinian society by the Zionist movement and the state it built have been well recorded. Zionism is an ideology and a political movement that subjects Palestine and Palestinians to structural and violent forms of dispossession, land appropriation, and erasure in the pursuit of a new Jewish state and society. As for other settler colonial movements, for Zionism, the control of land is a zero-sum contest fought against the indigenous population. The drive to control the maximum amount of land is at its centre.
> (Salamanca et al., 2013, p. 1)

Such practices are central to what postcolonial critic Achille Mbembe (2003) has called a state of permanent war, or the sustenance of necropower, where the technologies of destruction have become more tactile, more anatomical and sensorial and where the choice of the sovereign power is not simply the gauging and determining of what *kind* of life its subjects will live, but to take life away. For Mbembe, the most proficient contemporary execution of necropower is found in the Israeli occupation of Palestine: where vast populations are subjected to conditions of life conferring upon them the status of living dead (Ibid.).

THE STRUGGLE OVER NARRATIVES

Media and Zionism's exceptionalist claims

The role of media in supporting, enhancing, or legitimizing political, social, and cultural practices in diverse contexts other than Palestine/Israel has been amply discussed in the field of media and cultural studies. But the debate about whether this role can be ascribed to the 'concentrated symbolic power of media institutions' (Couldry, 2000, p. 192), to global capital, to the relationship between political entities and the media, or to the ability of some entities to cement their control through the media remains open and unresolved. For Nick Couldry, media power is not a tangible reality but a social process organized around distinctions between a manufactured 'media world' and the 'ordinary world' of ordinary people. One of the 'key roles of media is precisely to make this distinction seem entirely natural through legitimising their symbolic power as key institutions through which we can make sense of the world' (Freedman, 2014, p. 14). To comprehensively discuss the multiple debates in this field is beyond the remit of this chapter, but what most scholars agree on is that the media are to a certain extent implicated in the ways we come to understand the world as a web of narratives in which power and knowledge, as Foucault has argued, are part of one system.

In the context of Palestine/Israel, there is no doubt that how much we see or how much we hear about the conflict through Israeli or the mainstream Western media is inextricably linked to the ways in which particular narratives produce common assumptions which embed themselves in the media, the academy, and in other places. The power of narrative, in this sense, is its ability to act as a prism through which political relations are seen, thus restricting our vision of what we can see and learn. There is no doubt that addressing how epistemic systems are constructed via narrative (discourse and image) must take into account the asymmetric power relations and complex dynamics of economics, political, and cultural interactions that have shaped the histories of Palestinians and Jews. But there is also no doubt that in order to understand how these systems come to take hold of our imagination of spatialities and temporalities, we must acknowledge that what we know and what we see are the outcome of the repetition of specific narrative tropes that are sustained through particular 'configurations of space and various processes of differentiations along national, ethnic, racial, religious, gender and sexual lines' (Hochberg, 2015, p. 5).

Even a cursory consideration of the majority of news stories and images of the Palestinian-Israeli conflict in the mainstream Western media and public discourses over any period of time underlines how our knowledge of the conflict is limited and, therefore, how the media have been implicated in the re-production and the dissemination of narratives constituted by what Resende has called 'geographies of power' (2014) and control. Some of the images and narratives that are familiar to us as audiences include, among others, the now familiar photos and stories of sobbing Palestinian women, armed Palestinian militants, the aftermaths of suicide bombings on Israeli streets, and stone-throwing Palestinian youth, often juxtaposed against images of Israeli citizens going on about their daily lives in relative normality. Given the repetitive nature of these images and the dominant narrative frames they construct and disseminate – for example, the angry, extremist, terrorist, militant, and subjugated Palestinian – a restrictive narrative framework is constructed in which Israel's settler-colonial practices and occupation can only be seen through the recurrence of violence and in which the Palestinians are recognized through a narrative frame of destruction and violence. Furthermore, these restrictive narrative frames do contribute to the production of other narratives that, as Resende (2014) has argued, not only nourish the geographies from which they are derived but also sustain the maintenance of the imaginaries within which they inscribed. It is a matter of understanding, in this sense, that we are speaking of a world as being narrated from the perspective of the episteme of power (Ibid.), and certainly not from the perspective of the narrated.

The right to narrate

Who has the right to narrate, whose stories and memories enter the history books, and whose are dismissed as merely myth or unimportant are at the core of the Palestine-Israel conflict, its global narration, and appropriation, and to how it is understood and how it is to be dealt with culturally and politically. For the Palestinians, the right to narrate was evocatively noted by Edward Said in his article 'Permission to Narrate' (1984), in which he endeavoured to probe the potential power of telling, partly out of despair over the international response to the well-documented Israeli carnage of Lebanon in June 1982. In different ways, Said has consistently underlined the dynamics between narration and the power/knowledge nexus, particularly in his books *Orientalism* (1978), *Culture and Imperialism* (1994), *Covering Islam* (1997), and *The Question of Palestine* (2003), which constitute a seminal contribution to the expanding scholarship addressing the power to narrate as a crucial instrument of power colonial entities used to marginalize, or silence, the colonized.

Writing about marginalization and misrepresentation in the former colonies in the global south, cultural critic Stuart Hall also drew attention to one of the most dangerous and violent consequence of colonial

THE STRUGGLE OVER NARRATIVES

practices – the power of the colonizer to subjugate the controlled or the colonized through the production of knowledge. As he writes:

> They (the colonizers) had the power to make us see and experience ourselves as the 'Other'. . . . It is one thing to position a subject or set of peoples as the 'Other' of a dominant discourse. It is quite another to subject them to that knowledge.
> (Hall, 1994, p. 394)

Implicitly referring to how power is indirectly exercised through conditions of domination or through coercive consent, political scientist Charles Tripp, writing within a different historical moment, echoes Hall's sentiment in reference to the dominant Israeli narrative of Palestine, noting how this narrative had moulded the imagination of its subjects, particularly the Palestinians, because it was interwoven with and reinforced 'the material forms of power that are part of the landscape of domination' (Tripp, 2013, p. 253).

Since its creation and building on the meta-narrative connecting the birth of the nation with the struggle for national and (Jewish) survival, Israel has managed to mould the imagination of its subjects, the Palestinians, through seeking to prevent them from narrating their own stories and speaking for them. Of the many practices used to silence Palestinians, either in the Occupied Territories or on the global landscape, none have been as harsh as Zionist/Israeli measures of control in the West Bank, the Gaza Strip, Jerusalem, and for Palestinians within Israel, but none has been as potent as Israel's ability to propagate its version of reality in the mainstream media, particularly as historians 'are forced to tell the story of the powerless [. . .] in the words of those who victimized them' (Khalildi, 2007, p. 35).

In these contexts, any analysis of media's role in the production of knowledge and in the dissemination and normalization of exceptionalist narratives about Palestine/Israel cannot ignore the Zionist movement's persistent endeavours to intervene in, and to instrumentalize, culture, creating countless media genres, images and stories, productions, and publications that have legitimized its story about itself and limited the potential to look beyond them or cast a different light on various events and truths. In his book *The Idea of Israel*, Israeli historian Ilan Pappe argues that Israel's privileged place in the West is the result of Israeli-Zionist continuous efforts to manage and market an image of Israel as a state of what the West aspires for in the East – that of a modernizing and modern state championing Western-centric discourses of progress and civilization (Pappe, 2014).

As he writes, the narratives adopted by Zionist leaders and activists in the past and Israeli Jewish intellectuals and academics in the present, have presented Israel as the inevitable, successful implementation of the European history of ideas so that the 'idea must be packaged as a narrative, a story that begins with the birth of the state and its raison d'être. The nation is born as an ideal that becomes a reality that must be maintained and protected' (Pappe, 2014, p. 45).

The reasons why these narratives took hold for over almost a century in the global north and elsewhere are many, but there is no doubt that the control of the production of knowledge about the conflict took place within particular territorial boundaries or particular bounded spatialities and in extraterritorial geographies and global contexts. As Said has argued, Israel's narrative about itself underlines 'Zionism's sense of "the world as supporter and audience" that made the Zionist struggle for Palestine, one which was launched, supplied and fuelled in the great capitals of the West,' so successful (Said, 1978, p. 4) and the West's compliance and collusion. In a globalized world, this has meant that the imagination of Palestine and the Palestinians has as much to do with the relationship between structures and power as with the degree of visibility and access ascribed to the two parties in the conflict, the narrator and the narrated. But more importantly, what this also means is that ongoing violence that Israel carries out against Palestinians outside of highly mediated and visible bouts of violence, reported by the media, tends to remain invisible. As a result, 'everyday life under the Israeli Occupation fails to *appear* violent unless it is presented as a sudden (and often uncontextualized) eruption of what is quickly reframed and labeled exceptional and scandalous' (Hochberg, 2015, p. 14).

The role of the Western mainstream media in making visible and legitimizing Israel's exceptional narrative about itself and the Palestinians has been discussed extensively in diverse studies on media representations and dominant frames (see Philo and Berry's *Bad News from Israel* (2004) and *More Bad News from Israel* (2011) and Friel and Falk's research (2007) on the US media's reporting of the conflict). Other scholarship has discussed dominant frames that depict Israel as the 'righteous victim' of Palestinian violent actions and Israelis as victims suffering from long-term persecution, including by Palestinians (Piłecki and Hammock, 2014), ignoring socio-political contexts or tightening control as a result of increased militarization, securitization, and sovereign power. What the majority of this literature shows is that the media are a set of institutions that have been implicated in the transmission of ideas from the past often and their adoption as commonsensical, taken-for-granted hegemonic knowledge about the world. As Gramsci has argued, hegemony is never absolute and fixed, or as Williams has suggested:

> We have to emphasize that hegemony is not singular; indeed that is own material structures are highly complex, and have continually to be renewed, recreated and defended, and by the same token that they can be continually challenged and in certain respects modified.
>
> (Williams, 2005, p. 38)

As such, it is relevant to pay attention to discursive and visual narratives that trouble hegemony and subvert normalization practices. It is with this in mind that I turn to discussing some examples of emerging Palestinian self-narrations in diverse media and cultural spaces and what these mean.

Narrating the everyday

If visibility and narration are at the heart of the Palestinian-Israeli conflict, as argued above, then the diverse contemporary narration and memorialization of the Palestinian *Nakba* (catastrophe of 1948) and other important events in the conflict, represent a discursive and visual strategy through which to counter the Zionist narrative of 1948 and to combat perpetrator-induced amnesia vis-à-vis Palestinian claims for justice and recognition (see, for example, Abu-Lughod and Sa'di, 2007; Matar, 2010; Matar and Zahera, 2013). Critical interdisciplinary scholarship has also begun to address Palestinian cultural production and digital media (Khalili, 2007; Aouragh, 2011; Tawil-Souri, 2012), underlining the subversive potential of film, literature, comedy, music, and satire and other cultural forms to disturb, disrupt, and mobilize.

Hand in hand with this important shift in scholarship has been an exponential rise in self-narration by diverse actors, from filmmakers to artists, from activists to ordinary Palestinians in the margins or on the fringes of the mainstream. For example, in his films, *Chronicle of a Disappearance* (1996), *Divine Intervention* (2002), and *All that Remains* (2009), Palestinian director Elie Suleiman has consistently sought to tell the story of ordinary and forgotten Palestinians living within the Jewish state of Israel and in annexed Jerusalem. Other films, such as *Intimacy* (2007) and *Checkpoint* (2007), also tell stories about the daily lives of Palestinians under occupation, thus making clear that occupation is not a normal condition of life. While these new forms and genres will not liberate an occupied land, they can 'lay the groundwork for different ways of looking at power preparing through narrative and the imagination the resistance that may in the future materialize to shake a complacent order' (Tripp, 2013, p. 315), especially when combined with other developments, such as the growing global solidarity movement in support of Palestinian rights.

What is more relevant for the purpose of this chapter are the many creative ways in which ordinary Palestinians (the narrated) are telling their stories, or part-stories, in art, film, graffiti, news, and music in digital media platforms, underlining the centrality of narrative to the power/knowledge nexus and, also, the ways in which these platforms, in their accessibility and reach, can function as spaces for what Zayani has called 'digital cultures of contention' (2015, p. 12) that intervene politically. In what follows, I focus on some narrations of the everyday, which as Michel de Certeau has suggested in the *Practice of Everyday Life* is concerned with the way subjects negotiate their position of power, and therefore knowledge, within a particular episteme and system of power. Reiterating Foucault's conceptualization of disciplinary technologies in the production of knowledge, De Certeau focuses more on 'the network of an anti-discipline' that technologies of power (including media) create to help address how marginality is renegotiated and how subjects who are dominated re-appropriate spaces, discourses and practices using what he calls the 'art of the weak' (de Certeau, 1984, p. xiv). In this regard, the social practice of narrating, irrespective of the genre within which the narration is produced or the shape or the form the story takes, becomes an act of political agency that is inscribed in the narrating act. What is of interest in such articulations is that they draw attention to the potential of narrative to disrupt dominant discursive and visual fields and to generate new ways of knowing and seeing the 'narrated,' or spoken for.

The examples I use here range from documentary and satirical graphic novel turned animation production to a variety of online output. The examples I use are *Flying Paper* (2013), a documentary film that tells the story of a group of children in Gaza who proceed to break the Guinness world record in the number of kites flown simultaneously in the same place; *The Wanted 18* (2014), an innovative and satirical graphic novel authored by Amer Shomali and turned into a part-animation/part-documentary which uses the personal stories of 18 cows bought by Palestinians to produce milk during the first Palestinian intifada (uprising) in the West Bank town of Beit Sahour to bypass Israeli control; *Open Bethlehem*, a non-governmental organization that launched a campaign to free Bethlehem from the encirclement by the Separation Wall, which initially started as a film directed by Leila Sansour; *Dear World*, a Facebook campaign launched in 2012 to showcase stories written in a letter format and addressing the question of what it means to live one's life as a Palestinian; and *Love Under Apartheid*,

THE STRUGGLE OVER NARRATIVES

an online campaign launched in 2012 to make visible personal stories of Palestinians unable to exercise the right to love because of structural conditions and constraints of Israeli Occupation.

I begin with the Facebook page *Dear World* launched in 2012 explicitly to publicize and disseminate stories of Palestinian everyday lives, as it states, 'for people to understand us [Palestinians] and relate to us through our stories.' The stories are written in the form of an open letter in which diverse Palestinians in different locations tell stories, or part-stories, of daily experiences marked by separation, displacement, and a quest for belonging. The everyday comes across as an existential condition of spatiality and temporality, which comes across clearly in the post by Bassam Jamil, a young Palestinian from the Yarmouk refugee camp in Damascus, who tells the story of his continuous displacement following the outbreak of the Syrian Civil War in 2011. He writes:

> My name is Bassam Jamil, I am a Palestinian young man from the village of Hittin in Tiberias but was born in Damascus in 1984. I first learnt that I, along with my family, and our next door neighbours, were refugees after the expulsion of our grandparents from our homeland Palestine. . . . My peers and I belong to the third generation of refugees. I lived many events in my life which I consider unfamiliar or let's say does not meet the standards of the free world especially during my childhood and adolescence. We had to leave to any place away from the death and nights of anxiety and horror. I left Damascus to Lebanon four years ago, and the reality there was not much different from that of Damascus, as in Lebanon we live half a life with no dreams or sense of safely for a better tomorrow. I am not sure if it was the sense of belonging to a homeland that they try every day to prove to us that it's nothing more than a borrowed homeland.[1]

Most posts, including Bassam's, begin with a partially set phrase 'Dear World, my name is [. . .], I am a Palestinian' underlining the quest for belonging in contexts defined by continuous conflict and forced displacement. Similar posts and videos circulated by the online *Love Under Apartheid* page tell of the segregation of couples and families imposed because of the imposition of the Israeli citizenship law. The stories, in videos and text, speak of people unable to be together and unable to exercise the basic universal human right – the right to love. Other narrative tropes, including control of Palestinian everyday space and time, come across in the *Open Bethlehem* campaign which tells stories of people living in the shadow of the Separation Wall Israel build to 'deter terrorist acts.'

Interestingly, the popular narrative trope of 'victimization' used in the Palestinian national story and which has tended to normalize images of suffering and destruction is not at all evident in any of the stories. Indeed, none of these self-narrations in the various case studies position the Palestinians as the ultimate sufferers in the ongoing conflict with Israel because, as the *Dear World* Facebook page makes clear, the goal is not to look for pity but 'for people to understand us [Palestinians] and relate to us through our stories.' As such, while some themes emerging from these self-narrations could be theorized as resistance, assertion, empowerment, and defiance against a background of desperation, erasure, loss, violence, and crises, what comes across in most of these self-narrations is their attempt to summon audiences as involved co-witnesses of everyday social and political environments. In this sense, involvement, as Paul Anderson (2013, p. 478) argues, demands

> not a spectator, but a witness; others who will *identify* [my emphasis] with the speaker. . . . Witness is a kind of sociability where the audience lend their affect in order to realise the speaker's voice [. . .] The laments can only be performed effectively if the audience share the quality of empathy; in that case, they do not simply hear the speaker's narrative; they *witness* the speaker's radical and painful identification with their environment. What is then generated by this act is not simply critical or oppositional consciousness, or even a shared sense of victimhood, but a compelling sense of involvement: witnessed, echoed and re-enacted.

The overarching theme that comes across all the examples are 'everyday practices,' such as, for instance, flying kites in Gaza trying against the backdrop of rubble and destruction; coping with everyday life as in *The Wanted 18*; and with separation of families and couples as told in the many stories of the *Love Under Apartheid* campaign, all of which serve to contest the exceptionalist discourses about the Palestinians. In *The Wanted 18*, the 'cow' metaphor is used as a narrative mode and symbol through which everyday Palestinian lives become visible; the *Flying Paper* tells a poignant narrative of Palestinian lives through a seemingly ordinary, yet deeply personalized and moving story of Gaza's children who irrespective of the siege manage to enjoy their childhood and break the Guinness world record in the number of kites flown simultaneously in the same place and time. The fact that this childhood is not an ordinary one is then obvious only from a few yet no less influential statements throughout the film such as, 'If you fly kites about two kilometres that way, you get killed.' – 'We are not safe here. The Israeli checkpoints are only 700 metres away from us.'

Or 'During the days of war we used to see tanks over there where we were flying kites yesterday.' What remains important though is the fact that the latest Palestinian production offers promising efforts to counter the Israeli discursive practices and reinstate the Palestinian voice as an alternative to the current regime of representation that has long attempted to silence the Palestinian other.

Importantly, these narrative modes, this chapter argues, can subvert dominant frames of what Hallward (2009) has called 'commonplaces' – the frequently cited words, phrases, or events used to allude to Palestinians. The subversion of 'commonplaces' is also evident in the opening scene of *The Wanted 18* when one of the cows is heard stating: 'They are Palestinians. They do not work, they prefer to riot' – phrases often been used by Israel and its media to refer to the subjects it controls. This is also apparent in a particularly funny section when the cows are referred to as 'security threats' (a term Israel uses to refer to Palestinians it wants to target) that must be contained. In the first scene, the concept of security threat remains within its political context as an army officer talks about the intifada in a live interview; however, in the second scene of the film, the concept is completely detached from its usual usage and placed into the everyday life of farming and cow milking which suddenly strips it off its political acuteness and exposes its exaggerated nature vis-à-vis the Palestinian case. Furthermore, these examples underline the potential of narrative to challenge and disrupt prevalent regimes of representation even under conditions.

Importantly, in alluding to, while not clearly mentioning, Israeli settler-colonial practices, these narratives reflect a longing for normalcy, which as Salim Tamari notes, is simply a desire for solace in the midst of a prolonged conflict (Tamari, 2013) or a constant search for an opening to live a natural ordinary life that is not interrupted or disrupted, as it has been since 1948, by persistent violence, dispossession, and death. Ultimately, these narratives humanize the Palestinian 'Other' through stories of the everyday that are often touching personal snapshots of Palestinian children's lives, such as in *Flying Paper*, or community life, such as in *The Wanted 18*, and which enable the audience to relate to the Palestinians' lived experiences. They narratives underline how subjects negotiate knowledge and marginality through what De Certeau has called 'art of the weak' (1984, p. xiv). *The Wanted 18* negotiates marginality through using the 'cow' as a metaphor for how ordinary Palestinians negotiate structural power, but also produces knowledge about ordinary lives in conflict. The *Flying Paper* underlines how the 'art of the weak' is used as a strategy through which ordinary yet deeply personalized and moving narratives of a group of children in Gaza negotiate their restricted spaces, enjoy their childhood, and manage to break the Guinness world record in the number of kites flown simultaneously in the same place and time. It would be wrong to assume that the broader circulation of such marginal voices and narratives have transformed relations of power, but as Tripp has suggested in his study of resistance and power in the Middle East, a 'steady erosion that can take place as established authorities find themselves outflanked, superseded, mocked and derided' (Tripp, 2013, p. 261).

Conclusion

This chapter began with the premise that any discussion of the global south, as an imagined spatiality often defined by its perceived differences from the global north must also address how this imagined spatiality is interlinked with narrative, as image and discourse, and, as such, ask how narrative plays a role in the emergence and persistence of particular epistemic formations that are also sustained by material and structural conditions of power and resistance. It then used the Palestinian-Israeli conflict to address this premise and to consider the ways in which narrative, as Homi Bhabha (1994) has suggested, not only raises important issues on otherness, power relations, and contradictions/paradoxes but also re-inscribes the political in the narrative act.

In supporting the proposition set out at the beginning, the chapter addressed how the Zionist movement's narrative of itself has prevailed in the production of knowledge of Palestine and the Palestinians and how the media, as the space in which struggles over narrative are played out within and across borders, have played a role in normalizing this powerful episteme and, thus, in helping maintain the geographies and imaginaries within this episteme has been inscribed. This chapter advanced the argument that in order to understand how these systems took root and became normalized, we cannot simply analyze the conflict in terms of forcible seizure of land, competing national narratives, the removal of people, or structural practices of settler-colonialism but must recognize 'that the conditions through which the geographical arrangement of space and the classification of distinct identities in this conflict are themselves created and solidified through particular visual and discursive practices and distribution of visibility that tend to remain invisible' (Hochberg, 2015, p. 7). This argument is reflected in the ways in which Zionism sought to construct an exceptionalist narrative about Palestine and the Palestinians along with its narrative about itself, which was reinforced and reproduced through the media, through acts and publications. The power of such a narrative is that it 'can act as the prism through which political relations are seen. . . . Although by no means universal, a dominant consensus emerges, shaped by the institutions of knowledge, buttressed by prevailing political ideologies' (Tripp, 2013, p. 253). As the chapter has shown, however, ordinary

THE STRUGGLE OVER NARRATIVES

Palestinians have been engaged in alternative modes of narrating and telling stories about everyday lives, producing alternative ways of knowing and seeing that will ultimately help in de-colonizing the imagination and subverting powerful epistemic entities.

The argument made above is not intended to provide an overarching view of the conflict but to highlight the role of the various powerful forces that have been involved in the creation and sustenance of exceptionalist arguments based on the Zionist narrative about itself and to draw attention to the possibility of subverting these systems through narrative practices. As such, in the case of Palestine/Israel, as in the case of other conflicts involving occupation and ongoing violence, questions concerning the political function of narrative must be considered along with other structural conditions. The role and power of media cannot be ignored, but likewise neither can issues related to inequalities and structural relations of power. In fact, in order to challenge these inequalities, there is a need to focus more closely on how power is reproduced and maintained through narrative as well as in the operations of the state.

Note

1 Bassam Jameel, posted 4 June 2016 on www.facebook.com/frompalestine dearworld/.

References

Aouragh, M. (2011). *Palestine Online: Transnationalism, the Internet and the Construction of Identity*. London: I. B. Tauris.
Abu-Lughod, L., and A. Sa'di (2007). *Nakba, Palestine 1948 and the Claims of Memory*. New York: Columbia University Press.
Anderson, P. (2013). The Politics of Scorn in Syria and the Agency of Narrated Involvement. *Journal of the Royal Anthropological Institute*, 19, 463–481.
Bhabha, H. (1994). *The Location of Culture*. New York: Routledge.
Collins, J. (2011). *Global Palestine*. London: Hurst.
Couldry, N. (2000). *The Place of Media Power. Pilgrims and Witnesses of the Media Age*. London: Routledge. Dear Palestine (www.facebook.com/from palestinedearworld/).
De Certeau, M. (1984). *The Practice of Everyday Life*. (S. Randall, Trans). Berkeley: University of California Press.
Freedman, D. (2014). *The Contradictions of Media Power*. London, New York and New Delhi: Bloomsbury.
Friel, H., and Richard F. (2007). *Israel/Palestine on the Record*. London: Verso.
Hall, S. (1994). Cultural Identity and Diaspora. In Williams, P., and Chrisman, L. (Eds.). *Colonial Discourse and Post-Colonial Theory, A Reader* (pp. 222–237). London: Harvester Wheatshea,f.

Hallward, M. C. (2009). Creative Responses to Separation: Israeli and Palestinian Joint Activism in Bil'in. *Journal of Peace Research*, 46, 541–558. https://doi.org/10.1177/0022343309334612

Hochberg, G. (2015). *Visual Occupations: Violence and Visibility in a Conflict Zone*. Durham, NC: Duke University Press.

Khalidi, R. (1997). *Palestinian Identity: The Construction of Modern National Consciousness*. New York, NY: Columbia University Press.

Khalili, L. (2007). *Heroes and Martyrs of Palestine*. New York, NY: Columbia University Press.

Khalili, L. (2010). Palestinians: The Politics of Control, Invisibility and the Spectacle. In Ali Khalidi, M. (Ed.). *Manifestations of Identity: The Lived Realities of Palestinian Refugees in Lebanon*. Beirut: Institute for Palestine Studies.

Keilani, T. Love Under Apartheid. Retrieved from www.youtube.com/watch?v=ACfs8b7qv50

Landy, M. (1994). *Film, Politics and Gramsci*. Minneapolis, MN: University of Minnesota Press.

Makdisi, S. (2010). The Architecture of Erasure. *Critical Inquiry*, 36, 519–559. Retrieved from http://criticalinquiry.uchicago.edu/uploads/pdf/Makdisi,_Architecture_of_Erasure.pdf

Matar, D. (2010). *What It Means to be Palestinian: Stories of Palestinian Peoplehood*. London: I. B. Tauris.

Matar, D. (2016). Image Normalization. In Tawil-Souri, H., and Matar, D. (Eds.). *Gaza as Metaphor* (pp. 173–187). London: Hurst and New York: Oxford University Press.

Matar, D., and Zahera, H. (Eds.). (2013). *Narrating Conflict in the Middle East*. London: I. B. Tauris.

Mbembe, A. (2003). Necropolitics. *Public Culture*, 15(1), 11–40. https://doi.org/10.1215/08992363-15-1-11

Open Bethlehem. Retrieved from www.openbethlehem.org/our-vision – mission.html

Pappe, I. (2014). *The Idea of Israel: A History of Power and Knowledge*. London: Verso.

Piłecki, A., and Hammack, P. L. (2014). Victims Versus Righteous Victims: The Rhetorical Construction of Social Categories in Historical Dialogue Among Israeli and Palestinian Youth. *Political Psychology*, 35, 813–830. https://doi.org/10.1111/pops.12063

Philo, G., and Berry, Mike. (2004/2011). *More Bad News from Israel*. London: Pluto Press.

Resende, F. (2014). *The Global South Conflicting Narratives and the Invention of Geographies*. Retrieved from www.ibraaz.org/usr/library/documents/main/the-global-south.pdf

Rogan, E., and Shlaim, A. (Eds.). (2007). *The War for Palestine: Rewriting the History of 1948*. Cambridge: Cambridge University Press.

Salamanca, O. Jabary, Mezna Q., Rabie, K., and Sobhi Samour, S. (2013). Past Is Present: Settler Colonialism in Palestine. *Settler Colonial Studies*, 2(1), 1–8.

Retrieved from http://cmes.berkeley.edu/wp-content/uploads/2015/08/Past-is-Present-Settler-Colonialism-in-Palestine.pdf

Said, E. (1978). *Orientalism* (25th Anniversary Ed.). New York: Penguin.

Said, E. (1994). *Culture and Imperialism* (1st ed.). New York: Vintage.

Said, E. (1997). *Covering Islam: How the media and the Experts Determine How We See the Rest of the World*. New York: Vintage.

Said, E. (2003). *The Question of Palestine*. New York: Random House.

Said, E. (1984). Permission to Narrate. *Journal of Palestine Studies*, 13, Spring, 27–48. Retrieved from www.jstor.org/stable/2536688?origin=JSTOR-pdf

Swedenberg, T., and Stein, R. (2005). *Palestine, Israel and the Politics of Popular Culture*. Durham, NC: Duke University Press.

Tamari, S. (2013). Normalcy and Violence: The Yearning for the Ordinary in Discourse of the Palestinian-Israeli Conflict. *Journal of Palestine Studies*, XLII, 48–60. https://doi.org/10.1525/jps.2013.42.4.48

Tawil-Souri, H. (2012). The Necessary Politics of Palestinian Cultural Studies. In Sabry, Tarik (Ed.). *Arab Cultural Studies: Mapping the Field* (pp. 27–43). London: I. B. Tauris.

Tripp, C. (2013). *The Power and the People: Paths of Resistance in the Middle East*. Cambridge, MA: Cambridge University Press.

Williams, R. (2005). *Culture and Materialism. Selected Essays*. London: Verso.

Zayani, M. (2015). *Networked Publics and Digital Contention: The Politics of Everyday Life in Tunisia*. London: Oxford University Press.

12

HELPER AND THREAT

How the mediation of Africa-China relations complicates the idea of the global south

Cobus van Staden

Introduction

One of the strengths of the global south as a concept is that it emerged from an attempt to look at the global arrangement of power from the perspective of injustice and a lack of access to resources (Eckl and Weber, 2007). It stood in contrast with divisions on the base of geopolitical strategy (the three worlds division, both in its Western and Maoist iterations) and those based on a linear, Eurocentric idea of development (the division between so-called developed and developing nations) (Dirlik, 2004; Makki, 2004).

Despite fears that the north-south binary opposition locks the south into an eternal diminished status (Eckl and Weber, 2007), its coining at least opened the door to talking about what unifies the experience of being from, or in, the rest of the world – to talk about what constitutes 'southness.' That discussion necessarily also becomes a discussion about how to delineate the global south. Can the global south be geographically delineated? Can it be thought of as a collection of 'southern' nation states (many of which are located in the Northern Hemisphere)? Or should it rather be thought of as a state of being? In the latter case, what does that state constitute?

Jean and John Comaroff (2016) have pointed out that unlike the three worlds model that preceded it, the term *global south* is a polythetic term, where the members might share several, but not all and maybe not even most, of a wide range of characteristics. A key complicating factor, which distances the global south/north demarcation from earlier ones including the three worlds model and those structured around centre/periphery and developed/developing, is that several key members of the global south are not alienated from global capitalism but rather at its very heart. Africa, with its high growth rates driven by commodity booms during the 2000s, is one such example, albeit one that still locates Africa as the locus of extraction, in a seemingly straight line from the colonial era to the present.

However, this straight line – indicating both a horizon of impossibility in relation to African development and a demarcation line between Africa and Europe – is not as simple as it seems. As Etienne Balibar (2004) has argued, the demarcation lines traditionally dividing north and south are both fracturing and moving, calling into question the identity of the global north, as well as the global south.

China has emerged as a key disruptor of these distinctions. This isn't only because (like many other regions) China contains within itself zones of northness and southness. The yawning wealth gap between Shanghai and areas like Xinjiang echo global wealth gaps. However, in addition to containing this complexity, China's role as a global economic and geopolitical actor increasingly troubles the very essence of the global north/south system. As the Comaroffs argue, a key part of China's emerging global role lies in how it 'greatly profits from playing in the interstices between worlds' (2012, 46). In other words, China fundamentally disrupts the distinction between global north and global south because it has 'interpolated itself into *both* north and south, without being truly either' (Ibid., emphasis original).

China's key role therefore lies not only in containing contradictions but rather in grasping the agency to move within and between different zones of the global geo-economic and political system. To put this into different terms, Arif Dirlik has argued that 'the successes of the Chinese economy are attributable in the end to successful manipulation of a Neoliberal global economy, as are the problems it has produced' (2016, 149). The fact that China managed to manipulate the global neoliberal economy represents a level of agency rare in the rest of the global south and in the process troubles the entire system. This is the fundamental reason why the relationship between China and Africa reveals such key questions and conflicts: China's ability to 'play' between worlds raises fundamental questions about what it means to traverse the north/south divide, and whether other global south countries can also make that leap, possibly through engagement with (or through emulating) China.

These questions don't only play out in trade ministries – they play out in the media. Their mediation makes them crucial questions discussed on African streets. The China-Africa relationship is very wide, touching on all aspects of African life, from trade and geopolitics to migration, peacekeeping, UN reform, data network expansion, scandals around fake food and pharmaceuticals, and many others. Crucially, all of these are mediated, and the mediation shapes how we will think of the global south going forward.

In this chapter I look at two dominant tropes in the discursive construction of the China-Africa relationship in order to unpack how they complicate the concept of the global south itself. Discourse about the relationship, while expansive, has repeatedly returned to two dominant themes: solidarity between Africa and China and the dominance of Africa by China. I will examine each of these tropes in turn, before discussing their impact on the concept of the global south in the conclusion.

China as helper

The Chinese government has traditionally been one of the most ardent promoters of the idea that China stands in solidarity with Africa. However, while propaganda made up a sizable component of this message, it was also a wider mediation of the concept of the global south itself. A key moment of this mediation was the Bandung Conference of 1955. This meeting of decolonizing countries was an attempt to carve out a space between the competing spheres of influence that shaped the Cold War: those of the West, and the Soviet Union. China was a controversial attendee and worked hard to present itself as a benevolent partner in development, rather than a potential force for imperialism (Chakrabarty, 2010). This theme has continued in the Chinese government's conversation with Africa since. This is despite the fact that this discourse breaks down into two rough phases: the discourse of the Mao Zedong era, and that dating from China's 'going out' campaign, which reaches to the present.

In China-Africa discourse, the former era lasted roughly from the Bandung Conference to the death of Mao in 1976. During this era, China linked its aid to Africa to a discourse of revolutionary support. It positioned itself as a pioneer of a peasant revolution and chafed against the Soviet Union's self-characterization as the leader of the global anti-capitalist struggle. This only intensified after the Sino-Soviet split of 1960, after which China condemned the Soviet Union for 'revisionism' – backsliding towards collaborating with the West and abandoning the dream of a radical communist revolution led by peasants and workers. Together with this allegation of ideological impurity, Beijing also accused Moscow of being both blind to the racism suffered by Africa and of pursuing a racist neocolonial policy in Africa, akin to the West (Cooley, 1965).

Instead, China proposed itself as an alternative model. Not only was China a non-white country that suffered under Great Britain, it also presented an example of radical peasant-led revolution. China was simultaneously a leader in the revolution and a fellow revolutionary. However, it also offered the decolonizing world a promise that unlike the West and the Soviet Union, it is bound to a principle of non-interference. One of Premier Zhou Enlai's Eight Principles of Development Assistance to Africa, the commitment to not meddle in the domestic politics of its partners became a cornerstone of the China-Africa relationship, especially after Zhou's much-publicized African tour of 1963–1964 (Hutchison, 1975; Monson, 2010). Woven into China's discourse of revolution was a related discourse of development. Development was a dream of Bandung, and mutual cooperation to overcome the planned underdevelopment that characterized colonialism, and to surpass the West in development, was woven into Cold War discourse of solidarity. The emblematic project of this era was the TAZARA railway, which linked Tanzania and Zambia. This railway project was funded by the Chinese government and built by Chinese technicians (at a considerable loss of life). It became a potent symbol of China's commitment to mutual development (Monson, 2010; Poplak, 2016).

Dipesh Chakrabarty (2010) has pointed out that the discourse of Bandung and revolutionary development was split between dialogical and pedagogical styles of politics. The former focused on discussions of how a decolonizing world was to celebrate diversity without reimposing the mechanisms of racial othering that characterized imperialism. More pertinent to this discussion, pedagogical discourse uncritically accepted Western development models in prescribing a single trajectory of development. Similar to the model of developing/developed nations I mentioned above, this discourse tended to construct development as a single path, along which countries move at different speeds. Chakrabarty notes: 'The accent on modernization makes the figure of the engineer one of the most eroticized figures of the postcolonial developmentalist imagination' (53). The discourse of revolutionary solidarity functioned in tandem with discourses of development and personal discipline. However, these discourses would not have had widespread impact without mediation. During the Cold War, Chinese media played a crucial part in transmitting this message of solidarity, development and discipline to Africa.

Solidarity discourse and Chinese media in Africa

Research into the presence and nature of Cold War Chinese media in Africa is heavily dependent on Western sources. Up to the present I have found surprisingly few African or Chinese descriptions of this media, beyond general policy pronouncements. These Western accounts need to be treated with care because the only reason the Western sources I use below paid any attention to the issue at all was because of Cold War anxieties that China (and the Soviet Union) was winning the propaganda war in Africa. Yet, the strategic preoccupation with the success of Chinese media in Africa drove these authors to provide specific dates, numbers, and other details that I have so far not encountered in other sources.

Radio Peking (now China Radio International) began broadcasting to Africa in 1956 (Cooley, 1965; Lowenthal, 1963). The broadcasts started off in Cantonese (aimed at expatriate communities in Africa) and English-language Morse code. The latter proved a failure, and by 1959, it was replaced by a two-hour English-language program per week (Lessing, 1962). By the mid-1960s, this had increased exponentially:

> [i]n August 1961 Peking Radio's African service devoted 35 hours weekly to programmes in English, seven hours to Portuguese, seven hours to Cantonese, seven hours to Swahili, plus four hours to French programmes which were not directed solely at Africa, and an additional three hours to English which also did not have Africa as exclusive target.
>
> (Ibid. 125)

It also had an Arabic service. Hutchison (1975) estimates that by 1965 the total had risen to 108 hours of broadcasting per week. By then China had constructed short-wave transmitters in Somalia, Tanzania, Congo-Brazzaville, and Mali. It also conducted off-shore broadcasting (Ibid. 99, Hinton, 1968).

Radio and print formed the bulk of Chinese media in Africa during the Mao era. This was, among other reasons, due to the expense and logistics of producing film. That said, Larkin (1971) mentions that the Chinese Propaganda Department coordinated documentary productions with African governments (217). Films were shown at Chinese embassies (Ibid. 177, Hutchison, 1975, 99). Hutchison wasn't convinced of their appeal:

> Chinese embassies held parties, usually to celebrate anniversaries, at which, invariably films were shown extolling Chinese achievements. But there is little evidence that these efforts met with any great success. Embassy film shows, for example, have never been very popular with Africans. Firstly the films themselves are rather boring and secondly the Chinese do not serve alcoholic drinks at their parties.
>
> (99)

However one takes his description, the point is that Chinese film seemed to have enjoyed limited circulation in Africa, and when it was circulated, it seems that it was mostly confined to elites who managed to make it to the embassy for the screening. Compared to that, radio had a wider listenership.

So how fun was it to listen to Radio Peking? Here one runs into the crux of why relying on Western sources for this inquiry is problematic. One quickly senses from the writing that certain writers have a lot invested in talking up the threat that China (and the Soviet Union) posed to Western interests in Africa. One finds breathless descriptions of the power of Chinese propaganda: 'From experience I can testify that no other radio programmes can be heard as clearly in all parts of Africa as those of Peking Radio. And they are excellent – entertaining, instructive and interesting, well worth any listener's attention' (Hinton, 125).

Hutchison is more doubtful:

> It is more difficult to assess the impact of Chinese publications and radio broadcasts, but it seems reasonable to assume that the absence of any entertainment content must lessen their appeal. Pure propaganda is hardly of compelling interest to anyone, least of all to Africans, who are very politically conscious. Chinese broadcasts and publications give them neither entertainment nor information, nor well-informed comment about African affairs.
>
> (100)

I have found it challenging to verify this, because the media directed at African audiences have generally not been preserved. However, digital recordings of a few Radio Peking broadcasts aimed at a global audience during the same era are available. While they provide an imperfect comparison, Hutchison has pointed out that Chinese propaganda media of the era tended to follow a one-size-fits-all approach. Specific liberation movements were frequently not named, in favour of general terms like 'revolutionary peoples.' One can therefore argue that while these Southeast Asian examples are not a perfect comparison, they allow the listener a glimpse into what these broadcasts might have sounded like.

One clip starts off with a full orchestral rendition of *The Internationale*, followed by time signals and announcements that 'This is Radio Peking' repeated several times, interspersed with martial music. After several minutes, the program starts:

> We begin our program with a quotation from Chairman Mao Zedong. Our great leader Chairman Mao has said: 'Make trouble. Fail. Make trouble again. Fail again until [the] red dawn. That is the logic of the imperialists and all reactionaries the world over

when dealing with the people's cause. And they will never go against this logic.'

That quote is from a commentary that Chairman Mao wrote for the Xinhua News Agency in 1949, on the US State Department's white paper on US-Sino relations. We now repeat the quotation.

(YouTube)

One doesn't have to agree with Hinton that 'the content of Communist Chinese propaganda is strongly characterized by onesidedness, oversimplification, suppression, exaggeration, repetition, and the use of largely meaningless slogans' (155) to acknowledge that the coded nature of this discourse probably alienated many Africans. As a contemporary listener I had to marvel that anyone understood this discourse at all. It reminded me most of all of its parody – the arcane slogans chanted by the Mao-obsessed teenagers in Jean-Luc Godard's *La Chinoise*.

For all its dedication to popular global south solidarities, this discourse is essentially directed at an elite audience. I would argue that it supports the argument made by G. Thomas Burgess (2010) that Chinese post-Bandung public diplomacy in Africa in the 1950s and 1960s was strongly shaped by Chinese Party elites communicating a message of worker discipline to African Party elites. He argued that Chinese public diplomacy, especially in the form of official visits to China by African dignitaries, fostered stage-managed fantasies of post-Bandung futurism built on and via the politicized discipline and self-denial of ordinary workers.

The program I quoted above can be fully consumed (as opposed to simply endured) only if the listener submits him/herself to its very narrow structure. The Radio Peking broadcast demands full compliance from its listener – in essence, the act of listening becomes itself a form of labour, demanding discipline and self-sacrifice towards a collective goal.

The post-Bandung ideoscape was one where, in the terms of Vijay Prashad (2002), the third world was never a place but always a project. As Burgess argued, post-Bandung solidarity was fuelled by a collective fantasy of disciplined bodies achieving nationalist success through hard work and self-denial. As each country surges forward, the non-aligned movement, led by a China powered by the disciplined bodies of its own workers, would eventually challenge Euro-American aggression and imperialism globally. One sees in this narrative a succession from the personal to the national to the global, all powered through the energy of disciplined workers.

China's funding of the 1963 Games of the New Emerging Forces (a short-lived post-Bandung version of the Olympic Games), created a cultural arena where collective spectacle and the dream of modernity springing from previously colonized societies could be achieved through the reinstrumentalizing of the bodies of former colonial subjects, now reimagined as national subjects. The games were 'an explicit attempt to link sport to the politics of anti-colonialism and tangible evidence of the Third World's ability to mobilize itself through sport' (Field, 2014, 1853). The succession from the personal to the national to the global is explicit in the minutes of the Third Afro-Asian Peoples' Solidarity Conference, held in Moshi, Tanganyika (now Tanzania), in 1963. Commenting on the recently held Games:

> The Conferences [*sic*] shares the opinion that such Games in which sportsmen and women of the progressive countries of Africa, Asia, Latin America and the Socialist countries participate in sportsmanlike competitions, will defend the honour of their respective countries, and will constitute an extremely valuable contribution to further consolidate the solidarity and co-operation of all those forces and countries fighting against colonialism and imperialism.
> (Permanent Secretariat of the Afro-Asian Peoples' Solidarity Organization, 1963, 99)

This dream of solidarity resonates in the contemporary debates around the global south in complicated ways. In the first place, despite being separated from us by decades of talking about globalization and multilateralism, it chimes with the fact that, as Eckt and Weber (2007) pointed out, the conceptualization of the global south remains essentially state-based. This is also true for China-Africa relations as a whole. The Chinese government supports the African Union financially and rhetorically, but Africa-China relations are still overwhelmingly state to state.

In the second place, the performance of solidarity between China and Africa is both mediated and tends to take place at mass events funded by China. After the death of Mao Zedong in 1976, his successor Deng Xiaoping declared his country open for business. What followed was a dizzying rush towards development based on mass manufacturing and aggressive infrastructure development. By the early 1990s, the Chinese government realized that in order for this growth to continue, Chinese companies, many of them state-owned – needed outside exposure. Under its 'going out' strategy, the Chinese government encouraged companies to seek outside markets and to secure new sources of raw materials. The infusion of Chinese money into Africa's minerals and oil sectors, as well as China's financing and construction of infrastructure in Africa fundamentally reshaped both Africa's relationship with the outside world, and the concept of the global south itself (Young, 2012).

This process of moving into the world brought Chinese companies to Africa. Their engagement grew throughout the 1990s but really took off after the establishment of the Forum on China-Africa Cooperation (FOCAC) in 2000. Taking place every three years, FOCAC provides a forum for Chinese and African leaders to meet and discuss Chinese aid and investment on the continent. However, FOCAC is also a mass event that allows the staging of China-Africa solidarity. This is enabled by the rapid expansion of Chinese state media in Africa since 2012 (Van Staden, 2013; Gagliardone, 2013) but also by FOCAC's own function as a media conduit, posting positive stories about China-Africa relations on a daily basis, mostly to the news aggregator *AllAfrica.com*.

FOCAC and the Chinese state media's contemporary discourse of solidarity differs from the post-Bandung era, but key similarities remain. The main difference is that no trace of China's revolutionary fervour remains. In the place of exhortations to join China on their march to the red dawn, Africa is now invited to join China in working towards win-win development. This discourse is explicitly pro-business and links national and continental upliftment with capitalist success. In this sense it is the polar opposite of the discourse of revolutionary solidarity China employed in relation to Africa during the Cold War. However, in many other respects, it is similar. One of the themes that survived the passage from the Cold War is non-interference. Zhou Enlai's principal of non-interference has been repurposed to differentiate China from Western powers in the postrevolutionary era. For example, China has raised this principal in support of African countries' criticism of the International Criminal Court, in order to differentiate itself from Western attempts to promote progressive political causes in Africa.

A second theme that crops up again is a tendency towards elite communication. While public diplomacy enjoys more support from the Chinese government, FOCAC is inherently an elite forum, and the communication emanating from it also addresses elites. While I have so far focused on China as the origin of this discourse, it is oversimplified to think of it as unidirectional propaganda imposed on Africa. Rather, I would characterize it as a coded propagandistic conversation between Chinese and African elites, where certain discursive tropes are developed and repeated. A recent editorial by Lovemore Chikova, the news editor of the Zimbabwean progovernment newspaper, *The Herald*, demonstrates this process.

A discourse analysis of the article reveals a host of Chinese Communist Party tropes, some of which date from the Bandung era. For example: the first sentence is 'China's development assistance model, which emphasises on [*sic*] win-win cooperation, has the potential to help fellow developing countries out of poverty' (Chikova, 2016). Not only is win-win cooperation emphasized, but China is again positioned as both a developing country among many, and yet a leader among developing countries. Chikova goes on to cite China's non-interference doctrine ('China has a deliberate policy through which it treats other countries as equal partners and maintains a stance of non-interference in the sovereignty of other countries'), before criticizing the West and the Bretton Woods institutions for interventionism ('developing countries have to dance to the tune of Western countries for them to get assistance'). The article positions China as part of a global south experience of outside meddling and aggression ('China and Africa have a lot in common in terms of their historical links and how imperialists interfered with their internal affairs during colonisation. And this is why China understands Africa's development aspirations far better than Western countries do.'). Finally, the discourse echoes the Cold War era in linking individual, national, and global aspirations, in a view of the global south that remains stubbornly linked to the nation state ('China realises that there will be no world peace as long as other continents wallow in poverty. Recent interactions with top Chinese officials showed that the Asian country's aspiration is to see peace prevailing in the world to allow nations to concentrate on uplifting the lives of their citizens').

This discourse is unambiguously propagandistic but not unidirectionally so. Chikova manages to weave in some of the Zimbabwean government's preoccupations in with Chinese talking points. So we are reminded that

> relations between Zimbabwe and the IMF and the World Bank soured when Government embarked on the land reform program and after President Mugabe criticised homosexuality. Homosexuality is not accepted in many African countries. But Zimbabwe was blacklisted partly because of its stance against homosexuality.

This kind of discourse presents a deeply illiberal and state-centric aspect of global south relations, and China has come in for a lot of criticism for perceptions that it is supporting undemocratic governments in the global south. I unpack this counter-discourse below.

China as threat

The counter-discourse to the trope of China as helper is frequently referred to as China threat discourse. This is a broad genre, of which China-Africa discourse makes up a notable subset. In this subset, misgivings are expressed about the impact China might have on Africa, although those misgivings frequently also reveal anxieties about how China is affecting wider geopolitics. In many ways it can be characterized as the dark flip side of the helper discourse, in the sense that in many iterations, China helper discourse is repeated, only to be dismissed as a smokescreen that conceals China's supposedly nefarious intentions.

Similar to the helper discourse, contemporary aggressor trope shares certain overlaps with its Cold War antecedent, while having evolved to reflect new preoccupations. While China helper discourse overwhelmingly comes from the Chinese government and their African partners, China threat discourse morphs according to the speaker. In this chapter I will briefly look at examples from the West and Africa.

West

The West's China threat discourse is generally linked with Western anxieties about a loss of influence in Africa. This was true both during the Cold War and subsequently. As I showed in the previous section, Cold War Western commentators had vested interests in presenting the Chinese media presence in Africa as both formidable and popular. Presenting China as ascendant in Africa played on anxieties about the rise of outside influence in what has traditionally been seen as the West's natural sphere of influence. The difference between the Cold War and the present is the positioning of Africa itself. Cold War discourse clearly saw Africa in terms of Cold War strategic frameworks, with concern expressed about Africa (and Asia and Latin America) as acting as possible fertile ground for Maoism, in a way that could encroach on the West itself, while also complicating its access to raw materials (see Cooley, 1965; Wood Akers, 1968).

Some contemporary Western discourse, especially coming from right-wing sources, continues this discourse of strategic containment. For example, shortly after the election of US President Donald Trump, the Fox News commentator Richard Fowler wrote an open letter posted to the right-wing US website *The Daily Caller*:

> Dear President-elect Trump, I know there is a lot on your plate over the next couple months, but I wanted to bring your attention to a pressing issue that might not make it to the top of your radar during your transition: Africa. Some would argue that Africa shouldn't be at the top of your list when it comes to priorities, but I beg to differ. If you are committed to taking on China and averting their ability to 'eat our lunch,' then we should be concerned with their dominance in Africa and the impact they may have on our future hegemonic power.
>
> (Fowler, 2016)

This discourse is strikingly similar to Cold War writing about China in Africa, in that China-Africa relations is drawn as a direct threat to US hegemony. For example:

> Certainly Peking seeks to form its own sphere of influence, with the African continent part and parcel of this sphere. By expelling the United States entirely from Africa, Mao Tse-tung's planners could advance far toward their declared objective of isolating the United States on the world scene.
>
> (Cooley, 1965, 7)

Another strand of contemporary Western discourse about the rise of China in Africa tends to couch these concerns in the language of concern for Africa itself. Western commentators position the West as a concerned impartial observer, rather than (more realistically) as a participant in a global economy partly dependent on African raw minerals. The implication here is that the West is a much more responsible development partner for Africa, and that this relationship is under threat because of China's rapacious appetite for African minerals. This discourse dominated the Obama administration's stance on China-Africa relations, as well as that of the Cameron administration in the UK. At its most egregious, this discourse is blatantly racist both towards Chinese and Africans. For example, in a 2008 article titled 'How China Is Taking over Africa and Why the West Should Be VERY Worried,' the *Daily Mail* writer Andrew Malone breathlessly states that:

> More than a thousand miles of new Chinese railroads are criss-crossing the continent, carrying billions of tons of illegally-logged timber, diamonds and gold. The trains are linked to ports dotted around the coast, waiting to carry the goods back to Beijing after unloading cargoes of cheap toys made in China. Confucius Institutes (state-funded Chinese 'cultural centres') have sprung up throughout Africa, as far afield as the tiny land-locked countries of Burundi and Rwanda, teaching baffled local people how to do business in Mandarin and Cantonese.

This is a classic example of what Emma Mawdsley (2008) has described as Fu Manchu versus Dr. Stanley in the Dark Continent. It is steeped in classical racism, with Chinese portrayed as dishonest, Africans as 'baffled,' and Africa as packed with raw riches which will be lost by the West to the storehouses of the Orient (where they will be no doubt turned into monstrous idols for the non-baptized).

But even when not as nakedly racist, anxious Western discourse about China's presence in Africa runs the danger of moralizing in favour of Western aid, and implying that Africans are not capable of making their own way in the capitalist marketplace. For example, Deutsche Welle (2016) writes approvingly of networks that export second-hand European clothing and appliances to Cameroon, quoting a customs officer saying that: 'Most cherished electrical appliances are from Germany. Chinese goods are not very good. The goods look very bright but never last. When you buy Chinese products, you need to replace them after three months. But second and third hand goods from Germany are very solid.' At the end of the article, there is a brief acknowledgement that this charity-based second-hand trade is actually considered harmful to African economies, but there is no space in this discourse to discuss the trade in 'bright' Chinese products as one supplanting the traditional European guilt economy. Instead, one has to ask who is being reassured here and why. Why is it so important to state over and over that German products are oh so popular in its former colony?

An important trope in this discourse is that of 'the new scramble for Africa.' This phrasing has become a cliché of China-Africa reporting. A simple Google News search for the phrase turned up headlines using the phrase from *The Economist, Newsweek, The Guardian*, and The European Council on Foreign Relations just dating from the last three months before the time of writing. I lack space to unpack all of them here and will only note that the implication of the phrase is to exonerate the contemporary West by putting it in the position of morally condemning the 19th-century West. It indulges in a fantasy of being free from the historical crime of colonialism by recasting it as a drama starring China, one that is informed by a disbelief in Africa's ability to make its own choices. Moralizing the China-Africa relationship keeps these speakers from the harder task of interrogating the failures of Western modernism, liberalism, and aid in Africa.

Africa

'The new scramble for Africa' has also become a key trope in African reporting on the China-Africa relationship. Because of space constraints I can give only an extremely broad account of these debates. China threat narratives are constant in the African conversation about its relationship with China. However, it is not nearly the only discourse about China in Africa. Rather, it is frequently mixed with 'Africa rising' narratives. In other words, where Western accounts often use China-Africa as a stage for a drama about the morality of Western hegemony in the 21st century, African accounts tend to turn it into a narrative about African decision-making.

Different accounts tend to ascribe different levels of agency to Africa, with some taking a pessimist tone, characterizing Africa as a perpetual victim of outside aggression, mainly from the West, but now also from China. A 2013 *Financial Times* article by the Nigerian Central Bank governor Lamido Sanusi was an influential example of this discourse. Sanusi argued that 'China takes our primary goods and sells us manufactured ones. This was also the essence of colonialism. The British went to Africa and India to secure raw materials and markets. Africa is now opening itself up to a new form of imperialism.'

In the article, Sanusi calls for an Afro-centric model of development, where Africa's relationships with the rest of the world must always be viewed through the lens of what the effect will be on Africa. He calls for a hard-nosed view where 'Africa must recognise that China – like the US, Russia, Britain, Brazil and the rest – is in Africa not for African interests but its own.' This vision of Africa alone up against the world shows how troubling China-Africa relations really are for the concept of the global south. Sanusi's flattening of the differences between China, the United States, Britain, Brazil, 'and the rest' is a clear repudiation of the concept of south-south exchange as somehow morally (or developmentally) superior to north-south exchange. He and other China sceptics in Africa see both kinds of solidarity – north-south solidarity via aid, and south-south solidarity of trade among differentially developing southern powers – as potential traps. The only way out of those traps is to keep a beady eye on what is in it for Africa.

The south-ness of the global south

Once, while walking around in Beijing, it struck me that one can divide cities between those where dogs run around in the streets on their own, and ones where they are cared for behind closed doors. I then realized that both Beijing and Johannesburg (my home city) are both kinds of cities – depending on where you are in the city you will encounter both kinds of dogs.

The north-south divide can be applied only in the broadest of strokes. Once one tries to be more exact, or apply it on a smaller scale, it starts to fall apart. Sino-Africa relations is one such area of conceptual collapse. The way it collapses raises questions about the term and its use in the 21st century. As my bone-headed dog epiphany showed, the concept of the global south collapses because it fails to account for differential rates of development within global south countries and even cities. China-Africa relations trouble the south-ness of the global south, because China keeps switching sides. It acts both like a 'northern' power and a member of the global south.

Chinese government self-presentation, and the way it is echoed by state media in Africa, is structured around this contradiction: China is both still developing and yet a model of successful development. It is both a fellow victim of Western exploitation and an exploiter. China's slippage between south-ness and north-ness shows how the concept of the global south itself is an unstable one.

Sino-African relations become a useful case study in the wider debate about the concept of the global south because it functions like a Rorschach test, allowing us to track the various contradictions of north-ness and south-ness as they play out in the relationship. The mediation of this slippage is crucial to understanding the global south as a concept, a place, and a state of mind. The evolving role of Africa in the world lies at the heart of this understanding.

References

Balibar, Etienne. (2004). *Europe as Borderland: The Alexander von Humboldt Lecture in Human Geography*, University of Nijmegen, the Netherlands, November 10.

Burgess, T. G. (2010). Mao in Zanzibar: Nationalism, Discipline, and the (De)Construction of Afro-Asian Solidarities. In Lee, C. J. (Ed.). *Making a World After Empire: The Bandung Moment and its Political Afterlives* (pp. 196–234). Athens: Ohio University Press.

Chakrabarty, D. (2010). The Legacies of Bandung: Decolonization and the Politics of Culture. In Lee, C. J. (Ed.). *Making a World After Empire: The Bandung Moment and Its Political Afterlives* (pp. 45–68). Athens: Ohio University Press.

Chikova, L. (2016). *Unpacking the Beijing Consensus*. Retrieved from www.herald.co.zw/unpacking-the-beijing-consensus/

Comaroff, J., and J. L. Comaroff. (2016). *Theory from the South, Or, How Euro-America is Evolving toward Africa*. London: Routledge.

Cooley, J. K. (1965). *East Wind Over Africa: Red China's African Offensive*. New York, NY: Walker & Company.

Dirlik, A. (2004). Specters of the Third World: Global Modernity and the End of the Three Worlds. *Third World Quarterly*, 25(1): 131–148. https://doi.org/10.1080/0143659042000185372

——— (2016). *Alternatives? The PRC and the Global South. Global Mocernity: Modernity in the Age of Global Capitalism*. London: Routledge.

Eckl, J., and J. Weber. (2007). North-South? The Pitfalls of Dividing the World by Words. *Third World Quarterly*, 28(1): 3–23.

Field, R. (2014). Re-Entering the Sporting World: China's Sponsorship of the 1963 Games of the New Emerging Forces (GANEFO). *The International Journal of the History of Sport*, 31: 1852–1867. https://doi.org/10.1080/09523367.2014.922545

Fowler, R. (2016). *Opinion: Trump Needs to Be a Counterweight to China in Africa*. Retrieved from http://dailycaller.com/2016/12/13/trump-needs-to-be-a-counterweight-to-china-in-africa/#ixzz4Tm4IV0Lb

Gagliardone, I. (2013). China as a Persuader: CCTV Africa's First Steps in the African Mediasphere. *Ecquid Novi: African Journalism Studies*, 34(3): 25–40. https://doi.org/10.1080/02560054.2013.834835

Hinton, H. C. (1968). The Waking Dragon. In Lee, J. (Ed.), *The Diplomatic Persuaders: The New Role of the Mass Media in International Relations*. New York, NY: John Wiley & Sons.

Hutchison, A. (1975). *China's African Revolution*. London: Hutchinson.

Larkin, B. D. (1971). *China and Africa 1949–1970: The Foreign Policy of the People's Republic of China*. Berkeley, CA: University of California Press.

Lessing, P. (1962). *Africa's Red Harvest*. London: Michael Joseph.

Lowenthal, Richard. (1963). China. In Brzezinski, Z. (Ed.), *Africa and the Communist World* (pp. 142–203). Stanford, CA: Stanford University Press.

Makki, F. (2004). The Empire of Capital and the Remaking of Centre-Periphery Relations. *Third World Quarterly*, 21(1): 149–168. https://doi.org/10.1080/0143659042000185381

Malone, A. (2008). *How China Is Taking Over Africa and Why the West Should Be VERY Worried*. Retrieved from www.dailymail.co.uk/news/article-1036105/How-Chinas-taking-Africa-West-VERY-worried.html#ixzz4TmCmLFdd

Mawdsley, Emma. (2008). Fu Manchu versus Dr Stanley in the Dark Continent? Representing China, Africa and the West in British Broadsheet Newspapers. *Political Geography*, 27: 509–529. https://doi.org/10.1016/j.polgeo.2008.03.006

Monson, J. (2010). Working Ahead of Time: Labor and Modernization During the Construction of the TAZARA Railway, 1968–1986. In Lee, C. J. (Ed.), *Making a World After Empire: The Bandung Moment and Its Political Afterlives* (pp. 235–265). Athens, AL: Ohio University Press.

Permanent Secretariat of the Afro-Asian Peoples' Solidarity Organization. (1963). *The Third Afro-Asian Peoples' Solidarity Conference, Moshi, Tanganyika, February 4–11, 1963*. Cairo: Madkour Press.

Poplak, R. (2016). *The New Scramble for Africa: How China Became the Partner of Choice*. Retrieved from www.theguardian.com/global-development-professionals-network/2016/dec/22/the-new-scramble-for-africa-how-china-became-the-partner-of-choice

Prashad, V. (2002). *Everybody Was Kung fu Fighting: Afro-Asian Connections and the Myth of Cultural Purity*. Boston, MA: Beacon Press.

Sanusi, Lamido. (2013). *Africa Must Get Real About Chinese Ties*. Retrieved from www.ft.com/content/562692b0-898c-11e2-ad3f-00144feabdc0

Van Staden, C. (2013). Editor's Introduction. *African-East Asian Affairs: The China Monitor*, 1: 4–14. https://doi.org/10.7552/0-1-1

Welle, Deutsche. (2016). *Cameroon Basks in Cheap Second-Hand Clothes*. Retrieved from www.dw.com/en/cameroon-basks-in-cheap-second-hand-clothes/a-36111173

Wood Akers, R. (1968). An Indispensable Diplomacy. In Lee, J. (Ed.), *The Diplomatic Persuaders: New Role of the Mass Media in International Relations*. New York, NY: John Wiley & Sons.

Young, C. (2012). *The Postcolonial State in Africa: Fifty Years of Independence 1960–2010*. Madison, WI: University of Wisconsin Press.

YouTube. Retrieved from www.youtube.com/watch?v=GWRyVjaBeKU

INDEX

1919 Revolution 21

Adams, P. 75
aesthetic cosmopolitanism 80–82
Africa 2, 3, 7, 10–13, 15, 16, 34–36, 39, 41–43, 45, 48, 49, 52–54, 57, 58, 60, 66, 68–71, 81, 186–202
agency 5, 55–56, 65–68, 88, 90, 96–102, 105, 106, 110, 113, 115, 178, 187, 192, 199
Aguilar 142–144, 152
aid 188, 194, 198–199
Al-Andalus 26
al-Qais, Imru' 17–19, 31–32
Alvarez, J. and Passos, E. 108, 117
American dream 25
Anderson, P. 180
Andrade, L. A. 75
anthropofagic/anthropofag 146, 154
apartheid 11, 34–35, 40–41, 52, 178–180
artefacts 75, 120, 167
aspirational 55, 63
audiovisual 77, 80, 141, 158–161
avant-garde 10, 140–152

balance 19, 122–135, 140
Bandung Conference 188–194
Bar, F. 82
Barthes, R. 109
Batalha do Passinho 72–74, 81
Bhabha, Homi 5, 19, 182
biographies 164
blackness 50–51
black woman 56, 64–65

black womanhood 65
bodies 9, 39–52, 56–58, 65, 68, 79, 86–97, 108–114, 192–193
Brazil 3, 7–12, 72–83, 103, 105–107, 116, 140–155, 158–168, 199
broadcasting 77, 124, 163, 190
Brotas, D. 75
Burguess, J. 74, 77–79
Burke, Peter 26, 163

Campos 141–147, 152–154
cartography 19, 32
Castells, M. 75
celebrities 55, 66
celebrity 66
Chen, Steve 77
China 2–3, 11–12, 186–201
choice 2, 46, 61, 66–67, 141, 172
Chouliaraki, L. 109
cinema 159, 162
city 41, 45, 55, 58–67, 72, 82, 107–109
class 2, 12, 40, 45, 55–66, 77, 80, 87, 92, 107
colonial/colonialism 1, 8, 18–31
coloniality 88–92
coloniality of seeing 89–90
commonplaces 181
Comolli, J. L. 114, 117
concrete poetry 140–156
Conflito 16
construct/construction 42, 51, 161, 174, 182, 189

203

INDEX

consumers 11, 34–36, 42–43, 46, 49–51, 77
consumption 3, 7, 10, 34–36, 44–46, 50–51, 69, 157–158, 162–163, 166–167
Couldry, N. 75, 173
co-witnesses 180
cuir 9, 86–104
cuir visualities 86–104
cultural production 2, 94, 120, 177
cultural products 81, 120, 162, 167–168
culture of memory 157, 162–164

Dear World 178–183
Debord, Guy 112–113
De certeau, M. 178, 181
decolonial theory 90
Deleuze, G. and Guattari, F. 108
desires 55, 107–114, 167
Deutsche Welle 198
development 1–2, 32, 40, 75, 87–88, 142–143, 163, 186–200
Diadorim 116–117
Didi-Huberman, G. 147, 151
digitalized 55
discipline 4, 66, 87, 178, 189, 192
Domingos, E. 73–74, 79, 82, 106

East 11–13, 19–20, 25, 87, 175, 182
economy of image 107, 111, 114
Egypt 7, 12, 18, 20–26, 119–139
El-Ramly, Lenin 18, 28–32
entertainment industry 77, 159, 168
episteme 174, 178, 182
epistemic 8, 16, 90, 115–116, 170–173, 182–183
epistemic systems 173
ethical 35, 109, 119–121, 131–137
ethics 13, 120–136
everyday 6, 51, 55, 59, 72, 75, 84, 165–167, 171, 176–183
exceptionalist narratives 175
experience 6, 10, 41–42, 47, 56, 75, 77, 107–109, 113–114, 134, 144, 151, 167, 186, 191, 195
experimental 142, 148–151
expert interviews 125

fairness 122, 129–130
Fanon, Frantz 19, 24
favelas 74, 76, 79, 81, 83
femininity 55–56, 60, 63, 67
feminisms 91–92, 96
feminist 56, 86–94
Flying Paper 178, 180–181
FOCAC 194
forgetting 157–169
framing/framed 1, 9, 27–28, 109–110, 168
freedom 21, 30, 34, 60, 62, 67, 120, 122, 132–133, 162
Free Officers 20
Fundação Getúlio Vargas 84
funk carioca 83

Galloway, A. 75
gay 44–45, 92, 94, 102
gaze 62, 86, 90, 94, 110–111
gender 9–10, 35, 37–38, 52, 56–60, 87, 89, 91, 94, 96–97, 102–103, 162, 173
Germany 10, 140–155, 198
global capital 173, 186
globalization 3–4, 55, 60, 62, 135, 193
Global South 1–19, 32, 55, 66–88, 97, 120, 147, 151, 158, 170–182, 186–200
good-time girls 57–59
Gramsci 177
Green, J. O. 74, 77–79

Haesbaert, R. 76
hall 3, 41–42, 53, 174–175
Herschmann, M. 76, 165
heteronormative 55
historical theme 159
history 1–2, 16, 18, 20–23, 26, 29, 31–32, 34, 62, 79–80, 87–88, 97, 101–102, 140, 142–144, 147–148, 153, 158, 160, 163–164, 168, 174, 176
Hollywood 158, 162
Holocaust 149–151
Holzbach, A. 83
Hörspiel 141
Hurley, Chad 77

204

INDEX

hypervisibility 56, 60, 61, 65, 68
hysteria 90–95, 102

identities 10–11, 27, 36, 47, 60, 62–63, 80, 157, 166, 182
Ilan Pappe 175–176
imaginaries 6–7, 14, 17–33, 35, 52, 64, 86–103, 171, 174
imagined geographies 171
imagined spatiality 182
independent media 122–123
independent publications 88, 94
informational territories 8, 76, 82, 84
interracial 43–44, 46, 50, 53

Jenkins, H. 77
journalism cultures 119–139

Karim, Jawed 77
knowledge 5–9, 26, 29, 87–89, 101, 128, 130, 145, 170–182
Konkrete Poesie 147–148

lamentation 19, 26, 32
Lamido Sanusi 199
land 20–26, 30–31, 39, 64, 147–148, 160, 172, 177, 182, 195, 197
Latin America 2–3, 10, 13, 78, 81, 86–90, 97, 101, 196
Latour, B. 80
Lebanon 7, 12, 119–139, 174, 179
Lefebvre, H. 6
leisure 61, 63–64, 67, 69
Lemos, A. 75–76
liberty 20, 25, 27, 111
local 3, 8, 11, 55–56, 59, 67–68, 74–81, 97, 130, 159, 197
locative media 74–76
Lovemore Chikova 194
Love under Apartheid 178, 180
loyalist media 121
loyalist press 122

Mao Zedong 188, 191, 193
Maricarmen 90–101
Matar, D. 13, 170–184

materiality 109, 140
Mbembe, A. 172
McCarthy, A. 75
media organizations 119, 120, 123
media power 173
media technologies 35
medium 28, 65, 128, 142, 145, 151, 154
memory 7, 78, 140–143, 156–157, 160, 162–164, 167–169
Mexico 86, 91, 94, 97, 99, 103
military dictatorship 161–162
mimicry 56
Mitchell, W. J. 75
mobilizing media 121
modern 8, 20, 51, 57, 66, 69, 90, 100, 114–115, 138, 141, 153, 157, 160, 167, 169, 175, 184
modernity 57, 80–81, 85, 88–90, 112, 116, 158–159, 168, 192
Mon, F. 141, 147–151, 154, 197
Mondzain, J. M. 111
montage 28, 145, 149, 154
morality 56, 59–60, 63, 131, 198
Mu'allaqa 17, 32
multitude 107–108, 112–115
Muslim Brotherhood 122, 127

Nakba 20, 177
Naksa/Setback 20
narrative 1–18, 24–31, 56–58, 62, 65, 68, 105–107, 116, 151, 159, 161, 170–183, 198
Nasser/Nasserite 20
nationalist 20, 31, 192
nationalization 20
necropower 172
neo-colonialism 19
neoliberal 9–11, 56, 60, 63, 187
Noigandres 143–147
non-linearity 141, 151
normalization 171, 175, 177
North 3–7, 11–12, 16–33, 56, 86–88, 96, 140, 147, 151, 158, 170–171, 176, 182, 186–187, 199–200
Nostalgia 2, 7, 9, 31, 157–159, 161, 163, 165–169

205

INDEX

objectivism 120–121
occupation 20–22, 79, 89, 165, 172, 174, 176–177, 179, 183
opinion leaders 125, 127
organizational structures 120
other, the 8, 39
ownership 44–46

Palestine-Israel conflict 170, 174
pan-Arab 20
Passinho Dance-Off 72, 76, 78, 82, 84
Pereira de Sá, S. 10
performance 10, 18, 33, 64–65, 76–77, 79, 83–84, 96, 104, 108, 113, 118, 121, 193
period reconstitutions 161
peripheral cosmopolitanism 81
periphery 2, 26, 74, 81–82, 85, 96, 101, 146, 186, 201
permanent war 172
Pignarre, P. and Stengers, I. 115
Pignatari, D. 141–144
Pisani, F. 82
pleasure 42, 91
pluralist 124
polarized 42, 122–124
political parallelism 123
political production 107–113
politics of the visible 110
pornography 10, 34, 36, 39, 41, 43, 44–45, 51–54
post-Arab uprising 119
postcolonial/postcolonialism/postcolonialism 11–12, 18, 31, 57, 89, 151, 172, 189, 202
postmodern 11, 18
power 3–14, 18–19, 22, 34, 42, 45–46, 51, 54, 58–59, 66, 80–89, 96, 98, 110–123, 127–130, 134–136, 157, 170, 172–178, 181–186, 191, 196, 199
presence 8, 22, 45, 49, 56, 58, 60, 76, 90, 150, 189, 196, 198
professional 50, 63, 77, 119–121, 126, 129, 131–138, 163, 166
professionalism 120–124, 129–133
professional practices 119–120
propaganda 132, 137, 148, 188–192, 194

public 18, 36, 53, 56, 58–61, 63, 66, 91, 112, 123–125, 127–128, 131, 134, 142–143, 163–165, 170–173, 194
publishing market 163–164

queer theory 94, 97, 101

race 7, 10, 34, 35, 37–43, 46–53, 56–57, 147–148
racism 41, 47, 50, 53, 54, 56, 90, 94, 98, 102, 162, 188, 197
racist bias 46, 48
radio 55, 66, 69, 75, 123, 141, 142, 148, 156, 160, 165, 167, 190–192
Radio Peking/China Radio International 190–192
Rancière, J. 109
reality show 10, 28, 55, 61
reboots 162
Rede Globo 72, 158, 160–163
regime 20, 66, 109, 127, 136, 147, 181
remakes 162, 168
representation 5, 11, 14, 28, 53, 54, 58, 59, 66, 80, 87, 97, 108, 113, 114, 147, 148, 151, 165, 171, 172, 181
reruns 159, 160, 162
Resende, F. 1–16, 170, 174, 184
resistance 11, 20, 23, 31, 91, 99, 104, 111, 114, 115, 161, 170, 178, 180, 182, 185
respectability 61, 63, 65, 151
retrospective-synchronic view 144, 145
revolution 20, 21, 26, 32, 141, 188, 189, 201
right to narrate 170, 174
Riobaldo 105, 116, 117
risk 9, 105–110, 114–117, 126, 142
role perception 119–121, 126
Rosa, J. G. 102, 105, 116, 116, 118
Russell, B. 75

Sadat 23
Said, Edward 1, 18, 174
Santaella, L. 75
Santos, M. 6, 75

INDEX

Schafer, M. 154
Schechner, R. 30, 108
self-narration 171, 177
series 65, 66, 101, 107–110, 149, 157, 158, 160–162, 164, 167, 170
settler-colonial 171, 172, 174, 181
sexual difference 35
sexual diversity 91, 97
sexuality 34, 47, 52–54, 57, 59, 60, 70, 91, 92, 94, 97, 102
sexual preference 47–51
Sibilia, P. 112, 165
soap operas 11, 158, 160, 162, 163
Sobhy, Mohamed 24, 25
socialites 10, 55
social networks 107, 110, 164–166
sorcery 115, 116
South Africa 3, 7, 10–12, 34–36, 39, 41–45, 48, 49, 52–54
Soviet Union 188–189, 191
spatial/spatiality 18, 19, 31, 75, 87, 145, 158, 170
spectacle 41, 56, 58, 109, 111–114, 117, 118, 192
Starhawk 115
stereophony 149–151
stereotypes 28, 34, 40, 46, 58, 59, 67, 87
Sterling, B. 76
straw 25
structural conditions 170, 182

TAZARA railway 189
technology 2, 69, 75, 82, 83, 165
telenovela 162
television 10, 28, 39, 55, 56, 61, 65, 66, 68, 71, 78, 117, 137, 139, 142, 158, 160–163, 166, 169
territorialization 76
territory 1, 5–9, 13–14, 19, 22, 25, 27, 31, 53, 72, 75–77, 79, 89, 108, 109, 111–115, 142

transcrossing 9, 115, 116, 117
transformation 30, 42, 53, 94, 96, 108, 112, 116, 162
transitional system 121
Tripartite Aggression 20
Trump, Donald 196

universal values 129, 135, 137
Urabi, Ahmed 20
urban 32, 41, 55, 57–61, 68, 70, 75, 76, 83, 107
utopia 161

victimization 180
Virilio, P. 75
visibility 49, 57, 60, 65, 67, 72, 81–83, 96, 109, 111, 157, 165, 176, 177, 182, 184
visual culture 86–88, 90, 94, 103, 104
vixen 55, 61, 66

Wahba, Saad Eldin 18–24, 29, 33
Weber, M. 82, 186, 193
Weiser, M. 75, 85
Wertheim, M. 75, 85
West 2, 3, 9, 10, 19, 20, 21, 28–31, 33, 64, 65, 87, 175, 176, 178, 188, 189, 191, 195–199, 201
West-Pavlov 19
whiteness 40, 45, 51, 52, 53
women 10, 21, 42, 52, 55–71, 89, 92, 162, 174, 193

Youssef, Mahdy 18, 24, 122
YouTube 8, 10, 56, 68, 72, 74–85, 114, 192, 202
YouTube videos 79

Zaghlul, Saad 20
Zayani, M. 178
Zeffiro, A. 75
Zimbabwe 195
Zionism 171, 172, 173, 176, 182

207